Challenges of Command in the Civil War

Generalship, Leadership, and Strategy at Gettysburg, Petersburg, and Beyond

Volume I: Generals and Generalship

Richard J. Sommers

Savas Beatie
California

Library of Congress Cataloging-in-Publication Data

Names: Sommers, Richard J., author.
Title: Challenges of command in the Civil War: Generalship, Leadership, and Strategy at Gettysburg, Petersburg, and Beyond / by Richard J. Sommers.
Description: First edition | California: Savas Beatie, [2018] | Includes bibliographical references and index.
Identifiers: LCCN 2018008424 | ISBN 9781611214321 (hardcover: alk. paper) | ISBN 9781611214338 (ebook)
Subjects: LCSH: United States—History—Civil War, 1861-1865—Campaigns. | Command of troops—History—19th century—Case studies. | Generals—United States—History—19th century. | Generals—Confederate States of America. | Military art and science—United States—History—19th century—Case studies.
Classification: LCC E470 .S69 2018 | DDC 973.7/3—dc23
LC record available at https://lccn.loc.gov/2018008424

First Edition, First Printing

SB

Savas Beatie LLC
989 Governor Drive, Suite 102
El Dorado Hills, CA 95762
Phone: 916-941-6896
(web) www.savasbeatie.com
(E-mail) sales@savasbeatie.com

Our titles are available at special discounts for bulk purchases.
For more details, contact us at sales@savasbeatie.com.

Proudly printed in the United States of America.

To

MY OWN DEAR PARENTS, WALTER J. AND RUTH SOMMERS

From the elder of your two devoted sons,
In whom you inspired, by your own example,
Love of learning, love of country, love of family

Table of Contents

Table of Contents (continued)

List of Tables and Charts

Table of Contents (continued)

List of Maps

List of Photographs

Table of Contents (continued)

Table of Contents (continued)

Table of Contents (continued)

Preface

Military history has interested me for longer than I can remember. Memories from Third Grade mark my interest even then. In those early years, ancient and medieval military history—Alexander the Great, Julius Caesar, Joan of Arc, Richard the Lion-Hearted—appealed to me. (No, before anyone asks, when I was in Third Grade, the Third Crusade was not a current event!)

In Eighth Grade, the focus changed, thanks to my great good fortune to read Bruce Catton's *Mr. Lincoln's Army* and *Glory Road*—followed the following fall by *Stillness at Appomattox*. His felicitous, flowing narrative, enriched by keen insights, not only captivated but captured me. Ever since then, more than sixty years now, the Civil War has been my field of interest, study, and reflection.

Every Civil War book in my grade school and high school libraries, my hometown library in suburban Chicagoland, and the library of a larger nearby town in Indiana, plus even some from the Illinois State Library in Springfield were avidly read. At Carleton College, I wrote all fourteen term papers on military history—four of them on the Civil War itself. At Rice University, my dissertation covered the Siege of Petersburg.[1]

From 1970 until nominally "retiring" in 2014, I served on the faculty of the U.S. Army War College as the Chief Archivist-Historian of the U.S. Army Military History Research Collection, as the Assistant Director for Archives and later for Patron Services of the U.S. Army Military History Institute, as the General Harold Keith Johnson Professor of Military History at the War

1 "Grant's Fifth Offensive at Petersburg, A Study in Strategy, Tactics, and Generalship," Ph.D. Dissertation, Rice University, 1970.

College, and as the Senior Historian of the U.S. Army Heritage and Education Center. Even in "retirement," I teach one graduate seminar in the War College annually. This work in the Army History Program and Professional Military Education covered all of American military history, but again it emphasized the Civil War.

On my own time outside the work place, I also read, write, and speak on the Civil War. My opus, *Richmond Redeemed: The Siege at Petersburg* (first published by Doubleday in 1980-81 and brought back into print by Savas Beatie in an expanded 150th Anniversary edition in 2014), pioneered modern scholarship on that siege.[2] I delight in having addressed Civil War audiences from Boston to Austin, from Seattle to Atlanta, and scores of settings in between, and I have been active in the Harrisburg Civil War Round Table since 1971. Speaking to groups, conversing with individuals, teaching military professionals, encouraging researchers, visiting battlefields and historical sites, reading and writing and simply thinking—all these activities stimulate me to analyze the Civil War.

Some of these analyses have already been published in *Richmond Redeemed* and in articles, chapters, and entries on the Siege of Petersburg.[3] I have also published on Ulysses S. Grant,[4] on additional Federal and

2 The first edition of *Richmond Redeemed*, long out of print, now circulates only on the used-book market. The expanded 150th anniversary edition of the book, which Savas Beatie published in September of 2014, right in time for the sesquicentennial of my battles, remains readily reachable for readers.

3 In addition to those original and 150th anniversary editions of *Richmond Redeemed*, I wrote the following chapters, entries, and articles on the Siege of Petersburg and its battles and offensives: "Petersburg Besieged," in William C. Davis, ed., *The Image of War, 1861-1865*, v. VI, *The End of an Era*; "Petersburg Campaign, 15 June 1864-3 April 1865," in David and Jeanne Heidler, eds., *Encyclopedia of the American Civil War*, v. III; "Land Operations in Virginia in 1864," in William C. Davis, ed., *Virginia at War, 1864*, v. IV, *The Tightening Noose*; "1864," in William B. Styple, ed., *Writing and Fighting the Civil War*; "Fury at Fort Harrison," *CWTI*, v. XIX, no. 6; "Petersburg Autumn: The Battle of Poplar Spring Church," in Roman J. Heleniak and Lawrence L. Hewitt, eds., *The Confederate High Command*; "The Battles of Pegram's Farm and First Squirrel Level Road, September 29-October 2, 1864" and "The Battle of the Boydton Plank Road, October 27-28, 1864," *Civil War Magazine*, No. LXVII; "The Battle No One Wanted [Second Squirrel Level Road]," *CWTI*, v. XIV, no. 5; "The Dutch Gap Affair: Military Atrocities and Rights of Negro Soldiers," *Civil War History*, v. XXI, no. 1; and "Hatcher's Run, Battle of (October 27-28, 1864)," in David C. Roller and Robert W. Twyman, eds., *The Encyclopedia of Southern History*.

4 "Grant, Ulysses Simpson (1822-1885)," in Heidlers, eds., *Encyclopedia*, v. II.

Confederate generals,[5] on Northern and Southern military units,[6] and on various other aspects of the Civil War.[7] Many analyses, however, have not appeared in print until now. Most originated as addresses to Civil War audiences. Some were taped at the time; most were not. Now many of them are adapted for publication, preserved in print, and offered to a broader audience.

Challenges of Command concentrates on senior military leadership and on the generals who exercised it. The first volume focuses on "Civil War Generals and Generalship." Volume II covers "Civil War Strategy, Operations, and Organization." Within both volumes, each chapter is free-standing. Some chapters are grounded in extensive original research a la *Richmond Redeemed.*

5 My generalizations about generals appear in "The Men Who Led," in William C. Davis, ed., *Touched by Fire, a Photographic Portrait of the Civil War*, v. I. See also my entries on Generals George T. Anderson, Joseph R. Anderson, Richard H. Anderson, John D. Barry, Theodore W. Brevard, Thomas L. Clingman, John Dunovant, Stephen Elliott, William H. Forney, Birkett D. Fry, Martin W. Gary, Victor J. B. Girardey, Nathaniel H. Harris, William R. MacRae, William F. Perry, Matthew W. Ransom, William P. Roberts, John C. C. Sanders, and Alfred M. Scales in the six-volume *The Confederate General*, edited by Mr. Davis. For Federals, I authored entries on Generals Romeyn B. Ayres, Samuel W. Crawford, George W. Getty, Charles Griffin, Andrew A. Humphreys, Gershom Mott, Truman Seymour, Frank Wheaton, Orlando B. Willcox, and Horatio G. Wright in John T. Hubbell and James W. Geary, eds., *Biographical Dictionary of the Union*. My entries on Generals "Stonewall" Jackson, George G. Meade, and William T. Sherman appear in volume II of Andrew Roberts, ed., *The Art of War: Great Commanders of the Modern World*. See also my Foreword to Volume XI of Lynda L. Crist, ed., *The Papers of Jefferson Davis*, and my entry on Richard Heron Anderson in Roller and Twyman, eds., *Encyclopedia*.

6 I contributed thirty entries on Civil War military organizations to Patricia Faust, ed., *The Historical Times Illustrated Encyclopedia of the Civil War*, including six on Northern armies, eighteen on Federal corps, three on Yankee brigades, and three on Southern corps.

7 Some of my other writings bear directly on the themes of *Challenges of Command*. See the chapters on "Union Strategy in the Eastern Theater, 1861-1862" and "The U.S. Army and Military Thinking in 1861," in James I. Robertson, Jr., ed., *Military Strategy in the American Civil War*. Particularly pertinent to this book are entries on "Civil War Strategy" and "Civil War Tactics" in Faust, ed., *Illustrated Encyclopedia*. Other publications include chapters on "American Military History, 1816-1916" in John E. Jessup and Robert W. Coakley, eds., *A Guide to the Study and Use of Military History*; on the Battles of Cold Harbor, Trevilian Station, and Samaria Church in Frances H. Kennedy, ed., *The Civil War Battlefield Guide*; on "'They Fired into Us an Awful Fire:' The Civil War Diary of Private Charles C. Perkins, 1st Massachusetts Infantry Regiment, June 4-July 4, 1862," in William J. Miller, ed., *The Peninsula Campaign*, v. I; and on "Civil War Soldiers: The Henderson Brothers" and "Robert McQuin Black," in Richard L. Tritt, ed., *Here Lyes the Body: The Story of Meeting House Springs*. For all eleven years of publication, I edited and contributed to *Vignettes of Military History*, seven years of which later appeared as a three-volume book that I edited. See also the Foreword to the Arno/Crown and Barnes & Noble reprints of *The Official Military Atlas of the Civil War*.

Others bring readily available information together in new formulations and suggest new ways to consider it. Still others offer my own analyses and interpretations of oft-explored subjects, such as the generalship of U.S. Grant and Robert E. Lee and Confederate generalship in the Gettysburg Campaign. However, no effort is made to review and respond to the entire body of literature on these topics. Out of respect—and often friendship —for fellow historians, I leave it to them to express their interpretations in their writings. This book conveys my conclusions, grounded in sixty-three years of studying and thinking about the Civil War.

Readers may find helpful information and constructs in these chapters. Better yet, this collection of essays may stimulate readers to think or rethink about key dimensions of generalship and high command in the War of 1861-1865. If it does inspire readers to reconsider the Civil War and its generals, it will have succeeded. For my entire professional career—indeed, for my entire life—I have tried to help others who share my interest in this fascinating field of Civil War studies. In that spirit of helpfulness, *Challenges of Command in the Civil War* is offered to readers.

Acknowledgments

My dissertation at Rice University in 1970 acknowledged the staffs and services of the many repositories where I did research. The original edition of the resulting book, *Richmond Redeemed: The Siege at Petersburg* (Doubleday, 1980-81), included more research in more repositories, hence more acknowledgments. The expanded 150th anniversary edition of *Richmond Redeemed* (Savas Beatie, 2014) expanded the acknowledgments still further. I welcome this opportunity to reaffirm my gratitude to all those institutions and staff members who have been so helpful during the past half century. I especially appreciate the continuing cooperation of my long-time colleagues in the U.S. Army Heritage and Education Center of the U.S. Army War College.

Equally appreciated is the productive and helpful staff of Savas Beatie. My good relations with that publisher date back to 2013, when Ted Savas approached me about publishing the expanded 150th anniversary edition of *Richmond Redeemed*. He, moreover, committed to bring it out not just at any old time but right in time for the 150th anniversary of those operations of the Siege of Petersburg. The Richmond and Petersburg National Battlefield Parks had scheduled me as the principal battlefield guide for their sesquicentennial celebrations of those battles in September of 2014. Having *Richmond*

Redeemed again in print by then was highly desirable. True to their word, Ted and his staff, especially designer Lee Meredith, completed the book right on time in mid-September of 2014—perfect timing for the anniversary events.

Such strong support predisposed me to Savas Beatie two years later when Ted contacted me about writing another book. I proposed a much different approach: a collection of analytical essays on generals, generalship, strategy, and operations. Again, he readily agreed, and he promised that if the manuscript reached him by the end of January, 2018, he would publish it in time for the Gettysburg anniversary events in early summer. I knew him to be a man of his word—but little did I realize that he and his great production staff would really pick up the pace and finish the book by the anniversary of Chancellorsville! As a Civil War historian who had the privilege of studying under Frank Vandiver and who numbers "Bud" Robertson among his dear friends, I especially appreciate Savas Beatie for proceeding at the pace of "Stonewall" Jackson's foot cavalry! Even at such a gallop, my longstanding friendship with Ted has deepened immeasurably along the march. To Ted, Sarah Keeney, and the great production, marketing, author liaison, publicity, and administrative staff of Savas Beatie, I acknowledge my deep gratitude.

Even more do I express my boundless gratitude to my lovely wife, Tracy. Her understanding of reading and readers, her experience in desktop publishing, her longstanding knowledge of Civil War history, and her newfound talent for mapmaking and family-tree planting have made this book much the better. Her loving sharing of life's journey these past seven years has made my life much the better.

For ten times that long, I have benefitted from the enduring contributions of another group of people who also deserve acknowledgment here in *Challenges of Command*: my teachers from grade school to grad school. In those schools, I had many good teachers and also one truly influential teacher at each of the four levels.

At Lincoln Grade School in Calumet City, Illinois (back then almost out in the open farmland of far south-suburban Chicagoland), I think of Miss Esther Schrum in Fourth Grade, Mr. Paul Radziejewski in Seventh Grade, and particularly Miss Helen Stralko in Eighth Grade. Beyond those good teachers, the most influential teacher was Miss Josephine Walz in First and Second Grade. Her emphasis on phonics and fundamentals, her insistence on high standards, and her strict classroom discipline within the education discipline gave me a good start for studying, working, and living.

Then at Thornton Fractional North High School, also in Calumet City, I particularly recall freshman English teacher Miss Helen Brazzill and the Heinz brothers, Ray and Jack, from whom I took six semesters of mathematics. The elegant rigor of Euclidian plane geometry, as they taught it, so appealed to my sense of order that they almost inspired me to become a geometer or at least a mathematician. I might well have been another Kenneth P. Williams, who taught math and wrote Civil War books. My future did not unfold that way, but I still number them among my best teachers. Again, however, one teacher stands out for his enduring influence, my senior-year rhetoric and literature teacher, Dr. Herbert Grossberg. I went into his class already knowing how to write; he taught me how to write well. When he graded my first-semester term paper—on the Civil War, no less—worth only a "B+," I was so appalled that I fell ill. But he inspired me to work even harder, and when he awarded me an "A" for the second semester, I knew I had really earned it.

Someone else who insisted on good writing—and who demonstrated it in his own scholarship—was my graduate school dissertation director and mentor at Rice University, Dr. Frank E. Vandiver. His enduring influence on my own scholarship, my career, and my life I have repeatedly acknowledged in many fora, including the dissertation and *Richmond Redeemed*. Indeed, the first edition of that book is dedicated to him. It is a pleasure to reaffirm that gratitude here. Let me also recognize two other excellent Rice professors: Dr. William H. Masterson and Dr. Sanford W. Higginbotham, who respectively upheld the highest standards in teaching courses and in editing a scholarly periodical, *The Journal of Southern History*.

Between high school and graduate school came my undergraduate years at Carleton College from September, 1960, to June, 1964. The Carleton experience was wonderful in all respects: opening myself to broadening and deepening education, making enduring friendships, and learning opportunities and limits for living. However, this "Acknowledgments" section focuses on teachers, so let me highlight Mr. Carlton C. Qualey, Mr. Richard T. Vann, and especially Miss Catherine E. Boyd in the History Department, Mr. Reginald D. Lang in the International Relations Department, and Mr. Robert de Rycke in the French Department.

Yet there is another Carleton instructor, who towers as the most influential teacher I have ever had: Mr. Ronald R. Rader. A former U.S. Air Force officer who had not yet completed his own doctorate at Syracuse University, he was called to Carleton unexpectedly in the summer of 1960 to replace a professor who had just passed away. He and I thus began there together. Back then, all freshmen took European history; providentially, I was assigned to his section.

Although he was new to teaching, he was well grounded in human understanding. He recognized in this earnest, eager young freshman the makings of a historian, and he gave me the time and encouragement inside and outside the classroom to launch me on my life's work. He even allowed me to teach a lesson on the Battle of Borodino! By the end of the first semester of my freshman year, I knew that history was not just my avocation but my vocation. Not science, engineering, dentistry, international law, or even geometry but history—that would be my profession. Mr. Rader remained at Carleton for only two years until a permanent replacement was hired. He then returned to Syracuse, earned his Ph.D., and spent the rest of his professional career teaching at the University of Georgia. Yet my relatively limited contact with him fanned a flame that has burned brightly for a lifetime.

And, thus, to Miss Walz and Dr. Grossberg, to Mr. Rader and Dr. Vandiver, and to all those other good teachers over the decades, I say "thank you" for all that you contributed to make me a better historian, better student, and better person.

All these teachers, in turn, built on a foundation laid by my own parents, Walter J. Sommers and Ruth (Lewis) Sommers. They were born in the early 1900s and raised on Indiana farms, mother near Crothersville and father near Rensselaer. They moved to Hammond during or just after World War I, met, married—and, as the saying goes, the rest is history. They were not learned, but they respected and encouraged learning, and they welcomed my brother Walter and me pursuing professional careers. They liked to read; they read to us, and they encouraged us to read. They made sure we always did our homework. Father drilled us on multiplication tables and spelling exercises. He taught us, by his own example, the virtues of hard work and devotion to family. Mother personified family harmony, and she radiated love of nature and of animals. Both of them instilled in us personal virtue, civic virtue, and love of country. They insisted we uphold high moral standards and follow current events—as well as historical events. They included us in all their vacations from the 1940s to 1960s. In gratitude, my brother and I took them on vacations from the 1970s to their passing in 1992 and 1993.

Further to emphasize my most profound gratitude for all that they did for my brother and me, I devotedly dedicate this volume to our parents.

Richard J. Sommers, Ph.D.
Carlisle, Pennsylvania
December 28, 2017

Part I:
Grant and Lee

1. Gen. Ulysses S. Grant. *LOC*

2. Gen. Robert E. Lee. *LOC*

Chapter 1

The Generalship of Ulysses S. Grant and the American Civil War[1]

"Yours of this date, proposing armistice and appointment of commissioners to settle terms of capitulation, is just received. No terms except unconditional and immediate surrender can be accepted. I propose to move immediately upon your works."[2]

Those seven words, "no terms except unconditional and immediate surrender"—written February 16, 1862, outside Fort Donelson, Tennessee—made Ulysses S. Grant a national hero. They not only resulted in the surrender of Fort Donelson and most of its large garrison but also earned Grant promotion to Major-General of Volunteers. More importantly, they launched Grant on a course which marked him as the most successful general in the Union Army, one of the best generals in American history.[3]

1 This chapter is adapted from an address given in the "Perspectives in Military History" series at the U.S. Army Heritage and Education Center of the U.S. Army War College, February 16, 2011. That talk could have covered any aspect of the Civil War. The date determined the direction. The 149th anniversary of the Ulysses S. Grant's capture of Fort Donelson deserved a lecture dedicated to him.

2 *OR*, v. VII, pp. 160-61.

3 The two most senior Southern officers, Brigadier Generals John B. Floyd and Gideon J. Pillow, with two small brigades fled up Cumberland River just before the surrender. The brilliant cavalry commander, Colonel Nathan B. Forrest, escaped overland with nine mounted companies. Command devolved on Brigadier General Simon B. Buckner, who surrendered the remaining six brigades and the fort itself.

Grant's service before and during the Civil War is well known. It need only be summarized in this chapter. He was born in Point Pleasant, Ohio, April 27, 1822, and grew up in the Buckeye State. After graduating from the U.S. Military Academy in the middle of the Class of 1843,[4] he fought with the 4th U.S. Infantry Regiment during Zachary Taylor's battles in Texas and northern Mexico in 1846 and during Winfield Scott's drive from Vera Cruz to Mexico City the following year.[5] Postwar service in the peacetime army proved less promising. Like many other Regular officers of that era, Grant turned to the bottle. On July 31, 1854, he resigned from the Army under a cloud. Subsequent efforts to farm in Missouri were unsuccessful. By 1860, he was working as a clerk in his father's leather goods store in Galena, Illinois. From cadet to captain to clerk, Grant was fast sinking into oblivion. Had he died in 1860, he would rate no more than a footnote in Mexican War histories and a brief paragraph in West Point alumni directories.

The Civil War rescued Grant from such anonymity and afforded him opportunity to earn the highest military and civil offices that the United States can bestow. Although his initial efforts to re-enter the Regular Army in the spring of 1861 were ignored, he fared better in his adopted state of Illinois. Influential Republican Congressman Elihu B. Washburne repeatedly sponsored Grant as Galena's hometown hero (at the time, the only one it had).[6] Governor Richard Yates, moreover, welcomed help from the experienced professional Grant in raising volunteer regiments. On June 15, Yates appointed Grant colonel of the 21st Illinois Infantry Regiment. On

4 Seventy-three cadets were admitted in Grant's class in 1839. Only thirty-nine of them graduated four years later. He placed twenty-first among graduates.

5 Grant fought at Palo Alto, Resaca de la Palma, and Monterrey under Taylor and at Vera Cruz, Churubusco, Molino del Rey, and San Cosme Gate under Scott.

6 By war's end, nine residents of Galena had become generals. Grant, of course, was highest in rank and renown. The next most prominent were his Chief of Staff, Brevet Major General John A. Rawlins, and Brevet Major General John E. Smith, who rose to command a division in the XV, XVI, and XVII Corps. Brevet Brigadier Generals William R. Rowley and Ely S. Parker also served on Grant's staff. The remaining officers were also brigadier generals, Augustus L. Chetlain and Jasper A. Maltby in substantive grade and John O. Duer and John C. Smith by brevet. Chetlain was also breveted Major General. Those eight were a goodly group of citizen-soldiers who earned their stars during the war. Grant was the only professionally educated Mexican War veteran, which made him stand out to Washburne at the outbreak of the Civil War.

July 11, Grant led his regiment westward across the Mississippi River to operate against pro-Secessionist elements in northern Missouri.

Over the next twenty-four months—from Salt River to Cairo to Paducah to Belmont to Forts Henry and Donelson to Shiloh to First Corinth to Iuka to Second Corinth and on to victory at Vicksburg—Grant rose from Colonel of Volunteers to Major-General of Regulars, from commanding a regiment of ten companies to commanding a field army of sixteen divisions, from helping secure a border state to severing the Confederate States.

Grant captured Vicksburg, July 4, 1863. Fifteen weeks later, he was placed in command of the newly created Military Division of the Mississippi, responsible for almost the entire Western Theater of Operations. By late November and early December, his "army group" broke out from Chattanooga, sent the besieging Butternut brigades streaming back into Georgia, and then raised the Siege of Knoxville.[7]

From November, 1861, to November, 1863, Grant had gained tactical success everywhere, which usually translated into profound strategic success that secured Federal conquests, netted many Southern prisoners, and dealt devastating blows to the Confederacy. No Secessionist army or general in the West could withstand him. Only one Confederate army and one Confederate general continued enjoying success. Grant had earned the right to challenge that army and that commander. On March 10, 1864, he was promoted to General-in-Chief of all Federal armies, with the rank of lieutenant-general, the first U.S. officer holding that grade since George Washington. Grant promptly established his "Headquarters, Armies in the Field," commanding an army group, in the Old Dominion to operate directly against General Robert E. Lee and the Army of Northern Virginia.

Those two great opponents first came to grips in the tangled Wilderness of Spotsylvania, May 5-6, 1864. For the next eleven months they battled: Spotsylvania Court House, the North Anna, Cold Harbor, the prolonged Siege of Petersburg, Sailor's Creek. Their duel ended April 9, 1865, at Appomattox Court House, where Grant received the surrender of Lee and the battered remnants of his once mighty army. Within three months, all

7 *Challenges of Command* will repeatedly and unapologetically use the term "army group." Even though the anachronistic term was not in parlance during the Civil War, it so accurately describes the frequent formation—a group of armies, such as Grant led at Chattanooga and Petersburg as well as Henry W. Halleck at First Corinth and William T. Sherman in Georgia and the Carolinas—that using it makes sense.

other Southern armies surrendered, disbanded, or collapsed. The North had won the Civil War. The Union had been preserved.

Grant remained in charge of the Army for the next four years (at the grade of four-star General as of July 25, 1866—the first use of that rank in the U.S. Army). On March 4, 1869, the General-in-Chief became Commander-in-Chief as the eighteenth President of the United States. He served until 1877. He died in upstate New York, July 23, 1885, and is buried—appropriately enough—in Grant's Tomb in New York City.

To summarize sixty-three years of any one's life, especially Grant's, in just nine paragraphs as if it were a straight line of success cannot do justice to the many nuances, the many stops and starts and turns and searches for alternatives that marked the richly varied course of the commander's career. This author and many others have explored such nuances in detail elsewhere. In this chapter, these introductory paragraphs simply summarize Grant's service. The focus, as the chapter title suggests, is to highlight and analyze his generalship.[8]

Grant himself succinctly summed up his generalship as follows: "The art of war is simple enough; find out where your enemy is; get at him as soon as you can, and strike him as hard as you can, and keep moving on."[9] Within such summation, this chapter suggests thirteen hallmarks of his generalship. Why thirteen, the reader may wonder? On October 24, 1862, General Grant was assigned to command the newly created XIII Army Corps, the first officer in American history ever to command that corps. Thus "XIII" may be considered Grant's number, so this chapter will present thirteen facets of his leadership. (Now if only he had commanded the I Corps, this chapter would

8 Many books have been written by and about Grant, from accounts by his staff officers Adam Badeau (*Military History of Grant*) and Horace Porter (*Campaigning with Grant*) and his own *Personal Memoirs* through the mid-20th Century masterpieces by Lloyd Lewis (*Captain Sam Grant*) and Bruce Catton (*Grant Moves South* and *Grant Takes Command*) to works by present-day writers Michael Korda (*The Unlikely Hero*), Ronald C. White (*American Ulysses*), and Ron Chernow (*Grant*). Particularly useful are Brooks Simpson's books *Triumph over Adversity* and *Let Us Have Peace*. The indispensable complement to these memoirs and biographies is the 32-volume *Papers of Ulysses S. Grant*, edited by John Y. Simon and John C. Marszalek. See also Francis B. Heitman, *Historical Register and Dictionary of the United States Army, 1789-1903*, v. I, p. 470, and Ezra J. Warner, *Generals in Blue*, pp. 183-87. Chapters 3, 4, 5, and 9 of this volume of *Challenges of Command* and Chapter 17 of Volume II give this author's analyses of Grant's generalship. See also his *Richmond Redeemed: The Siege at Petersburg*.

9 John H. Brinton, *Personal Memoirs*, p. 239.

end in just one more page, and if he had commanded the XXV Corps, the chapter would fill the entire volume. However, Grant's corps was the XIII, so thirteen it is.) All of these qualities are important. They are not offered in any particular priority but simply flow from one into the next:

1. Undaunted persistence: Grant never turned back, and he never looked back. He did not brood over past problems and setbacks but focused on present and future challenges and opportunities.

2. Such future focus reflected the reality that Grant had unshaken confidence in ultimate success. This was different from the arrogance of Philip H. Sheridan, the boastfulness of Joseph Hooker, the braggadocio of George Armstrong Custer. Rather did Grant feel a calm, comfortable confidence in his ability to do the job. Such self-confidence and certainty of success gave him military peace of mind, which freed him from the doubt, fear, anxiety, and torment that vexed so many other Union and Confederate army commanders and which thus enabled him to focus on winning campaigns and eventually on winning the war. This confidence usually came through in his actions and decisions, but occasionally he articulated it in letters to his wife. For instance, on June 22, 1864, just as the Siege of Petersburg was beginning, he wrote her that, "Our work here progresses slowly and I feel will progress securely until Richmond finally falls; the task is a big one and has to be performed by someone."[10] Six months later, on Christmas eve, he again wrote her, "I know how much there is dependent on me and will prove myself equal to the task. I believe determination can do a great deal to sustain one, and I have that quality certainly to its fullest extent."[11]

3. This confidence gave him insight. Where others saw calamity, Grant saw opportunity. This was certainly true in July of 1864, when Jubal Early's incursion through Maryland to the very ramparts of Washington, D.C., produced panic in many Union civilian and military leaders. Grant, in

10 Simon, op. cit., v. XI, p. 110.

11 Ibid., v. XIII, p. 163.

contrast, perceived it as a great opportunity to cut off and annihilate the exposed Southern invaders.[12]

4. Such insight was part of his broad strategic vision for waging war against the entire Confederacy. Striking up the Tennessee River toward the strategic railroad intersection at Corinth; striking down the Mississippi River against Vicksburg; recognizing Mobile as a more strategic target than Brazos Santiago at the mouth of the Rio Grande all reflect his breadth of strategic understanding. The most obvious and effective example came in the spring of 1864. As General-in-Chief of the entire Federal Army, he prioritized major fighting fronts, heavily reinforced armies already there or created new armies for those fronts, and ordered all those armies to advance simultaneously in early May. Such an approach seems elementary—but it had not yet been done. Until then, the Graycoats had been able to draw troops from quiet fronts to defeat one or another Yankee army in detail. Grant's simultaneous attacks on all fronts denied the Secessionists that opportunity. Bringing the North's superior numbers to bear proved crucial to turning that advantage into achievement.

5. Another factor producing that same result, in Virginia and in most of his campaigns in the West, was that Grant dominated the strategic initiative. He did not allow Butternuts the luxury of choosing when and where to attack but rather forced them to react to him.

6. Relatedly, Grant understood the importance of logistics as the necessary under-girding of strategy and tactics. For most of his campaigns, he operated so as to remain in supply—and thereby assure that the great materiel advantage of the United States could actually reach and thus benefit his forces in the field. Again, the value of this seems obvious—until one recalls many other Civil War generals who envisioned grandiose grand strategy oblivious to the logic that it was logistically ludicrous.[13]

12 How Grant, as theater commander for the East, responded strategically to Early's operations will be covered in Chapter 17, "'That Maryland Raid Upset My Plans,'" in volume II of *Challenges of Command*.

13 The Tennessee, Cumberland, and Mississippi Rivers proved unbreakable supply lines for his operations from February, 1862, to July, 1863. So did the great tidal rivers emptying into Chesapeake Bay—the Potomac, Rappahannock, York-Pamunkey, and James—for his Virginia Campaign from May, 1864, to April, 1865. Only thrice in the war did he have to rely on tenuous rail lines rather than mighty rivers. Once, when he raised the Siege of Chattanooga in November, 1863, and again, during the pursuit to Appomattox in April, 1865, there was no alternative. In late 1862, during his first advance against Vicksburg, his

7-8. The previous six qualities were rendered more effective by two more hallmarks of Grant's generalship. Within his "persistence," or great fixity of purpose, he displayed great flexibility of methods. That quality is well known in his quest for victory at Vicksburg between October of 1862 and July of 1863. It was equally true of his operations in Virginia in 1864-1865. Such flexibility, in turn, reflects his facility to recognize, understand, learn from, and apply the lessons of experience. Grant was not a military genius, who could discern solutions in an instant—with a "coup d'oeil," or "blow of the eye" [i.e., a glance], as the 19th Century term went. But he could learn, and that helped him to win. He learned even from defeat. More than that, he wove such defeat into the fabric of victory. In his Virginia operations, especially in the spring, he was checked on every field, tactically, but he advanced from every field, strategically, and he drove ever more deeply into the Old Dominion. In a very real sense, Grant succeeded through a succession of setbacks.[14]

9. In those 1864 operations, Grant came to wage a "war of attrition"—a term that is often applied to his generalship but really misapplied. There is no more egregious canard in all the Civil War than to call Grant a "butcher," a modern Xerxes who heedlessly sent his men to their deaths by the thousands in hopes of killing a few score Confederates. Cold Harbor on June 3, 1864, no more characterized the generalship of Grant than Malvern Hill typified the generalship of Lee. After all, Grant's combat experience from Belmont through Fort Donelson, Shiloh Monday, Champion Hill, and Big Black Bridge to Orchard Knob, Lookout Mountain, and Missionary Ridge demonstrated that frontal attacks succeeded. It thus is hardly surprising that the approach which had served him and the Union so well in the West he continued to apply in the East. But the East was not the West; the Army of

overland operations along the Mississippi Central Railroad came to grief when Graycoat cavalry raiders hit his forward supply base at Holly Springs and his rear railroads in West Tennessee. That setback led him to transfer his axis of advance and line of communications to the Mississippi River. In contrast to Grant's understanding of strategic logistics stand Major Generals George B. McClellan, John C. Fremont, and Benjamin F. Butler, who proposed preposterous operations early in the war—appealing arrows of advance on a map but utterly unsupportable logistically. Even such a brilliant strategist as Confederate General P.G.T. Beauregard was given to grandiosity in some of his conceptualizations.

14 Grant's ability to understand and apply the lessons of experience is explored more fully in Chapters 3 and 4 of this book: "Success through a Succession of Setbacks" and "Winged Victory."

Northern Virginia was not the garrison of Fort Donelson; and Robert E. Lee was not Braxton Bragg. Grant learned that lesson the hard way—but here again he did learn. Hardly had the Siege of Petersburg begun in mid-June before Grant peremptorily, explicitly, and repeatedly forbade frontal attacks against well defended, fortified positions.[15]

Grant's war of attrition was not waged tactically but strategically. He pinned the Secessionists in place around Petersburg and Richmond, denied them the strategic initiative, ate away at their communications, attenuated their lines, wore them down physically and psychologically—and relied on other Blue-coated armies to devour the rest of the Confederacy. "My own opinion," Grant wrote to his trusted subordinate and friend Major General William T. Sherman on December 18, 1864, "is that Lee is averse to going out of Virginia and if the cause of the South is lost, he wants Richmond to be the last place surrendered. If [Lee] has such views it may be well to indulge him until we get everything else in our hands." That is the essence of strategic attrition.[16]

10. In all these operations throughout the entire war, Grant showed courage—not just physical courage, which most Civil War commanders possessed, but that rarer, more crucial moral courage to give and maintain battle, to launch and continue campaigns. He found this courage right at the start during his initial operations against elements of Brigadier General Thomas A. Harris's Second Division of Missouri State Guards near the hamlet of Florida, Missouri, in mid-July, 1861: "As we approached . . . Harris' camp . . . ," Grant recalled,

> my heart kept getting higher and higher until it felt to me as though it was in my throat. I would have given anything then to have been back in Illinois, but I had not the moral courage to halt and consider what to do; I kept right on. When we reached a point from which the valley below was in full view I halted. The place where Harris had been encamped a few days before was still there and the marks of a recent encampment were plainly visible, but the troops were gone. My heart resumed its place. It occurred to me at once that Harris had been as much afraid of me as I had been of him. This was a

15 Grant's explicit prohibitions against attacking well defended, fortified positions are quoted in Chapter 3 of this book. Those quotes come from *OR*, v. XL, pt. 2, pp. 268-69, and pt. 3, p. 180, and v. XLII, pt. 3, pp. 36, 331-32, and v. XLVI, pt. 2, p. 806.

16 Ibid., v. XLIV, pp. 740-41.

view of the question I had never taken before; but it was one I never forgot afterwards. From that event to the close of the war, I never experienced trepidation upon confronting an enemy, though I always felt more or less anxiety. I never forgot that he had as much reason to fear my forces as I had his. The lesson was valuable.[17]

11. From that first operation in Missouri all the way to Appomattox, Grant demonstrated a willingness to work with the resources at hand and GIVE IT A TRY. While other army commanders on both sides waited for perfection—and thus often waited forever—Grant acted with what he had, usually with good results.[18]

12. He also worked well with his Navy counterparts. In the Civil War, there was no unified command. Army and Navy commanders were co-equal: at best allies, all too often feuding rivals. No such discord marred Grant's relations with the five senior Navy officers with whom he campaigned. From Belmont to Richmond, he and they cooperated harmoniously to produce victory.[19]

13. Even more importantly, his uncomplaining and effective conduct of operations earned him the confidence and trust of the War Department and the President. His ability to work not only for but with the civilian leadership—and certainly not against it –was one of the greatest strengths of Ulysses S. Grant (and, for that matter, of Robert E. Lee). It is an enduring

17 Grant recounted this revealing incident in his *Personal Memoirs*, v. I, pp. 248-51. Carefully reading his account, John Simon, op. cit., v. II, pp. 66-73, and sometimes contradictory "Returns of C, D, F, and H/21st Illinois, June-August, 1861," RG 94, M594, NA suggest that Grant left camp at the Salt River railroad bridge on July 16, bivouacked on the road that evening, reached Florida the next day only to find Harris gone, spent the night there, and returned to his own camp at the railroad bridge on July 18.

18 The author gratefully acknowledges this contribution by one of his students in the U.S. Army War College Class of 2008, Colonel Flem B. Walker (now, 2017, Major General Walker, Commanding General of the 1st Sustainment Command). In seminar dialogue, he articulated the insight that Grant was willing to work with whatever resources were at hand.

19 His U.S. Navy counterparts were Commander Henry A. Walke at Belmont, Flag Officer Andrew H. Foote at Forts Henry and Donelson, Flag Officer Charles H. Davis on the Mississippi River from May to October of 1862, Rear Admiral David D. Porter at Vicksburg and again from October of 1864 to the end of the war, and Rear Admiral S. Phillips Lee in the first part of the Siege of Petersburg. Although only very junior officers within Foote's naval squadron worked with Grant at Shiloh, Lieutenant Commanders William Gwin and James W. Shirk, they rendered invaluable service in shelling the Confederates.

truth of American history that in a republic at war the President can never be a "meddler." By constitutional prescription, the President is "the Commander in Chief of the Army and Navy of the United States and of the Militia of the several States when called into the actual Service of the United States."[20] The Constitution itself thus gives him the right to be involved. Great war Presidents, such as Franklin D. Roosevelt in World War II and George H. W. Bush in the First Gulf War, knew where to draw the line on their involvement. Others, such as James Knox Polk and Lyndon Baines Johnson, did not. Sometimes, as in the Mexican War, the United States won despite such Presidential involvement; other times, as in the Vietnam War, the United States did not win. Yet each President had the right to draw that line. Truly successful commanders understand this reality, work with their Presidents—and thus are accorded latitude to apply their professional military abilities. Officers, in contrast, who bridle at such involvement, no matter how accomplished they are professionally, are reined in, shunted aside, or relieved. Union Major Generals George B. McClellan and William S. Rosecrans and Confederate Generals Joseph E. Johnston and P.G.T. Beauregard are some of a sorry series of senior soldiers stretching from Winfield Scott through Douglas MacArthur to William Fallon and Stanley McChrystal who failed to understand that relationship (Stan McChrystal might have been the greatest general who ever lived. Such superlative ability, if it existed, remains unknown—because he defeated himself.) Ulysses Grant and Abraham Lincoln, in contrast, form a model example of the proper wartime relationship of uniformed General-in-Chief and constitutional Commander-in-Chief.[21]

Yet to highlight these hallmarks is not to suggest that Grant was a perfect general, any more than that he was a perfect man. He had shortcomings, as

20 U.S. Constitution, Article II, Section 2.

21 Scott was the greatest American general between George Washington and U.S. Grant, one of the greatest in American history. Yet Scott diminished his ability to contribute by repeatedly quarreling with Presidents and Secretaries of War in the Mexican War and the 1850s. One hundred years later, Douglas MacArthur—despite his tremendous achievements in the two World Wars and the first part of the Korean War—was removed from command in 1951 because of continuing conflicts with President Harry S. Truman. The same consequences befell both Admiral William J. Fallon in 2008, who was perceived as publicly opposing the Middle East policies of President George W. Bush, and also General Stanley A. McChrystal, whose staff openly ridiculed Vice President Joseph R. Biden and indirectly President Barack H. Obama himself in 2010.

all people do. For one thing, his judgment of subordinates and staff officers was mixed. He identified and elevated some good officers—Major Generals William T. Sherman, Philip H. Sheridan, James B. McPherson, Edward Ord—and he got rid of some poor ones, such as Major Generals John A. McClernand, Stephen A. Hurlbut, and Charles S. Hamilton. But he also targeted some good officers, whom he perceived as rivals—Major Generals William S. Rosecrans, George H. Thomas, Gordon Granger—and he overvalued the abilities of some U.S. Military Academy classmates, such as Major Generals William B. Franklin and Joseph J. Reynolds.[22]

Nor was Grant an inspiring leader of men in the mold of the magnetic McClellan or the electric Sheridan. Soldiers rarely cheered Grant when he rode past, and they did not love him. But he loved them, in his own quiet way, not in the hot, effusive, shouting love of parades and rallying cries but in a calm, dedicated determination to provide for them, to care for them, to uphold their rights when captured even after military necessity made him cancel prisoner exchanges, to use them in battle when necessary but never to squander their lives needlessly. The so-called "Grant the Butcher" was far too devoted to his soldiers ever to risk their lives without good reason.

Then, too, Grant's confidence in ultimate success at some place at some point in the future occasionally caused him to overlook opportunities awaiting him right here, right now in the battle at hand.

Yet such strategic success would eventually come to Federal arms—and it came, in good measure, because of the Generalship of Ulysses S. Grant in the American Civil War.

22 As late as mid-1864, Grant contemplated assigning Franklin to major commands. On July 1, the senior officer considered putting the Pennsylvanian in charge of the Army of the James. Seventeen days later, the General-in-Chief proposed placing him in command of what would become the Middle Military Division to deal with Jubal Early's continuing threat. However, on July 21, Chief of Staff Henry W. Halleck warned Grant that "General Franklin would not give satisfaction. The President ordered him to be tried for negligence and disobedience of orders when here before [September 5-6, 1862], but General McClellan assumed the responsibility of his repeated delays in obeying orders." On August 1, the lieutenant general assured Lincoln "nor do I insist upon General Franklin commanding.... General Franklin was named because he was available, and I know him to be capable, and believe him to be trustworthy." Yet nothing in Franklin's record from First Bull Run to Sabine Cross Roads justified such promotions. One surmises that Grant's regard and respect for Franklin was based primarily on the fact that the latter officer graduated at the head of Grant's Class of 1843 at West Point. *OR*, v. XIX, pt. 2, pp. 188-90, and v. XXXVII, pt. 2, pp. 374, 408, and v. XL, pt. 2, pp. 558-59, and pt. 3, p. 436.

3. Abraham Lincoln. *LOC*

4. William T. Sherman. *LOC*

5. Philip H. Sheridan. *LOC*

6. George H. Thomas. *LOC*

Chapter 2

The Generalship of Robert E. Lee and the Civil War in the East[1]

Robert E. Lee endures as one of the most significant soldiers of the Civil War. He had already achieved high reputation in the Old Army even before that conflict erupted. Second in his Class of 1829 at West Point, he earned three brevets for service in the Mexican War; he was tapped for Superintendent of his alma mater, the U.S. Military Academy, in 1852; he was catapulted from Captain of Engineers to Lieutenant Colonel of the new 2nd U.S. Cavalry in 1855; and during the secession crisis he was elevated to Colonel of the 1st U.S. Cavalry.[2]

That final promotion came, March 20, 1861. It did not keep him in the U.S. Army. Despite his deep devotion to that army and to the United States, his greater loyalty lay with his native Virginia. One month after that promotion, he resigned from U.S. service. Three days later, Virginia made him Major General, commanding the land and naval forces of the Old Dominion. As of May 14 of that year, he was also commissioned a brigadier

1 This chapter is adapted and updated from a presentation first given at the Robert E. Lee Seminar of the Central Pennsylvania Civil War Round Table, March 28, 1992, and most recently delivered to the Harrisburg Civil War Round Table, December 15, 2017.

2 When Edwin V. Sumner was promoted to Brigadier General as of March 16, 1861, he vacated the Colonelcy of the 1st U.S. Cavalry, and Lee was elevated to that slot. The Virginian never assumed actual command of that regiment in the field in Kansas and Colorado before resigning from U.S. service.

general in Confederate service, and as of that June 14 he was elevated to full General in the army of the new nation, the third ranking officer in that grade.[3]

On July 28, 1861, he left desk duty in Richmond to "coordinate" efforts to retrieve the rapidly deteriorating military situation in western Virginia. His operations there proved unsuccessful. Nor did his next assignment, commanding the Department of South Carolina, Georgia, and East Florida, starting on November 8, result in the recapture of Port Royal Sound, which the U.S. Navy had seized the previous day and which became the base for the South Atlantic Blockading Squadron's operations against Charleston and Savannah for the rest of the war.[4] Despite such disappointing beginnings, President Jefferson Davis retained confidence in Lee and ordered him back to the capital on March 3, 1862, to serve as his senior military advisor.

Lee was thus readily available when command of the Army of Northern Virginia fell vacant at the Battle of Seven Pines.[5] Davis assigned Lee to that command, June 1, 1862. For the next thirty-four months, he led that army in raising the Siege of Richmond, recovering almost all of Virginia, twice carrying the war north of the Potomac, maintaining the strategic stability of the Rapidan-Rappahannock military frontier, and prolonging the war another eleven months from the Wilderness through Petersburg to Appomattox.

True, those operations did end at Appomattox with his surrender. Even so, they mark him as one of the most brilliant generals, not only of the Civil War but of American military history. His battles and campaigns are well

3 Generals Samuel Cooper and Albert Sidney Johnston ranked ahead of Lee. The other two full Generals in 1861 were Joseph E. Johnston and P.G.T. Beauregard. Officers to reach that grade later in the war were Braxton Bragg the following year, and Edmund K. Smith and John B. Hood in 1864.

4 On November 3, Lee was ordered to go south to meet the imminent threat sure to strike somewhere on the lower Atlantic coast. By the time he arrived five days later, the blow had already fallen. It was not his fault that the Federals captured Port Royal Sound, nor was he to blame that the Confederacy lacked the means even to try to retake it from the U.S. Navy and the strong Army division that secured it.

5 Joseph Glatthaar correctly points out that General Lee did not coin the name "Army of Northern Virginia" when he assumed command of it on June 1, 1862. The name had been used before then but was not in common parlance. What Lee accomplished was to make that name synonymous with success over succeeding months and thus immortalize it during and after the Civil war. See his *General Lee's Army*, pp. 128, 494.

known to students of the Civil War. They need not be detailed here. Rather will this chapter analyze Lee's generalship and highlight its hallmarks.[6]

As a military engineer by professional training and experience, Lee understood the military geography of war—tactical, operational, and strategic. On the battlefield itself, Lee used terrain to strengthen the defense by damming creeks to form impassable moats, by relying on bramble-infested bottomlands as natural abatis, and especially by constructing field fortifications to heighten defensive capabilities.[7] He also

6 The literature on Lee is legion. His son and nephew wrote on him: Robert E. Lee, Jr., *Recollections and Letters of General Robert E. Lee*, and Fitzhugh Lee, *General Lee*. So did his staff officers Walter Taylor (*Four Years with General Lee*), Armistead Long (*Memoirs of Robert E. Lee*), and Charles Marshall (*An Aide-de-Camp of Lee*). Books have been published on him ever since. One looks forward to Dr. JoAnna M. McDonald's forthcoming re-interpretation "R. E. Lee's Grand Strategy and Strategic Leadership: A Paradoxical Paradigm," projected for publication by Lexington in 2018. Of all Lee books, the three that have most influenced my own understanding are Douglas Southall Freeman's *R. E. Lee: A Biography* and *Lee's Lieutenants*, and Joseph L. Harsh's *Confederate Tide Rising: Robert E. Lee and the Making of Southern Strategy, 1861-1862*. Dr. Freeman's deep roots in Southern culture and his pervasive connections with the First Families of Virginia complemented his professional education as an historian to afford him profound understanding of the Confederate war effort and of Lee and the other generals who waged it. His magisterial presentations endure as magnificent works of scholarship. This author had the privilege of meeting Dr. Freeman's widow and his long-time comrade in arms in battlefield preservation, Mr. J. Ambler Johnston, Sr., but not the great biographer himself. Joe Harsh, on the other hand, was my graduate school classmate and close friend at Rice University, where both of us earned our doctorates under the mentorship of Frank E. Vandiver in 1970. Many was the time that Joe and I talked the night away about Civil War generalship. His keen perceptions and original insights came through clearly back then. They are preserved in print in his brilliant *Confederate Tide Rising* and *Taken at the Flood*. Another Rice graduate school alumnus—and good friend—Thomas L. Connelly was the foremost modern critic of General Lee, especially in his *Marble Man*. Lawyer Alan Nolan argued his case against the general even further in his *Lee Considered*, and Grady McWhiney's *Attack and Die* challenged Lee's style of warfare. This chapter makes clear that my perspective on Lee's generalship differs from theirs. Respectful and honest disagreement among scholars is to be expected. I expressed such disagreement to them in their lifetimes, and I convey it again now. At the same time, I welcome this opportunity to aver my respect for their scholarship in so many aspects of the Civil War and to affirm my friendship for Tom, Alan, and Grady personally. Their contributions to history endure in their writings. Their friendship remains in my memory—just as it does for my dear, departed friend, Joe Harsh.

7 Hatcher's Run and Indian Town Creek were streams his army dammed to create impassable water barriers. Virginia's tangled, swampy creek bottoms were notorious impediments to advancing troops. Lee began using field fortifications as soon as he succeeded to command the Army of Northern Virginia in June of 1862. Some of those preliminary parapets were later strengthened to become Richmond's permanent defenses. Lee continued using field works over the winters of 1862-63 and 1863-64, throughout the

used tactical terrain to sharpen the offensive by moving concealed forces along backroads, woodland trails, and ravines to launch surprise flank attacks on unsuspecting Unionists. Such flank attacks offset his disparity of manpower and often enabled him to beat the Bluecoats in detail.[8]

Operationally, Lee recognized how the Shenandoah Valley represented a natural covered way for carrying the war north of the Potomac. He also understood how the lateral, west-to-east rivers of Virginia—the York-Pamunkey, the North Anna, and especially the Rappahannock-Rapidan—were formidable, defensible barriers against Federal invasion. And he perceived how President Abraham Lincoln's understandable solicitude for saving Washington became a Union vulnerability which he could exploit by threatening or just seeming to threaten the Union capital. No matter how many Northern troops served in the Eastern Theater, Lee knew that at least some of them—often many of them—would remain idle in D.C.'s defenses rather than operate in the field against him.[9]

Those operational insights bordered on understanding strategic geography as well. It was in the domain of strategy and grand strategy where Lee excelled. Yet in recent decades, some excellent historians have criticized him in this regard and have asserted that he was a parochial Virginian who cared only about the Old Dominion or at most the Eastern Theater but who ignored the West. Indeed, some historians have even identified the West as the "Confederate Heartland," and they blame Lee for failing to protect that claimed core of the Confederacy.

The West unquestionably was important. It deserved the attention of Confederate strategists in the Civil War. It deserves the attention of all who

---

overland operations from the Wilderness to Cold Harbor, and especially during the Siege of Petersburg. Earl J. Hess has written extensively on this topic in *Field Armies and Fortifications*, *Trench Warfare under Grant and Lee*, and *In the Trenches at Petersburg*.

8 Chancellorsville, the Wilderness, First and Second Weldon Railroad, Poplar Spring Church, and First Hatcher's Run reveal how Lee's soldiers used superior knowledge of terrain to launch surprise flank attacks on more numerous but unwary Unionists.

9 The most pronounced instances of Lincoln retaining excessive forces to guard Washington came in 1862. In March of that year, he withheld the I corps from the Peninsula Campaign to help cover the capital. Then in September, the equivalent of three corps languished in D.C.'s defenses, while only six corps took the field against Lee's invasion of Maryland. Even in mid-1863, when six brigades did leave the capital to reinforce the Army of the Potomac and fight at Gettysburg, over 18,000 other soldiers remained in the Department of Washington. *OR*, v. XXVII, pt. 3, pp. 635-38.

study the Civil War today. But going beyond recognizing the West's importance to strategists and scholars and criticizing Lee for supposedly neglecting or even undercutting the West is, in this historian's judgment, unfair and unfounded. In the more immediate sense, for most of the war Lee was responsible for only the Eastern Theater. Not until February 6, 1865, did he become General-in-Chief of the entire Confederate Army—too late for him or anyone to reverse the course of the war. Before then, Lee understandably focused on his area of responsibility. He would not have welcomed Western Generals Edmund K. Smith, John C. Pemberton, or Braxton Bragg telling him how to conduct his operations in the East, and he can hardly be blamed for not telling them how to conduct their operations further west.

Beyond that immediate point looms the more marked misrepresentation that Lee's talents were wasted on Virginia, a mere "headland" far from the heart of the Confederacy. That Heartland supposedly lay in the West—say, Tennessee, Mississippi, Alabama, and Georgia. To defend that Heartland, critics claim, the Confederates should have abandoned frontier "headlands" such as Missouri, Kentucky, and Virginia and concentrated their forces in the center. There such massed forces could have beaten off all Yankee efforts to overrun the Heartland.

This effort to apply to the Civil War early 20th Century concepts of Geo-Politics, which identified Czarist Russia as the "Heartland" of the Eurasian land mass, is interesting—but inappropriate and inaccurate, in this author's judgment. Militarily it would have been impossible to supply and support a grand army in, say, northern Alabama or western Georgia for prolonged periods. The Confederate logistical infrastructure was so primitive and the Confederate supply system—especially the Subsistence Department for foodstuffs—was so inept that the South was overtaxed even to supply its various field armies in their respective theaters. Supplying a Napoleonic-type Grande Armee in the "Heartland" for any considerable time was totally beyond Confederate capabilities. Even if the Subsistence Department had been reorganized early in the war—as it finally was February of 1865—the paucity of usable rail and water transportation would have handicapped efforts to sustain that Grande Armee in the "Heartland."

There is, moreover, even a more fundamental flaw in the Heartland interpretation: It mis-locates the Heartland! Just as the human heart is not in the physical center of the body, so a geostrategic heartland is not necessarily in the geographic center of the nation or land mass. Rather in the geostrategic sense is the Heartland located in the center of resources and capabilities for waging war and thereby protecting the nation, its government, its economy, its culture, and its most populous areas.

What constituted war resources in the 1860s? The answer is clear: able-bodied manpower (white men to fight, slaves to raise crops and dig entrenchments), natural resources (especially iron, lead, salt, and saltpeter), war industry, horses and mules for cavalry and draft animals, other animals and crops for food, and militarily usable logistical lines of communication (navigable rivers, good roads, and especially railroads connecting strategic cities within one state and among several states).

Equally clear is that such resources were most abundant in Virginia. It was the most populous Confederate state.[10] It raised more mounted cavalry than any other Confederate state.[11] It contained the amazingly fertile

10 The U.S. Census for 1860 shows the three most populous future Confederate states as Virginia (1,596,318), Tennessee (1,109,801), and Georgia (1,057,286). Even subtracting the 376,388 residents of the future state of West Virginia still leaves the Old Dominion with the largest number: 1,219,630. Many West Virginians, moreover, remained loyal to the Confederacy and sent organized companies, battalions, and even regiments into Southern service. Over 31,000 white Tennesseans and even one battalion of white Georgians, on the other hand, fought for the Union and thus need to be subtracted from their states' totals, along with their families. Admittedly, significant portions of each state's populations were slaves: 490,865 in Virginia (including 18,371 in future West Virginia), 462,198 in Georgia, and 275,719 in Tennessee. Those bondsmen were a potential liability who could cause unrest on the home front and provide intelligence, guides, laborers, and even soldiers to the Union Army. On the other hand, slaves who raised crops, drove wagons, dug earthworks, and worked in military hospitals and war industry were a war resource to the Confederacy, especially if Federal forces could be prevented from disrupting the slave economy. Even with all these caveats and adjustments, Virginia remained the most populous state.

11 Virginia raised twenty-six numbered and one unnumbered cavalry regiments, two mounted infantry regiments, and seven cavalry battalions—the equivalent of thirty-four regiments. No other Confederate state came close to that total except, understandably, for Texas. The Lone Star State had forty-six numbered cavalry regiments (including four Arizona outfits and three Partisan Ranger units), nine unnumbered regiments, and at least five battalions. It also had four regiments and four battalions of state cavalry. Together, all of them were equivalent to at least sixty cavalry regiments. The key distinction, however, is that all thirty-four Virginia units were mounted throughout the entire war. For Texas, in contrast, fifteen outfits served the entire war dismounted; five more fought on foot in 1862 and were mounted only later in the war; and at least twelve more were dismounted in 1865. Eight of those regiments lacked horses. The others were intentionally dismounted because the army needed more foot soldiers than horse soldiers, especially in the Trans-Mississippi Department. Thus, Texas had more units called "Cavalry," but the Old Dominion had more outfits serving as cavalry. Lee A. Wallace, *A Guide to Virginia Military Organizations, 1861-1865*, pp. 38-80, 179; Marcus J. Wright and Harold B. Simpson, *Texas in the War,*

Shenandoah Valley, the "Breadbasket of the Confederacy." Not far west of that valley lay the crucial lead mines of Wytheville and the Confederacy's only major inland saline deposits at Saltville.[12] Richmond itself contained the Confederacy's foremost iron works, Tredegar. That city, moreover, was the national capital. In theory, the Confederacy could have kept its capital in Montgomery, but moving it to Richmond in late May and early June of 1861 proudly proclaimed the new nation's confidence in winning the war. Then saving it from siege a year later endued Richmond with an aura of invulnerability. It remained the symbol of Confederate independence.

For all these reasons—strategic, supply, and symbolic—Virginia was not a mere headland at all. It was the true Heartland of the Confederacy. To lose Virginia was to lose both head and heart. To lose Virginia was to lose the war.

Robert E. Lee understood this. He defended the Old Dominion not simply because he was a son of that state, not even because it lay in his area of responsibility, but primarily because the commonwealth was crucial to the Confederacy. His defense of Virginia thus reflected not only his tactical skill and operational dexterity but also—and mainly—his strategic vision.

Presenting him in that light precludes the proposition that he was parochial. Lee unquestionably was conscious of his Virginia heritage and of his bonds to the Old Dominion. Yet he remained the professional soldier of his nation. Prewar, that nation was the United States. While in U.S. service, he helped build Forts Monroe and Calhoun in his native Virginia, to be sure. But he also helped build Fort Pulaski below Savannah, Forts Hamilton and Lafayette in New York harbor, and Fort Carroll in Baltimore harbor. Moreover, he surveyed the Michigan-Ohio boundary and at least attempted (though unsuccessfully) to bridge the Mississippi River at St. Louis. He made his reputation in Mexico; he later served as Superintendent at West Point; and he fought Comanches in Texas. Of his thirty-six years in U.S. service, he spent twenty-five neither assigned to nor residing in Virginia. Wherever duty called, there Lee went to serve to the best of his ability—and

---

1861-1865, pp. 23-35, 110-30; *OR*, v. XXXVIII, pt. 3, pp. 639, 645, and v. XLI, pt. 4, pp. 1141-44, and v. XLVIII, pt. 1, pp. 1392-93, 1407.

12 Confederates attempted to extract salt from seawater, but such coastal work risked disruption by the U.S. Navy. The largest, safest, most productive salt works lay in southwestern Virginia at Saltville.

such service earned him the reputation as one of the most promising officers of the Old Army.[13]

In 1861, he became the professional soldier of a new nation, the Confederate States of America. In service to that nation, he was often assigned to the Old Dominion—but not just to his native Tidewater. Early in the war, duty took him deep into the mountains of the commonwealth, into an area that in 1863 became the state of West Virginia. Later in 1861, he was assigned to duty along the lower Atlantic coast. Far from resigning in protest at having to leave his beloved Virginia, Lee accepted that assignment and served there as well as possible. In March of 1862, he returned to Virginia—not because he angled for such re-assignment but because President Davis valued his ability and wanted him near at hand to help meet the imminent Union offensive there. Thereafter Lee served in the Eastern Theater, centered on the Old Dominion, for the rest of the war—because that was his place of duty.[14]

Had he been assigned elsewhere—to Tennessee, say, or Georgia or even Texas—there is no doubt in this historian's mind that he would have gone there and done his duty as well as he could. Whether with fewer soldiers and less able subordinates he could have accomplished as much there as he did in Virginia is highly questionable. But the point remains that he would have gone and would have tried; duty demanded that he do so. But as the war actually developed, duty kept him in the East. There his operations protected his home state, to be sure, but they also protected his nation, because Virginia was essential to the Confederacy.

Operating in the Eastern Theater, admittedly, constricted Lee's latitude for strategic maneuver because the theater itself was small. He could fall

13 From when he entered West Point in July of 1825 until he resigned in April of 1861, Lee spent almost thirty-six years in U.S. service. Of those years, barely three and one half involved direct duty in the Old Dominion. For an equal time, he was assigned to Washington but at least resided in Arlington House. And for at least three and one half more years, he was back in Virginia on leave, including over two years devoted to settling his father-in-law's estate. For the remaining twenty-five years of his U.S. Army career, he served and lived outside his native state.

14 That early in March, the most likely threat in Virginia was that Major General George B. McClellan's large Army of the Potomac would strike straight from the Washington area against the main Confederate position around Centreville, Fairfax, and Manassas Junction. He, indeed, advanced there but encountered no resistance since the Secessionists had fallen back behind the Rappahannock. Only in mid-month did he transfer his axis of advance to the Peninsula, where Lee would eventually fight him.

back from the Potomac to the Rappahannock-Rapidan, to the North Anna, to the Chickahominy, even to the James-Appomattox. However, he could not fall back into the Carolinas, Georgia, or Alabama for all the reasons already given: the fatal folly of forsaking Virginia's war-making resources, the risk of forfeiting Virginians' loyalty to the Confederacy, and the logistical inability to supply a grande armee in the Deep South.[15]

Such constraint was not contrary to Lee's style of warfare. Lee did not fall back; Lee fought back. When the Yankees moved out against him, he moved out against them. He did not equate probable disadvantage with certain loss but instead strove to overcome threatening dangers and to redirect the military situation to his advantage. By fighting back strategically, he redirected the military situation in Virginia in "Stonewall" Jackson's Valley Campaign of 1862, the Second Manassas Campaign, and at least the June-August phase of Jubal Early's Valley Campaign of 1864. Chancellorsville, the Wilderness, and the various combats of the Siege of Petersburg (from First Weldon Railroad to Dinwiddie Court House) comparably illustrate how he redirected the military situation operationally and tactically.

Attacking and counterattacking, moreover, represented more than the consequences of constricted strategic geography. They reflected Lee's fundamental approach to warfare, the "audacity" which contemporaries considered his key characteristic.[16] They also proved a requirement in

15 In the dynastic wars of 18th Century Europe, monarchs could abandon borderland peasants in order to concentrate forces elsewhere for military advantage. A republic at war, in contrast, feels obliged to protect all citizens. If it withdraws protection from them, they may withhold service and even loyalty from it. The growing disaffection of Arkansans after Butternut troops left that state in April of 1862 in order to join the concentration in Mississippi demonstrates this danger. Risking similar sullenness among Virginians if their commonwealth was comparably conceded to capture might have caused the collapse of the Confederacy.

16 Lee's audacity was the subject of conversation between the insightful, analytic Lieutenant Colonel E.P. Alexander and Colonel Joseph C. Ives of President Davis's staff in mid-June of 1862, shortly after Lee assumed command of the Army of Northern Virginia: [Ives] "reined up his horse, stopped in the road, and, turning to me, said: 'Alexander, if there is one man in either army, Confederate or Federal, head and shoulders above every other in *audacity*, it is Gen. Lee! His name might be Audacity. He will take more desperate chances and take them quicker than any other general in this country, North or South; and you will live to see it, too.' It is needless to say [Alexander added] that I did live to see it many times over." *Military Memoirs of a Confederate*, pp. 110-11. Slightly different wording and fuller

battling a foe much stronger in men and materiel. Both Frederick the Great and Napoleon had relied on attacking and counterattacking to offset comparable disparities that they suffered. Lee operated very much in their approach to warfare.

As with those soldier-monarchs, Lee strove to control the initiative strategically, operationally, and tactically. Such control is among a commander's greatest assets. It determines when, where, whether, why, and how to attack. It controls the course of operations. And it sets the pace for the battle, the campaign, and the war.

Without the initiative, Lee would have been at the mercy of the Federals, who could have used their superior logistics both to mass their superior manpower and materiel into an overwhelming force against him strategically and operationally and also to deliver devastating attacks tactically. But with the initiative, Lee could disrupt Yankee combinations, destroy their supply lines and bases, defeat them in detail strategically before they could concentrate against him, and defeat them through surprise flank attacks tactically before they could bring their full force to bear on the battlefield. The Valley in 1862 and mid-1864, Second Manassas, Second Bristoe Station, and even Antietam and Gettysburg were campaigns where Lee used the strategic initiative to good advantage, at least initially. The Seven Days, Chantilly, Harper's Ferry, Second Winchester, and Second Bristoe Station were battles where he attacked, almost always victoriously, and even at Gettysburg Butternut attacks prevailed on the first two days.[17]

Such tactical and strategic success came to the Graycoats because Lee controlled the strategic initiative in the East from June to September of 1862, in June and early July of 1863 and again in October of that year, and even for a few weeks in July of 1864. Maintaining mobility was essential to such control, and to achieve that mobility Lee strove to keep the Bluecoats far from Richmond. For a year and a half after he raised the first siege of that city in mid-1862, he succeeded to maintaining the military frontier in central or northern Virginia or even north of the Potomac. Ulysses S. Grant changed all

---

commentary about Ives appear in Gary Gallagher's edition of Alexander's *Fighting for the Confederacy*, pp. 89-93.

17 Second Bristoe Station, as a campaign, was a Confederate offensive victory that forced the Unionists to retreat from Culpeper County to the Heights of Centreville. As a battle, however, Second Bristoe Station resulted in bloody repulses of Southern attacks.

that. From the Wilderness to Appomattox, the Federal commander dominated the strategic initiative. He drove the military frontier from the Rapidan to the James and confronted the Confederates with the confining constriction of the close and constant coverage of their capital. With Richmond and her communications center, Petersburg, besieged, Lee was reduced to contesting the operational initiative with the Northerners. Losing the strategic initiative proved a major factor in losing the war.[18]

Even so, such defeat was a long time coming. Lee continued fighting for the operational and tactical initiative in those final eleven months just as he had done earlier in the war. Even when the Northerners initiated battle, Lee did not sit supinely to suffer their strikes, but he often struck back—at the very least to restore defensive stability and often to wrest the initiative from the Unionists. Antietam, Fredericksburg, Spotsylvania, Cold Harbor on June 1, the Crater, Second Deep Bottom, and Fort Harrison illustrate how he counterattacked to retain his position. Greater success attended the Secessionists at Second Manassas, Chancellorsville, Mine Run, the Wilderness, First Weldon Railroad, Second Reams's Station, Poplar Spring Church, and First Hatcher's Run, where Lee's counterattacks not merely stopped the Unionists but hurled them back and sometimes drove them from the field.

Yet not all of Lee's attacks and counterattacks succeeded. Malvern Hill and Pickett's Charge were the most conspicuous failures. Most of the other Seven Days battles, for that matter, also saw him repulsed tactically—although cumulatively those combats succeeded both operationally in raising the Siege of Richmond and also strategically in reversing the course of the war for over a year and a half.[19] The attacks that he initiated at Second

18 Grant's generalship in Virginia, 1864-65, is analyzed more fully in Chapters 1, 3, 4, and 5 of this book.

19 Chapter Three of this volume explores how, from the Wilderness through Cumberland Church to Appomattox, General Grant "succeeded through a succession of setbacks." That same concept may be applied to General Lee's operations in the Seven Days. The first of those fights the Federals actually initiated, Oak Grove on June 25, and they gained limited advantage there. The next five combats Lee launched. He was bloodily repulsed at Beaver Dam Creek and Malvern Hill, checked at Savage's Station, and thwarted in his greatest opportunity at Glendale. Only Gaines's Mill did he win, and even there his breakthrough came so late in the day that he could not exploit it before night fell. Despite such battlefield batterings, Lee in the Seven Days succeeded operationally in raising the Siege of

Bristoe Station, First Darbytown Road, and Fort Stedman also came to grief, as did his counterattacks at the North Anna, First and Second Bethesda Church, First Deep Bottom, and Second Hatcher's Run. Even his efforts to follow up initially successful counterattacks—as at Globe Tavern and Poplar Spring Church—produced only higher casualties but not greater gains.

Some critics have castigated Lee for exposing his army to such losses. They showcase Fredericksburg and Cold Harbor on June 3 as the ideal way to fight: bloodily repulsing Yankee frontal assaults while suffering few casualties. Such an ideal is idle. It would have forfeited all options to the Federals and then depended on them obligingly choosing the most foolish and fatal option: making those frontal assaults, wave after wave, battle after battle, campaign after campaign until the battered and bloody Bluecoats finally grew weary of suffering such slaughter and abandoned the war. Such an assumption is absurd. Even Ambrose E. Burnside learned the terrible lessons of Fredericksburg and in his next effort attempted to outflank Marye's Heights rather than assault it. It was hardly his fault that the skies opened, the rains fell, and his army bogged down in the Mud March before it could turn Lee's left. An even keener student of experience was Ulysses S. Grant, one of whose greatest strengths was his ability to learn and apply the lessons of war. June 3 at Cold Harbor held such a lesson for him; so did the disastrous repulse of his grand assault on Petersburg on June 18. Thereafter Grant expressly forbade such frontal attacks against defended, fortified positions. Grant simply refused to fight the kind of battle which Lee's critics have idealized.[20]

Lee had the good judgment to understand that he could not count on the Northerners to fight the type of warfare that most favored him. It was far more prudent to presume that they would try to act to their own best advantage, not his. Their great superiority of manpower, materiel, and mobility, moreover, made it even easier for them to conduct their style of warfare. Rather than simply sit in some ideal defensive tactical terrain—

Richmond. Even more significantly, he wrested the strategic initiative from the Yankees and reversed the course of the war for the next twenty-two months.

20 Grant's explicit prohibitions against attacking frontally well-fortified and well-defended positions are quoted in Chapter 3 of this book. Those quotes come from *OR*, v. XL, pt. 2, pp. 268-69, and pt. 3, p. 184, and v. XLII, pt. 3, pp. 36, 331-32, and v. XLVI, pt. 2, p. 806.

whether atop Marye's Heights, Seminary Ridge, or Turkey Hill—Lee realized that he needed to move, strike, catch the Unionists off guard, hit their flank, defeat them in detail—in sum, to attack them tactically, operationally and when practicable strategically.

Time was not on the South's side. If it did not win the war early on, then sooner or later the North would find a general who comprehended how to apply its many advantages to overpower the Confederacy. Rather than give the Federals time to identify such a commander, Lee strove to beat them sooner—and to do that, he had to attack them in battle and campaign. Some critics have branded that approach "Attack and Die." It would better be termed "Attack and Live," because it was essential to the life of the Confederacy.[21]

Lee became General-in-Chief too late to apply his strategic vision nationwide. As an army commander, he certainly pursued it in his theater strategy. Civil War army commanders, after all, were primarily strategists. More than many of his contemporaries, however, Lee also involved himself in operations and even tactics, especially as the quality of his subordinates declined.

Those domains customarily fell to corps and division commanders, and Lee largely allowed his responsible subordinates to exercise the responsibilities of their offices. That was the command style of the Civil War. To ask why he did not relieve James Longstreet, Richard Ewell, A.P. Hill, and "Jeb" Stuart on the battlefield at Gettysburg for not following his orders is to expect him to violate that command style. Civil War army commanders simply did not deal with senior subordinates that way.[22]

Lee the Commander has been the focus of this chapter so far. Yet to understand Lee the Soldier, attention must also be given to Lee the Man. Duty, dignity, nobility, magnanimity, an aura of greatness, yet all the while an absence of arrogance, pridefulness, boastfulness, and hubris—these were

21 This analysis of Lee's generalship, as reflected in the Gettysburg Campaign, is explored more fully in Volume II of this book in Chapter 14 "Penetrating the Void" and Chapter 15 "Strategic Imperatives and Tactical Realities."

22 Union Major General Philip H. Sheridan's summary relief of Brevet Major General William W. Averell right after Fisher's Hill and Major General Gouverneur K. Warren right after Five Forks was all the more glaring because it was so contrary to common practice among Civil War commanders.

his hallmarks. To a Civil War readership, there is no more need to elaborate on them than to chronicle his campaigns.

Yet such qualities are more than just moral precepts, which make him an exemplar for youth and an ornament of national history of whom all Americans in this reunited country may feel proud. Rather are they also martial virtues which carry over into the military realm. Lee's qualities helped inspire—not compel but inspire—the loyalty of his officers. Those qualities helped deserve the devotion of his soldiers. And they helped explain the esprit, perseverance, and combat effectiveness of the Army of Northern Virginia.

And it was through that army, in turn, that Lee excelled. The army was the instrument he wielded—tactically, operationally, strategically—to wage war in the East.

That war was going badly for the Confederacy when Lee took command on June 1, 1862. The main Bluecoat army was at the outskirts of the capital. Four other Federal columns threatened to overrun the rest of the Old Dominion. Through his masterful use of the strategic and tactical initiative, Lee defeated all five of those columns, raised the Siege of Richmond, virtually cleared Virginia of the Yankee presence, and carried the war north of the Potomac. Thereafter he repeatedly beat back Union invasions and thereby preserved the true Confederate Heartland, located in the Eastern Theater.

Ultimately, of course, Lee failed, because he met a foeman who would not stay beaten but who kept coming and who understood how to turn the North's advantages into achievements. Ultimately, too, Lee failed, because his country failed and was eaten up all around him. Was such failure inevitable? Perhaps so—but perhaps not. To the extent that the Confederacy had any chance at all, Lee gave it that chance, and at Chancellorsville and at Gettysburg—and in a certain respect even at Petersburg—Lee produced the Secessionists' best prospects for success.

Yet for the past half century, some historians have criticized Lee—indeed, have asserted that the South could not afford him and his style of offensive warfare. As much as this author admires the fine work which those authors have done in other regards, he cannot agree with such criticism.

Rather has this chapter suggested why Lee waged war as he did: to explain how the hallmarks of his generalship were governed not only by his own character and preferences but also by the geographic and strategic imperatives of the Confederate war effort. The South not be able to afford

Lee? To the contrary, the South could not afford to do without Lee. Truly, the achievements of the Confederacy and the prospects for independence of the Confederacy were largely the result of "The Generalship of Robert E. Lee in the Civil War in the East."

7. Jefferson Davis. *LOC*

8. Thomas "Stonewall" Jackson. *LOC*

9. James Longstreet. *LOC*

10. James E. B. Stuart. *LOC*

Chapter 3

Success Through a Succession of Setbacks: Ulysses S. Grant and the Virginia Campaign of 1864-1865[1]

Ulysses S. Grant was neither a natural genius at war nor a deep student of war. Yet he was a great general because of his perseverance, his resourcefulness, and—particularly—his ability to learn from experience and adapt accordingly. For Grant, failure was not a fatal flaw but simply part of the learning process through which he eventually attained the avenue to achievement.

His various efforts, between October of 1862 and July of 1863, to capture Vicksburg stand as a pre-eminent example of perseverance. Important as victory at Vicksburg was, however, it did not win the war. The conflict continued for almost two more years. In that later period, too, Grant's operations in Virginia between May of 1864 and April of 1865 illustrate his ability to learn from setbacks. Those operations are often parsed into at least three, sometimes six segments, but they are better understood as a unitary Virginia Campaign, spanning the eleven months from the Wilderness to Appomattox, and they will be so considered in this chapter.[2]

1 This chapter is based on a presentation originally given at Pamplin Historical Park, October 21, 2007, at a symposium on the overall theme of "Infamous Episodes and Disastrous Endeavors of the Civil War."

2 The three major segments of the Virginia Campaign are the Overland Campaign, the Siege of Petersburg, and the Appomattox Campaign. That first campaign is sometimes broken down into its component battles: the Wilderness, Spotsylvania, the North Anna, and

By the time he waged that campaign, Grant was the Lieutenant General of the Army, serving as General-in-Chief of all Union land forces. Yet he did not remain in Washington, as had his predecessor, Major General Henry W. Halleck, but took the field in Virginia. There he served as Eastern Theater commander and as commander of the army group operating directly against Robert E. Lee and the Army of Northern Virginia. For the next eleven months, he commanded at all three levels of responsibility—national, theater, and fighting front. That third level, his command of an army group, is where his ability to learn from setbacks will be explored.[3]

His first seven weeks of Virginia fighting he found full of such lessons. His initial intent, on striking south from Culpeper County in early May, was to hasten through the Wilderness of Spotsylvania and bring the Confederates to battle in more open country south of there. Although he did not expect to achieve a victory of annihilation of Napoleonic proportions—Grant, after all, never succumbed to the illusory allure of Napoleonic victory on the battlefield—he was confident he could beat the Butternuts so badly that they could not keep the field against him and would have to retreat behind Richmond's ramparts. Once there, they might prove as vulnerable as Brigadier General John B. Floyd's forces at Fort Donelson and Lieutenant General John C. Pemberton's army at Vicksburg.

Lee, however, was not Floyd or Pemberton. The Army of Northern Virginia was not one of those western armies. The Graycoats did not obligingly play along with Grant's plan but immediately challenged him for

---

Cold Harbor. Officers in the Army of the Potomac grandiosely styled those four components "epochs." They further called the first three offensives at Petersburg, through July 30, the "Fifth Epoch." This author prefers considering these segments and "epochs" simply successive phases within one unitary campaign covering eleven months.

3 As reiterated throughout *Challenges of Command*, the term "army group" was not in parlance during the Civil War. Yet because it accurately describes the force structure—a group of armies—it will unhesitatingly be used in this book. Henry Halleck at First Corinth, U.S. Grant at Chattanooga, and Major General William T. Sherman in Georgia and the Carolinas commanded army groups. During operations covered in this chapter, Grant's army group in May of 1864 consisted of Major General George G. Meade's Army of the Potomac and Major General Ambrose E. Burnside's IX Corps. From June of that year to Appomattox the army group contained Meade's army (including the IX Corps) plus the Army of the James (under Major General Benjamin F. Butler until January 8, thereafter under Major General Edward Ord). Major General Philip H. Sheridan's cavalry command became a third co-equal component within Grant's army group during the Ninth Offensive at Petersburg and the pursuit to Appomattox.

control of the initiative. They did not risk fighting the big open-field battle that he preferred but instead forced him to fight in the Wilderness itself, where tangled terrain diminished his numerical advantage of manpower and artillery. The resulting battle, May 5-6, was at best a stalemate. Really, it was a tactical defeat for the Yankees.

Here was Grant's first failure: he did not get through the Wilderness unchallenged; he did not have everything his own way; and he suffered a tactical setback. Yet, unlike Major Generals John Pope, Ambrose E. Burnside, Joseph Hooker, even George G. Meade at Mine Run, the Illinoisan did not let this check kill his campaign by retreating across the Rappahannock or Rapidan Rivers to recuperate and refit. Instead, he converted this small setback into strategic success by continuing southward on May 7 and sustaining his drive ever more deeply into the Old Dominion. He thereby assured himself control of thc strategic initiative—an overriding advantage which he would retain (except for a few weeks in early July) all the way to Appomattox.[4]

The strategic story stayed the same for the next four weeks. At Spotsylvania, at the North Anna, and at Cold Harbor on June 1, the Confederates contained Grant's temporary tactical advantages. He achieved no major battlefield victories comparable to Champion Hill or Chattanooga. Even storming the Muleshoe on May 12 netted many prisoners but no big breakthrough. And, of course, June 3 at Cold Harbor proved disastrous—an aberration, it must be added, as atypical of Grant's generalship as Malvern Hill was uncharacteristic of Lee's leadership. Time and again, Grant was beaten on the battlefield. Such failure influenced but did not foil his campaign. Strategically, he continued dominating operations.[5]

4 After being beaten at Second Bull Run, Pope fell back across that stream to the Heights of Centreville and then into the defenses of Washington. Burnside after Fredericksburg and Hooker after Chancellorsville withdrew across the Rappahannock. And Meade after Mine Run retired across the Rapidan. In the latter three instances, months of quiescence continued before the Bluecoats launched another major campaign. The interval was less in September of 1862 but only because the Butternuts forced the pace by invading Maryland.

5 Sources on the tactics and operations of the Overland Campaign, May 4-June 12, 1864, and of the ensuing Siege of Petersburg, June 15, 1864-April 3, 1865, are provided in Chapter 4 of this book.

On May 11, Grant had vowed "to fight it out on this line if it takes all summer."[6] "Fight it out" he would indeed do. After June 3, however, he would no longer do so "on this line" that led straight south from Culpeper County to the Confederate capital. And just as, earlier in the Civil War, he had tested varying venues to Vicksburg, now he sought a new route to Richmond.[7] Rather than try fighting his way across the Chickahominy swamp only to face the city's fixed fortifications, he swung boldly by his left, crossed James River, and struck for Petersburg, communications crossroad for the Confederate capital.[8]

Strategically, it was one of the most elegant and daring strikes of the entire war. Tactically, however, it failed: Major General William F. Smith's XVIII Corps overran Petersburg's outer defenses, June 15, but failed to capture the Cockade City itself. The Yankees made only limited gains over the next two days. Their great onslaught, June 18, was completely repulsed. Grant waited four days, then again led with his left (as he had done ever since leaving Culpeper). He had already cut two railroads leading into Petersburg from the east. Now he attempted to sever the third, which connected southward with Wilmington, Charleston, and Savannah—the Atlantic ports to which blockade runners brought desperately needed supplies. The resulting First Battle of the Weldon Railroad, June 22-23, was one of the worst Union defeats of the entire campaign. The Yankees were routed, with heavy loss of prisoners. Raiding Federal horsemen were similarly scattered

6 *OR*, v. XXXVI, pt. 1, p. 4.

7 Grant first attempted to capture Vicksburg in the autumn of 1862 by moving southward along the Mississippi Central Railroad. Early the following year, he transferred his axis of advance to the Mississippi River. From there, he tried to reach favorable terrain east of that river via the DeSoto and Duckport Canals, Lake Providence, Yazoo Pass, and Steele's Bayou. Not until late April, 1863, did he finally find the route that led to the left bank below Vicksburg—and victory.

8 The City Point Railroad from the northeast, the Norfolk Railroad from the southeast, the Weldon Railroad and connecting lines from the south, and the Southside Railroad from the west all ran into Petersburg. From there, a single line ran northward to Richmond. Only one route, the Danville Railroad running southwestward from the capital to the Carolina piedmont, did not pass through Petersburg. The Cockade City (the nickname for Petersburg) thus proved essential for connecting Richmond with the rest of the Confederacy.

at First Reams's Station a week later. The tracks stayed securely in Secessionist hands.[9]

The dual setbacks at Petersburg, June 18, and on the Weldon Railroad in late June taught Grant painful lessons. He had the strength, character, and perceptivity to learn and apply those lessons.

First, he now realized that the tactical offensive, which had served him so well in the West—from Belmont to Missionary Ridge—did not work against Robert E. Lee and the Army of Northern Virginia. Thereafter he explicitly and emphatically forbade frontal assaults against fortifications that were thought to be well manned. His orders over the next ten months of the Virginia Campaign abound with language such as:

"My desire is that Petersburg be enveloped as far as possible without attacking fortifications."[10]

"I would not permit any attack against the enemy, in an entrenched position."[11]

" . . . make no attack against defended fortifications."[12]

"I do not want any attack made by you against intrenched and defended positions. . . . Let it be distinctly understood by corps commanders that there is to be no attack made against defended intrenched positions."[13]

" . . . the object to be gained by attacking intrenchments is not worth the risk to be run."[14]

9 Two Union cavalry divisions raided through Southside Virginia, June 22-July 2. They damaged the Weldon, Southside and Danville Railroads but were repulsed in trying to destroy the bridge over Staunton River on June 25. Worse defeat befell them four days later at the First Battle of Reams's Station. Their raid, including those two battles, was part of Grant's Second Offensive at Petersburg, which also included First Weldon Railroad.

10 Grant to Meade, June 21, 1864, at the very beginning of the Siege of Petersburg. *OR*, v. XL, pt. 2, pp. 268-69.

11 Grant to Meade, July 12, 1864, forbidding such an attack even during a reconnaissance southwest of Petersburg. Ibid., pt. 3, p. 180.

12 Grant to Meade, October 2, 1864, terminating the first phase of the Fifth Offensive rather than attack fortifications. Ibid., v. XLII, pt. 3, p. 36.

13 Grant to Butler, October 24, 1864, governing attacks in the upcoming Sixth Offensive. Ibid., pp. 331-32.

14 Grant to Meade, March 3, 1865, prohibiting a proposed attack on Petersburg's works on learning that they were still well manned. Ibid., v. XLVI, pt. 2, p. 806.

Just as significantly, Grant recognized that his subordinates and his soldiers were exhausted, physically and emotionally. They just could not keep going in the hot, dry, debilitating climes of Southside Virginia or in the miasmatic swamps of the Peninsula. They needed rest—not through disengagement into summer quarters but through a change in pace of operations. The mobile warfare of spring thus stagnated into the slowdown of summer, and the Siege of Petersburg began.[15]

It was not a tactical siege, in the classic European sense in which the besiegers attempt to breach, undermine, or storm the defenders' works. Rather was it a strategic siege, waged from Grant's great entrenched camp east of Petersburg. That camp afforded needed rest—after a fashion—yet pinned the Secessionists in place strategically. It also served as a secure base, from which Grant launched a series of "offensives" aimed at severing the remaining supply lines into the city and at capturing Richmond. The Siege of Petersburg was waged on both sides of James River. Operations in Henrico and Charles City Counties, north of that stream, were every bit as much part of the siege as were operations in Prince George and Dinwiddie Counties, south of Appomattox River, with Chesterfield County a potential third sector if either side was so foolhardy as to lower its guard there.[16] Both Grant and Lee understood that reality. How the lieutenant-general sought to exploit it represents the next phase of how he tried—and failed, and learned from experience in his unending quest to win the war.

Grant waited over a month before attacking again—partly because his men needed rest, primarily because his attention and some of his troops (eventually seven divisions) were diverted to deal with Lieutenant General Jubal A. Early's incursion north of the Potomac and his continuing threat

15 On June 25, Grant notified Washington that "I shall try to give the army a few days' rest, which they now stand much in need of." Ibid., v. XL, pt. 2, p. 402.

16 Chesterfield County lay between Richmond and Petersburg on the right bank of James River and north of the Appomattox. It had witnessed extensive military operations during the Bermuda Hundred Campaign in May and the June operations against Petersburg. As the siege progressed, however, little fighting flared in Chesterfield because the tactical terrain was too difficult. The Bluecoats seemed secure inside the well-fortified Bermuda Hundred peninsula, but they were blocked from moving westward by the Confederate Howlett Line. Yet even with such tactical stasis, neither side could lower its guard or remove all its forces from that sector.

from the Shenandoah Valley.[17] When the Illinoisan did resume attacking in late July, he launched a series of two-pronged strikes over the ensuing thirteen weeks. In each onslaught, his right wing delivered the first blow north of James River. It sought major goals for their own sake. Even if they were not attained, moreover, these strikes were sure to lure so many Graycoats to the Peninsula to counter them that Grant's second prong, his left wing south of Petersburg, would have better prospects of achieving its objectives.[18]

His first such onslaught, the Third Offensive, erupted July 27, as Major General Winfield Scott Hancock's II Corps and Major General Philip H. Sheridan's Cavalry Corps sortied from the Deep Bottom bridgeheads onto the Peninsula to try to cut the Virginia Central Railroad connecting Lee and Early. The Northerners got nowhere near those tracks and were hard-pressed to beat off heavy Confederate counterattacks. All that Hancock and Sheridan achieved, before they recrossed to the Southside, July 29, was to draw four divisions to the Richmond sector. Their transfer made Petersburg vulnerable when Burnside detonated his mine, July 30—and thus made his IX Corps' complete fiasco all the more glaring.[19]

The Third Offensive was a total failure. Yet Grant learned two key lessons from it. He no longer conducted any major attacks directly against Petersburg itself until the final day of the siege—and he no longer entrusted any operations to Ambrose E. Burnside.[20]

17 To counter Early, Meade initially sent the Third Division of the VI Corps to Maryland in early July and then the other two divisions of that corps in mid-month. The First Cavalry Division joined them in early August and the Third Cavalry Division in mid-August. In addition to those five divisions from the Army of the Potomac, two divisions of the XIX Corps, arriving from Louisiana in July to reinforce Butler, were diverted to oppose Early, instead.

18 The ensuing pages of this chapter highlight how Grant learned from setbacks that beset his use of two-pronged attacks. His overall operational approach during the Siege of Petersburg is explored in greater depth in Chapter 4 of this book, "Winged Victory."

19 The Third Offensive is the subject of Michael A. Cavanaugh's *The Horrid Pit* and James S. Price's *The Battle of First Deep Bottom*.

20 From August 5 to 12 and again from August 29 to September 9, a court of inquiry sought reasons for the Union failure at the Battle of the Crater. The court found Burnside and four of his subordinates "answerable for the want of success" in that battle. Four weeks before the verdict was rendered, Grant gave Burnside a twenty-day leave of absence. As that leave expired, the General-in-Chief kept extending it because he did "not deem it best to return you [Burnside] to the command of your corps at present...." Burnside left the front late on

Disgusted but not daunted by the Crater fiasco, Grant waited two weeks, then launched his Fourth Offensive, August 14. Again, Hancock led the way out of Deep Bottom. He succeeded in his short-term objective of forcing the recall of one of the three divisions Lee was sending toward the Valley. Again, he came under heavy attack. Again, he remained on the Northside only briefly, then withdrew to Prince George County, August 20-21. And again, he drew two divisions from Petersburg to the Peninsula. This time the Bluecoats capitalized on that transfer. On August 18, while Hancock was still in Henrico, Major General Gouverneur K. Warren's V Corps struck west from the Jerusalem Plank Road and cut the Weldon Railroad at Globe Tavern. From then to the 21st, Warren reeled under devastating counterattacks by General P.G.T. Beauregard and Lee himself but retained his clutch on the tracks. Cutting the Weldon Railroad makes the Fourth the most successful of all Grant's offensives at Petersburg until his final offensive in the spring of 1865.[21]

Another month went by, punctuated by the inglorious rout of Hancock at Second Reams's Station, August 25, and by the humiliating Cattle Raid, September 14-17.[22] Such tactical setbacks did not eclipse the reality that Grant controlled the strategic initiative. He decided when the next big attack would come: the Fifth Offensive, September 29. This time Major General Benjamin F. Butler himself led virtually the entire Army of the James onto the Peninsula. His troops broke through the outer defenses at Fort Harrison, forced the evacuation of New Market Heights (which had stopped Hancock

---

August 13, hours before the Fourth Offensive was launched. His senior division commander, Brigadier General Orlando B. Willcox, temporarily replaced him. The following day the IX Corps Chief of Staff, Major General John G. Parke, took charge of the corps. He led it for the rest of the war. Burnside remained on leave until he resigned his commission six days after Appomattox. *OR*, v. XL, pt. 1, pp. 128-29, and v. XLII, pt. 2, pp. 153-56, 177-78, 603, 641, 1076, 1136.

21 John Horn's *The Battles for the Weldon Railroad, August, 1864* covers the Fourth Offensive.

22 The Second Battle of Reams's Station was the final phase of the Fourth Offensive. The Cattle Raid was a separate foray, September 14-17, in which daring Confederate cavalry raiders penetrated far into the Union rear, captured the Yankee cattle herd at Coggins' Point, and brought the nearly 2,500 beeves back into Secessionist lines. Not only was the episode mortifying to Federal commanders, but also it raised concerns that, next time the Graycoats raided into the Union rear, they might go all the way to City Point and make off with Grant himself. To guard against that danger, the garrison and fortifications of City Point were greatly increased.

twice), and threw Richmond herself into the direst danger of being captured by a Federal field army which the city ever faced to the day of her downfall. Heroic resistance by the Graycoats as well as Union failure to exploit opportunities saved the capital. On September 30, however, the Northerners repulsed efforts to recapture Fort Harrison.

That same day, while heavy fighting still raged in Henrico, the Army of the Potomac punched through outer Confederate defenses on Peebles's Farm, just west of Globe Tavern, and came close to cutting the last supply lines into Petersburg. Indeed, Lee, who had transferred nine brigades from the Southside to the Peninsula and ordered four more to follow, was prepared to abandon Petersburg that day if necessary to save Richmond. But again, Yankee hesitancy and Secessionist heroism saved those communications and the Cockade City herself. Tactically, the Bluecoats made nice gains on both sides of James River. Strategically, however, the Battles of Chaffin's Bluff and Poplar Spring Church must rank as Union defeats because they failed to attain the great prizes, Richmond and Petersburg, so nearly within their grasp.[23]

Once more, Grant turned such failure to Federal advantage. The road net radiating from Peebles's Farm provided the launching area for his Sixth Offensive, October 27, and all subsequent offensives in Dinwiddie. Correspondingly, Butler (unlike Hancock) stayed on the Northside and sallied from his sector during the Sixth Offensive that same day. Again, though, opportunities went unrecognized and unrealized, and the Butternuts took advantage of these shortcomings. The Army of the Potomac and the Army of the James both attacked simultaneously. Both were beaten

23 The Fifth Offensive included not only the two big battles of September 29-October 2 but also three follow-on fights. At First Darbytown Road on October 7, Butler beat off the Southerners' final effort to drive him from his conquests on the offensive's opening day. At Second Darbytown Road six days later, the Butternuts parried Union probes against their new defense line that sealed off the gaping breach in Richmond's outer defenses which the September 29 onslaught on the Peninsula had caused. In between those last two combats on the Northside, Meade fought the Second Battle of the Squirrel Level Road south of Petersburg on October 8. That little combat confirmed what he and his Confederate counterparts already knew: fighting a big battle there and then was not worthwhile. The Fifth Offensive is covered in this author's *Richmond Redeemed*. For Second Squirrel Level Road, see also his "The Battle No One Wanted," *CWTI*, v. XIV, no. 5.

simultaneously at First Hatcher's Run and Second Fair Oaks, respectively. The Sixth Offensive, like the Third three months earlier, was a total failure.[24]

Yet again, Grant acknowledged and applied the hard lessons of experience. Ever since July, his offensives had involved two-pronged strikes on both sides of the James. He had persisted in that approach all summer and fall and had simply modified the timing: from the sequential strikes of the Third Offensive to the simultaneous sorties of the Sixth. Even with the change of timing, that approach brought only limited gains at best. They sometimes failed tactically to accomplish anything and always failed strategically to net a big prize. The price for diverting Butternut battalions to the Peninsula was diverting Bluecoat brigades there as well.

That proved too high a price to pay. Thereafter Grant made a fundamental change: to deliver no further attacks on the Northside and to concentrate forces for massive first-strikes by his left, below Petersburg. That approach enabled Warren to destroy more of the Weldon Railroad in the Seventh Offensive, December 7-12.[25] That approach also enabled Meade to extend all the way to Hatcher's Run in the Eighth Offensive, February 5-7. And that approach finally produced victory at Petersburg in early April.

Yet the path to victory was fraught with failure. The Seventh Offensive, for all its accomplishments, could not destroy the Meherrin River bridge or cross that stream to capture Hicksford, which became the new railhead from which supplies were transshipped to Petersburg. Intercepting those wagons became a major objective of the Eighth Offensive. It, however, netted only twenty-five wagons, and for its troubles, the V Corps took quite a drubbing at Dabney's Steam Saw Mill. The starkest setback came at Fort Stedman on March 25. In a serious security slip—inattention bred of inaction—the Union position east of the city suffered severe severance when Secessionists

24 Hampton Newsome's *Richmond Must Fall* covers the Sixth Offensive. See also this author's "The Battle of the Boydton Plank Road, October 27-28, 1864," *Civil War Magazine*, No. LXVII.

25 Although the Yankee clutch-hold on the Weldon Railroad at Globe Tavern denied the Secessionists unrestricted use of that line since mid-August, they still brought supplies by rail northward to the new railhead at Stony Creek Depot and then transshipped them by wagons to the Boydton Plank Road and thence to Petersburg. Raiding Federal Cavalry broke up that railhead on December 1. Warren's expedition the following week tore up tracks all the way south from Jarratt's Station to the Meherrin River. Such destruction impeded using the Weldon Railroad, but it remained in service to the new railhead at Hicksford on that river.

stormed Stedman. This time, however, they were the ones who failed to exploit their advantage. Not only were they contained and then driven out of the IX Corps' lines with heavy loss, but also the Federal left, far from recoiling to recover the center, actually advanced and captured the fortified Confederate picket line facing the II and VI Corps. The failure of security at Fort Stedman Grant converted into handsome gains, which would lead to total victory eight days later.

In just half that time, he unleashed his final offensive. The Butternuts battled back bravely. Time and again, they achieved temporary triumphs: at Lewis's Farm, March 29; at the White Oak Road, the Crow House Redoubt, and Dinwiddie Court House, March 31. This time, though, the Northerners kept coming. They overran the last Southern mobile reserves at Five Forks, April 1. Then came the decisive day. By April 2, the military situation had developed so favorably over the first four days of fighting, Grant judged, that "I believe with a bombardment beforehand the enemy will abandon his works.... [The IX and VI Corps] can open with artillery and feel with skirmishers and sharpshooters, and if the enemy is giving way push directly after him."[26] By that day, direct attacks against Graycoat fortifications, which had been forbidden for so many months, at last seemed justified. Yet even on that fateful—for the Southerners, fatal—Sunday, it took far more than shelling and sharpshooting to supplant the Secessionists. Indeed, most Union assaults failed, from Bermuda Hundred to the Jerusalem Plank Road. But two succeeded. At Sutherland's Station, the Bluecoats finally cut the last rail line into the Cockade City from outside, the Southside Railroad. And at Boisseau's Farm came the decisive breakthrough, which doomed Petersburg—and with her, Richmond herself.

Even that day, the victorious VI Corps made one serious mistake, for which it would not have been fair to criticize those victors at the time but which stands out clearly in hindsight. On penetrating Brigadier General James H. Lane's lines on Boisseau's farm, the Northerners—perhaps drawn to where resistance remained robust—turned leftward and fought their way to Hatcher's Run. They thereby bagged two Butternut brigades.[27] How much

26 *OR*, v. XLVI, pt. 3, pp. 398-99.

27 Brigadier General William McComb's Tennessee Brigade and Brigadier General Joseph R. Davis's Mississippi Brigade were cut off by advancing Yankees and captured in a

greater a prize might have been theirs if they had turned rightward and pressed for Petersburg herself! Possibly they could have captured the Cockade City before first Brigadier General Nathaniel H. Harris's Brigade from Bermuda Hundred and then Major General Charles W. Field's Division from the Peninsula could have arrived athwart their advance. But history did not unfold that way. Those Graycoats arrived just in time, put up a good fight and a bold front – and retained Petersburg for one last day.[28]

To fight further on the fall line would be fatal, so they fell back. On April 3, Grant's men occupied Petersburg and Richmond without resistance. At long last, he had those two cities—but not their defending army. Unlike with Floyd's forces at Fort Donelson or Pemberton's forces at Vicksburg, Grant had failed to capture Lee's army. Overnight April 2-3, the great Virginian succeeded in disengaging and extracting all his troops—from Richmond, across the Peninsula, down through Chesterfield to Petersburg, beyond Hatcher's Run, all the way west to beyond Five Forks. The Unionists had failed to detect, intercept, or interfere with this withdrawal.

Once more, Lee was at large—but not for long. Although he inflicted several setbacks on the Yankees—at Farmville, April 6, and at Cumberland Church, the next day—his strategic situation swiftly deteriorated. At Jetersville, April 5, the Federals blocked his escape toward North Carolina. At Sailor's Creek, April 6, they ripped his rear. At Appomattox Station, April 8, they headed off his retreat westward. Then at Appomattox Court House, April 9, they doomed his campaign, his corps, his country, and his cause.[29]

The route from the Wilderness through Cold Harbor and Petersburg to Appomattox had been long, bloody, and difficult for Grant and his men. Time and again his projections had failed to materialize; his plans had failed

---

big bend in Hatcher's Run. Only Brigadier General John R. Cooke's North Carolina Brigade escaped across the run before the trap closed.

28 A. Wilson Greene's *Breaking the Backbone of the Rebellion* is the foremost work on the Ninth Offensive, the final fighting of the Siege of Petersburg.

29 The last week of the Virginia Campaign, from the fall of Petersburg to Appomattox, is the subject of many books. Among them may be mentioned Christopher M. Calkins' *The Appomattox Campaign*, Perry D. Jamieson's *Spring 1865*, William Marvel's *Lee's Last Retreat*, Noah Andre Trudeau's *Out of the Storm*, and Elizabeth Varon's *Appomattox: Victory, Defeat, and Freedom*. All students of the Civil War must remain awestruck by the resounding echoes of Bruce Catton's *A Stillness at Appomattox*.

to mature. The "opening battle in the open country" south of Spotsylvania failed to be fought. The tactical frontal assaults against field works in central Virginia, from mid-May to mid-June, failed to achieve breakthroughs. The two-pronged strikes on both sides of James River during the Siege of Petersburg, from late July to late October, failed "at one or the other place to let us in," as Grant had anticipated.[30] Even the capture of the Cockade City and the Confederate capital on April 3 failed to bag the Army of Northern Virginia.

Such repeated failures no more daunted Grant than had his series of setbacks in the Vicksburg Campaign. With great fixity of purpose, he persevered in his great objective of capturing Richmond, conquering the Army of Northern Virginia, and crushing the Confederate States of America. With great flexibility of methods, he sought the proper approach to attaining that objective. He learned from experience and adapted his approaches accordingly. Even failures he forged into the fabric of victory. Although his offensives at Petersburg were always blunted and often beaten—until April 2 belatedly brought the big breakthrough at Boisseau's—he still made those operations contribute toward his broader objectives: to tighten his grip on the Southerners grand tactically and strategically, to wear them down physically and psychologically, and to wage a strategic siege which fixed them in Virginia while other Federal forces devoured the rest of the Confederacy. In that sense, setbacks slowed but did not slay the search for success. Quite to the contrary, in his great Virginia Campaign of 1864-1865, Ulysses S. Grant secured success through a succession of setbacks.

30 Grant expressed this anticipation to Meade, September 30, 1864, in ordering his left wing into action at Poplar Spring Church while his right wing remained heavily engaged at Chaffin's Bluff during his Fifth Offensive.

Chapter 4

"Winged Victory:" Ulysses S. Grant and the Search for Success in the Siege of Petersburg[1]

Ancient Greeks called her "Nike." Ancient Romans called her "Victoria." She was the Goddess of Victory. Sculptors often represent her with wings—but not because such feathered features were essential for flight. Ancient gods were quite capable of flying without wings; after all, they were gods! Rather do Nike's appendages affirm the variability of victory. One time it may alight on one army; the next time it may settle on the other side. Thus, the term "Winged Victory" has passed into popular parlance right down to the present day.

That term will be used here but differently than in antiquity. This chapter will instead focus on how Lieutenant General Ulysses S. Grant used the wings of his army group to strive for strategic success in the Siege of Petersburg.

Grant commanded in three capacities during the final fourteen months of the Civil War. As General-in-Chief of the whole Union Army, he coordinated the grand strategy of the entire war effort on land. As Eastern Theater commander, he oversaw all land operations in Virginia, West Virginia, Maryland, Pennsylvania, the District of Columbia, and eastern North Carolina. And as commander of "Army Group Grant," he coordinated

1 This chapter is adapted from a presentation originally given at the Chambersburg Civil War Seminar, held in Henrico County, Virginia, July 24, 2015. The seminar focused on the Siege of Petersburg.

the campaign directly against the Confederate capital, Richmond, and its defenders, General Robert E. Lee and the Army of Northern Virginia.[2]

In this capacity as army group commander, Grant drove ever more deeply into Virginia—from the Rapidan River to the Appomattox River—during the first seven weeks of campaigning. Always he led to his left: from Culpeper County to the Wilderness, to Spotsylvania, to the North Anna River, to Cold Harbor, across the Chickahominy River and the James River, to Petersburg.[3] His initial assaults, June 15-18, overran outer defenses but failed to capture the Cockade City itself (as Petersburg was nicknamed).[4] Again Grant led leftward to try to cut the railroads leading into Petersburg and Richmond from the south and west. Two of his infantry corps were routed at the First Battle of the Weldon Railroad, June 22-23. Disaster also befell two of his raiding cavalry divisions at the First Battle of Reams's Station, June 29. With these dual defeats, the mobile warfare of spring—with its almost non-stop fighting—stagnated into the slowdown of summer, as the Siege of Petersburg began. Neither Grant nor anyone else knew it at the time, but the siege would last for virtually the rest of the war, until April of 1865.

Why the armies stopped and stayed at Petersburg sheds light both on the city and the soldiers. How Grant sought success there reflects his evolving generalship.

One reason that the armies stopped at Petersburg was because it was so important. It was the seventh largest city of the Confederacy. It was the site of the Confederate States Lead Works, the principal factory for making

2 This term "Army Group" is an anachronism not in parlance in the Civil War. Nevertheless, this descriptive term so accurately conveys the group of forces that Grant commanded—the Army of the Potomac and the separate IX Corps in May of 1864, the Army of the Potomac and the Army of the James from June of that year to April of 1865—that it will be used in analyzing Grant's generalship.

3 Gordon Rhea's five volumes provide the best overall coverage of the initial operations of Grant versus Lee, May 5-June 15, 1864. William D. Matter's *If It Takes All Summer* and J. Michael Miller's *Even to Hell Itself* concentrate on Spotsylvania and the North Anna, respectively.

4 Thomas Howe's *Wasted Valor* covers fighting at Petersburg, June 15-18.

bullets in the South. Most critically of all, it was the rail center for Richmond.[5]

Four railroads entered Petersburg from the Southside: from City Point on James River to the northeast, from the fertile farmlands of Southside Virginia to the southeast, from the lower Atlantic coast with its three great ports for blockade runners to the south, and from western Virginia with its vital lead mines and salt works to the west.[6] The resources of men, munitions, materiel, and food that passed through Petersburg on those four railroads were carried on to Richmond on a fifth railroad that ran northward through Chesterfield County. Only one railroad linking the capital to the rest of the Confederacy did not pass through Petersburg: the line which ran southwestward from Richmond through Danville to the Carolina piedmont. Even that Danville Railroad would become vulnerable to Federal cavalry raids if Petersburg fell. Petersburg thus proved the key to Richmond. Holding the Cockade City was crucial to holding the capital itself. Capturing that rail center would gravely imperil Richmond.

Such strategic reasons help explain why both sides fought so long and so hard for Petersburg. So does the fact that they had already fought so long and so hard before reaching Petersburg. Even the veteran soldiers in Blue and Gray had never before endured the almost incessant combat that raged between May 5 and June 23, 1864. By the time they reached Petersburg, they were exhausted, both physically and psychologically—enlisted men, officers, senior commanders alike.[7] The slower pace of siege warfare

5 A. Wilson Greene's *Civil War Petersburg* is the benchmark book on the Cockade City throughout the war.

6 The City Point Railroad ran northeastward to James River. The Norfolk Railroad ran southeastward from Petersburg. The Weldon Railroad and connecting lines linked the Cockade City [hence, Richmond] to the more southerly ports of Wilmington, Charleston, and Savannah, to which blockade runners brought badly needed supplies. And the Southside Railroad ran westward to Lynchburg and on to East Tennessee. Near the latter rail line were the crucial lead mines at Wytheville and saline works at Saltville, on whose resources the Confederacy depended.

7 In the fifty days between May 5 and June 23, soldiers were engaged in fighting, much of it heavy, on thirty-two of them. Another seven days were spent marching from one battlefield to the next. Even the brief interlude after Cold Harbor, June 4-11, afforded little rest amid the heat, humidity, and rotting corpses of that fatal field.

afforded relief and respite—at least to some degree.[8] No longer did major battles erupt every week, yet the Graycoats could not ignore the continuing threat of such combat. Daily sharpshooting and shelling and the looming presence of all those Yankees so near the city underscored the relentless pressure Grant kept applying.

Such relentless pressure reflected the reality that Grant dominated the strategic initiative in the Eastern Theater for the final eleven months of the Civil War. Yet for one brief period he temporarily lost it: July of 1864. From July 5, when Lieutenant General Jubal Early's Southern army erupted at Shepherdstown on the upper Potomac, to July 30, when Early's cavalry burned Chambersburg, Pennsylvania, the Butternuts wrested the strategic initiative from the Bluecoats.[9] To counter their threats to Washington and to deal with the continuing danger that they posed to the North, Grant had to send three infantry divisions and two cavalry divisions from the Army of the Potomac and to divert to the Shenandoah Valley front two more infantry divisions from Louisiana and one infantry brigade from South Carolina that were intended for the Army of the James.[10] Losing these twenty-one

8 On June 25, Grant informed Chief of Staff Henry W. Halleck in Washington that, "I shall try to give the army a few days rest, which they now stand much in need of." The following day, the General-in-Chief told Army of the Potomac commander George G. Meade, "Whilst this exceedingly hot and dry weather lasts, we will give the men all the rest we can." *OR*, v. XL, pt. 2, pp. 402, 430.

9 Jubal Early's incursion down the Shenandoah Valley through Maryland to the outskirts of Washington, D.C.; his continuing presence in the lower valley, and Grant's strategic response to it are covered in Chapter 17 of Volume II of this book: "That Maryland Raid Upset My Plans."

10 The Third Division of the VI Corps from the Army of the Potomac reached Maryland in time to fight Early at Monocacy, July 9. The other two divisions of that corps arrived in time to skirmish with him at Fort Stevens, July 11-12. Meantime, the XIX Corps from Louisiana, sailing into Chesapeake Bay en route to the Army of the James, was redirected to the capital instead. Its vanguard disembarked there on July 11. Most of its First Division joined them over the next few days, but follow-on forces temporarily continued to the Army of the James as originally intended. Not until August 17 were all seven brigades of the XIX Corps reunited in the Shenandoah Valley. That same day, the Third Cavalry Division from the Army of the Potomac reached Winchester in the Valley. The First Cavalry Division from Meade had already arrived ten days earlier. Finally, two brigades from the Department of the South reached Chesapeake Bay in August. The first one joined the Army of the James, but the other one went to Washington that month and then to the Valley in late September. Thus, eight brigades intended for the Army of the James were diverted to the Valley, and Meade transferred thirteen of his own brigades there. Losing those twenty-one brigades seriously weakened Grant's army group.

brigades from his own army group so early in the operation against Petersburg hindered Grant's ability to continue the mobile warfare of springtime. His reduced force was better suited to siege warfare than to swinging southwestward.

The ensuing siege was not tactical. It did not involve the saps and parallels and breaching batteries that had been hallmarks of siegecraft since the 17th Century. Yet Petersburg unquestionably was a siege in the broader, operational sense. The Federal army group literally beleaguered Petersburg—that is to say, it camped against the city, which is the essence of a siege. Grant's great entrenched camp east of Petersburg posed an immediate potential threat to the city, against which defenders needed always to be on guard. Even more significantly, that camp pinned the Secessionists in place at Petersburg and denied Lee the operational and strategic mobility that he had used to such good advantage earlier in the war. Such pinning in place assumed grand strategic proportions by December, as Grant fixed the foe in Virginia while other Federal forces under Major Generals William T. Sherman, Philip H. Sheridan, and George H. Thomas devoured the rest of the Confederacy.[11]

The entrenched camp, moreover, provided a safe and secure center from which Grant could launch attacks against the vulnerable railroads leading into Petersburg from the south and west and against the well-fortified but lightly garrisoned sector north of James River. That Richmond sector north of the James was an integral part of the Siege of Petersburg, as was the intervening Bermuda Hundred sector in Chesterfield County, every bit as much as were the sectors east and south of Petersburg itself. Since the 1930s, two excellent national parks have been responsible for parts of those sectors.[12] No such separation existed in 1864. From northwest of Richmond

11 The grand strategic importance of pinning Lee in place in the Siege of Petersburg comes through clearly in Grant's letter to Sherman, December 18, 1864: "My own opinion," wrote the General-in-Chief, "is that Lee is averse to going out of Virginia, and if the cause of the South is lost he wants Richmond to be the last place surrendered. If he has such views it may be well to indulge him until everything else is in our hands." *OR*, v. XLIV, pp. 740-41.

12 The U.S. Army, which was the original custodian of many Civil War battlefields, created the Petersburg National Military Park in 1926. That park was transferred to the National Park Service seven years later. In 1962, the park was renamed the Petersburg National Battlefield. It currently covers City Point, Battery 5, Fort Stedman, the Crater, Fort Wadsworth, many other Federal forts and a few Confederate forts east, south, and west of the city, and Five Forks. More Confederate strongholds (from Fort Alexander to Fort Maury

all the way around through Henrico, Chesterfield, Prince George, and Dinwiddie Counties to the southwest of Petersburg was just one siege, just one field of operations.

The attacks that Grant launched from the security of his center against these various sectors are called "Offensives."[13] The two initial offensives actually preceded the siege proper. They have already been discussed: the original assaults on the city, June 15-18, formed the First Offensive, and the disastrous defeats at First Weldon Railroad and First Reams's Station, June 22-29, thwarted the Second Offensive.[14]

Seven more offensives punctuated the remainder of the siege—four of them two-pronged, the other three first-strike. Looking at them even briefly offers insight into Grant's evolving generalship as he searched for success at Petersburg.[15]

---

as well as Fort Darling and Parker's Battery) survive in the Richmond National Battlefield Park, established by the National Park Service in 1936. That park pays much attention to sites of the Peninsula Campaign of 1862 and Cold Harbor, but it does preserve some earthworks from the Siege of Petersburg. Besides the previously mentioned forts, the park includes the Union fortifications from Fort Burnham [formerly Fort Harrison] to Fort Brady.

13 This author originated the concept of calling Grant's onslaughts throughout the Siege of Petersburg "offensives." The term was first propounded in 1970 in his dissertation at Rice University, "Grant's Fifth Offensive at Petersburg." Ten years later, it was introduced to a broader readership in the first edition of *Richmond Redeemed: The Siege at Petersburg*. Over the ensuing decades, the concept has been accepted in Civil War parlance by the National Park Service and fellow historians as a useful way to understand the siege. That dissertation and the 1980 book designated the Kautz-Gillmore Fiasco of the Ninth of June "the First Offensive." Reconsideration by this writer now regards that operation as the final phase of the Bermuda Hundred Campaign. The term "First Offensive" better applies to Grant's initial effort to capture the city, June 15-18. This reinterpretation appears in many of the author's published works since then, most recently in the Savas Beatie 150th Anniversary Edition of *Richmond Redeemed*, pp. xvi-xvii.

14 Following footnotes in this chapter cite some books on specific offensives. Good, one-volume histories of the entire Siege of Petersburg are Noah Andre Trudeau's *The Last Citadel* and Earl J. Hess's *Into the Trenches at Petersburg*. Edwin C. Bearss and Bryce A. Suderow have co-authored the two-volume *The Petersburg Campaign*. The entire community of Civil Warriors eagerly anticipates A. Wilson Greene's three-volume *A Campaign of Giants*, the first volume of which is scheduled for publication in mid-2018.

15 Grant's generalship is analyzed in Chapters 1, 3, and 5 of this volume and in Chapters 16 and 17 of Volume II of *Challenges of Command*. See also the author's *Richmond Redeemed* and "Grant, Ulysses Simpson, 1822-1885," in David and Jeanne Heidler, eds., *Encyclopedia of the American Civil War*, v. II.

Almost a month elapsed between his Second and Third Offensives. Preliminary skirmishing by two brigades of the X and XIX Corps north of James River, July 21-26, drew one Graycoat division there. Heavier fighting erupted on that Richmond sector, July 27, as Grant's Right Wing under Major General Winfield Scott Hancock, consisting of the II Corps and three cavalry divisions from Petersburg plus two local brigades, sallied out of the Deep Bottom bridgeheads. Cutting the Virginia Central Railroad running to Early's army in the Valley and perhaps reaching the capital were Hancock's goals. He was stopped far short of them and could count himself fortunate to beat off heavy Confederate counterattacks before he withdrew to Prince George County overnight, July 29-30. At least, this First Deep Bottom fighting drew four more of Lee's divisions from Petersburg to the Peninsula. Their absence left the Cockade City even more vulnerable when Major General Ambrose E. Burnside detonated his mine on July 30. The ensuing attack by Grant's Left Wing was expected to penetrate into Petersburg itself. Instead, that Battle of the Crater proved one of the most disastrous Union defeats of the entire war.[16]

Disgusted but not daunted by that debacle, Grant waited two weeks and then launched his Fourth Offensive. Again, Hancock led the Right Wing (the II and X Corps plus the Second Cavalry Division) from the Deep Bottom bridgehead on August 14. Two days later, he broke through at Fussell's Mill but could not exploit it, and within hours the Secessionists restored their lines. This time, the Right Wing remained on the Peninsula potentially threatening Richmond until August 20. By then, the Left Wing (the V Corps under Major General Gouverneur K. Warren) was already in action. Warren struck westward from the entrenched camp and cut the Weldon Railroad at Globe Tavern, August 18. Heavy fighting continued through August 21. Though badly battered by Butternut blows, the Bluecoats (bolstered by two divisions of the IX Corps) kept their clutch on the Weldon Railroad. However, when Hancock with three divisions sought to exploit the Left Wing's gain by tearing up the tracks south of Globe Tavern, he was routed at Second Reams's Station, August 25.[17]

16 Michael A. Cavanaugh's *The Horrid Pit* and James S. Price's *The Battle of First Deep Bottom* cover the Third Offensive.

17 The standard work on the Fourth Offensive is John Horn's *The Battles for the Weldon Railroad, August 1864*.

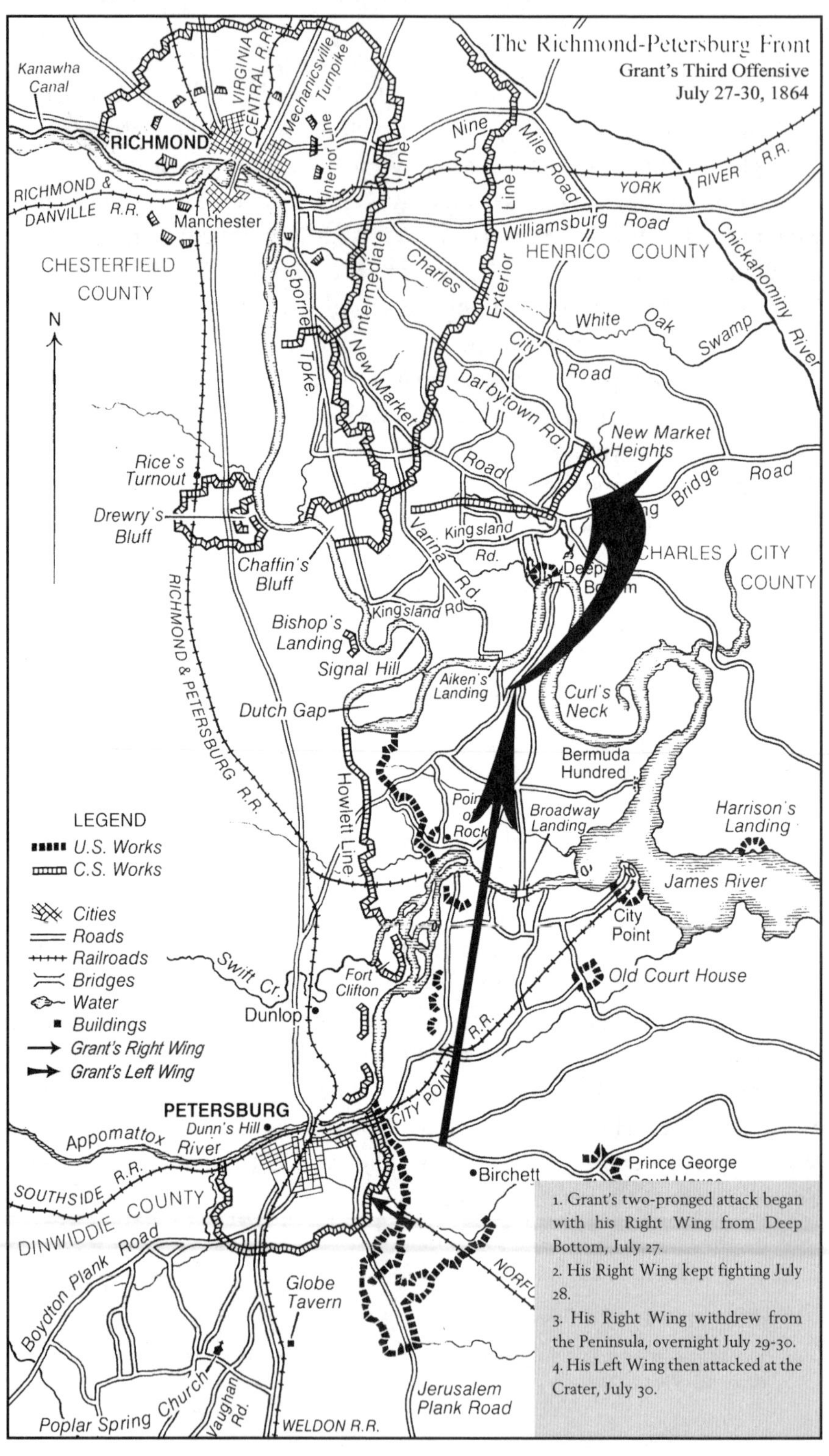

1. Grant's two-pronged attack began with his Right Wing from Deep Bottom, July 27.

2. His Right Wing kept fighting July 28.

3. His Right Wing withdrew from the Peninsula, overnight July 29-30.

4. His Left Wing then attacked at the Crater, July 30.

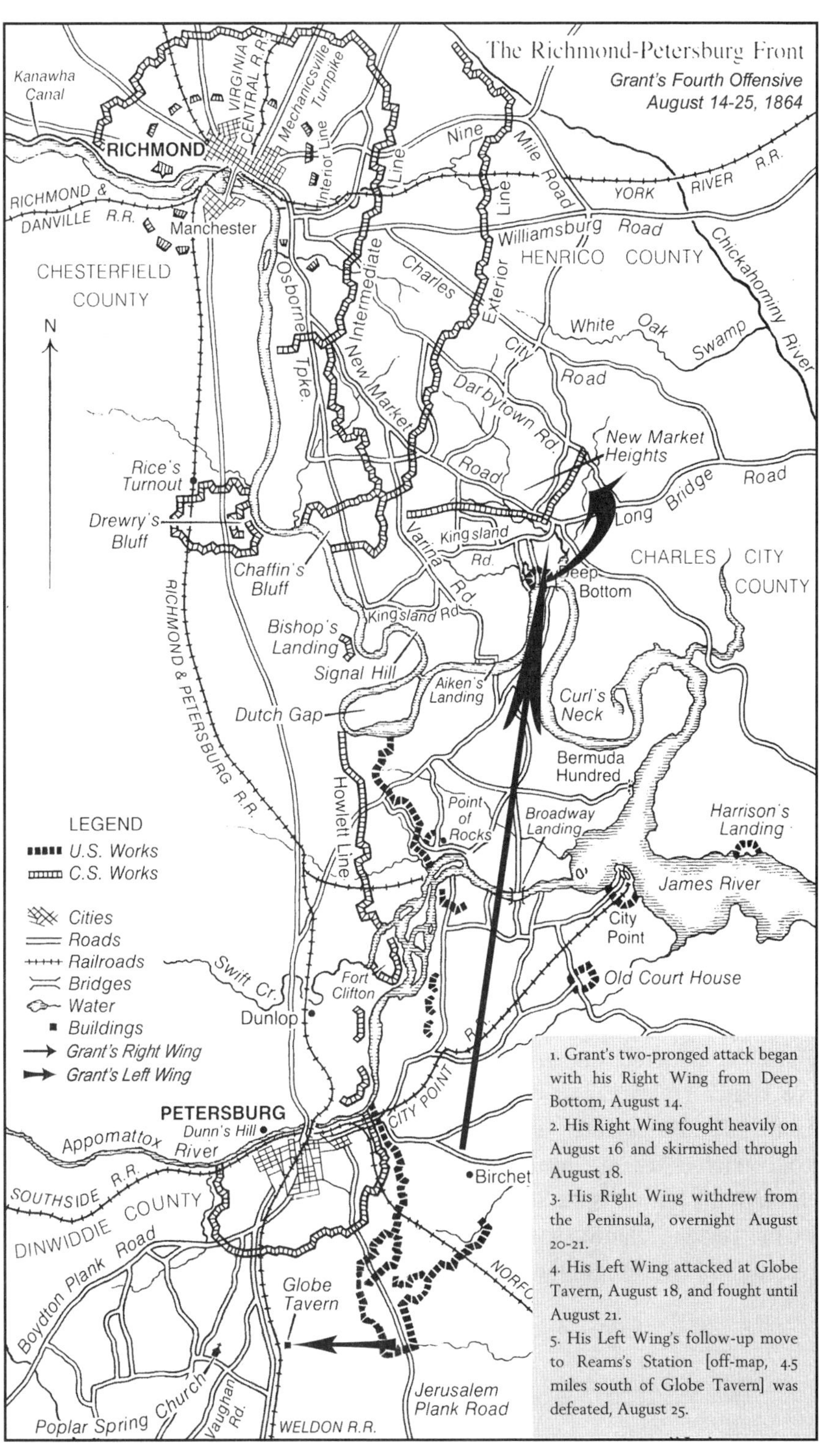

1. Grant's two-pronged attack began with his Right Wing from Deep Bottom, August 14.
2. His Right Wing fought heavily on August 16 and skirmished through August 18.
3. His Right Wing withdrew from the Peninsula, overnight August 20-21.
4. His Left Wing attacked at Globe Tavern, August 18, and fought until August 21.
5. His Left Wing's follow-up move to Reams's Station [off-map, 4.5 miles south of Globe Tavern] was defeated, August 25.

Another month went by, and Grant launched his Fifth Offensive on September 29. Again, the Right Wing struck first. This time it consisted of virtually the entire Army of the James, led by army commander Major General Benjamin F. Butler himself. His Yankees broke through the outer defenses at Fort Harrison, forced the evacuation of New Market Heights (which had stopped Hancock in the Third and Fourth Offensives), threatened the James River bridges above Chaffin's Bluff, and threw Richmond into the greatest danger of capture by a field army that the city endured on any day in the entire war. Yet because the Unionists failed to recognize and exploit their opportunities and because the Butternuts battled back so bravely, the great prize eluded Butler, and the Confederates kept their capital for another six months. Heavy fighting resumed at Fort Harrison on September 30, as the Federals repulsed savage Southern counterattacks.

While such combat continued on the Richmond sector, the Left Wing (the V and IX Corps of Major General George G. Meade's Army of the Potomac) punched through outer Confederate defenses on Peebles's Farm, south of Petersburg, on September 30 and nearly reached the vital supply lines along the Boydton Plank Road. Major General Wade Hampton's cavalry and Lieutenant General A.P. Hill's infantry stopped the Yankees short of that key artery, but the Southerners failed to recapture Peebles's Farm on October 1. Fighting fizzled out the next day, with the Confederates covering the plank road and the Bluecoats keeping the crucial road junctions west of Poplar Spring Church.

Those Battles of Chaffin's Bluff and Poplar Spring Church ended on October 2, but the fall of Fort Harrison had generated such strategic instability that the Fifth Offensive continued into mid-month. Repulsed in his efforts to recapture that stronghold directly on September 30, Lee tried to flank the Federals out of their new position on the Richmond sector one week later. He was again defeated in the First Battle of the Darbytown Road, October 7. Reluctantly reconciled to the loss of his outer works, he now concentrated on sealing off the breach that the Northerners had ripped through his ramparts on September 29. He easily fended off their follow-up in the Second Battle of the Darbytown Road on October 13. Meantime Meade and Hill fought the little Second Battle of the Squirrel Level Road on

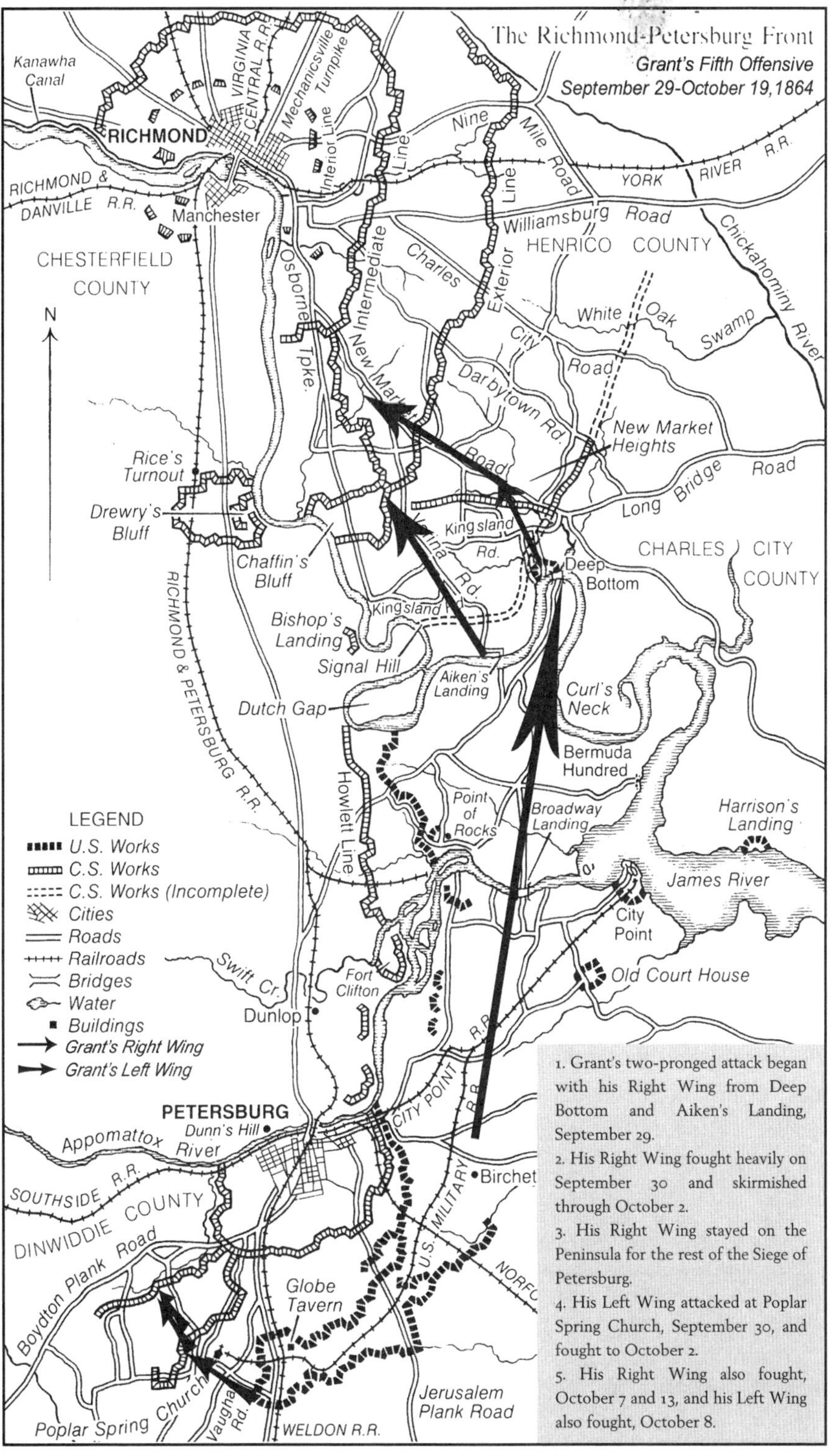
The Richmond-Petersburg Front
Grant's Fifth Offensive
September 29-October 19, 1864
RICHMOND
Manchester
CHESTERFIELD COUNTY
HENRICO COUNTY
CHARLES CITY COUNTY
DINWIDDIE COUNTY
PETERSBURG
James River
Appomattox River
Deep Bottom
New Market Heights
Chaffin's Bluff
Drewry's Bluff
Bermuda Hundred
City Point
Globe Tavern
Poplar Spring Church
LEGEND
U.S. Works
C.S. Works
C.S. Works (Incomplete)
Cities
Roads
Railroads
Bridges
Water
Buildings
Grant's Right Wing
Grant's Left Wing
1. Grant's two-pronged attack began with his Right Wing from Deep Bottom and Aiken's Landing, September 29.
2. His Right Wing fought heavily on September 30 and skirmished through October 2.
3. His Right Wing stayed on the Peninsula for the rest of the Siege of Petersburg.
4. His Left Wing attacked at Poplar Spring Church, September 30, and fought to October 2.
5. His Right Wing also fought, October 7 and 13, and his Left Wing also fought, October 8.

October 8 to reassure themselves that fighting a big battle was not then worthwhile.[18]

Big battles proved quite worthwhile on October 27, as Grant launched his Sixth Offensive. This time both wings struck simultaneously. On the Richmond sector, Butler's Right Wing, which had stayed on the Peninsula all month, moved northward and then westward to try to get around the Confederate left and reach Richmond. Meantime Meade's Left Wing sought to turn the Secessionist right southwest of Petersburg and cut the Boydton Plank Road, perhaps even the Southside Railroad, the last line linking Petersburg with the rest of the Confederacy. Both attacks failed. For the Right Wing in this Second Battle of Fair Oaks, the X Corps was checked on the Darbytown and Charles City Roads, and the XVIII Corps was bloodily repulsed on the Williamsburg Road. Meantime, for the Left Wing in this First Battle of Hatcher's Run, Graycoat works stopped the V and IX Corps. Farther left, the II Corps did reach the plank road near Burgess's Mill, but only Hancock's mastery of defensive tactics in this his final battle in the Civil War saved his command from capture by counterattacking Confederates. The Yankees did not launch the Sixth Offensive in order to extricate the II Corps from disaster. They launched it to achieve big gains on both sectors. Instead, they failed before Richmond and below Petersburg. On October 28, both Butler and Meade recoiled into the positions they had captured in the Fifth Offensive a month earlier.[19]

From late July to late October, Grant had unleashed four offensives. Each was two-pronged, involving his Right Wing north of James River and his Left Wing south of Appomattox River. Each offensive sought major gains on the Richmond sector. Even if they were not attained, moreover, Grant hoped to draw so many Secessionist soldiers there as to render Petersburg and its vital supply lines vulnerable to the second strike by his Left Wing. Such constants characterized all four offensives.

18 This author's *Richmond Redeemed* explores the Fifth Offensive, especially its two big battles, September 29-October 2, 1864: Chaffin's Bluff and Poplar Spring Church. A revised and redesigned edition was printed by Savas Beatie in 2014. For the Second Battle of the Squirrel Level Road, see his "The Battle No One Wanted," *CWTI*, v. XIV, no. 5.

19 The Sixth Offensive is covered in *Richmond Must Fall* by Hampton Newsome. See also this author's "The Battle of the Boydton Plank Road, October 27-28, 1864," in *Civil War Magazine*, No. LXVII.

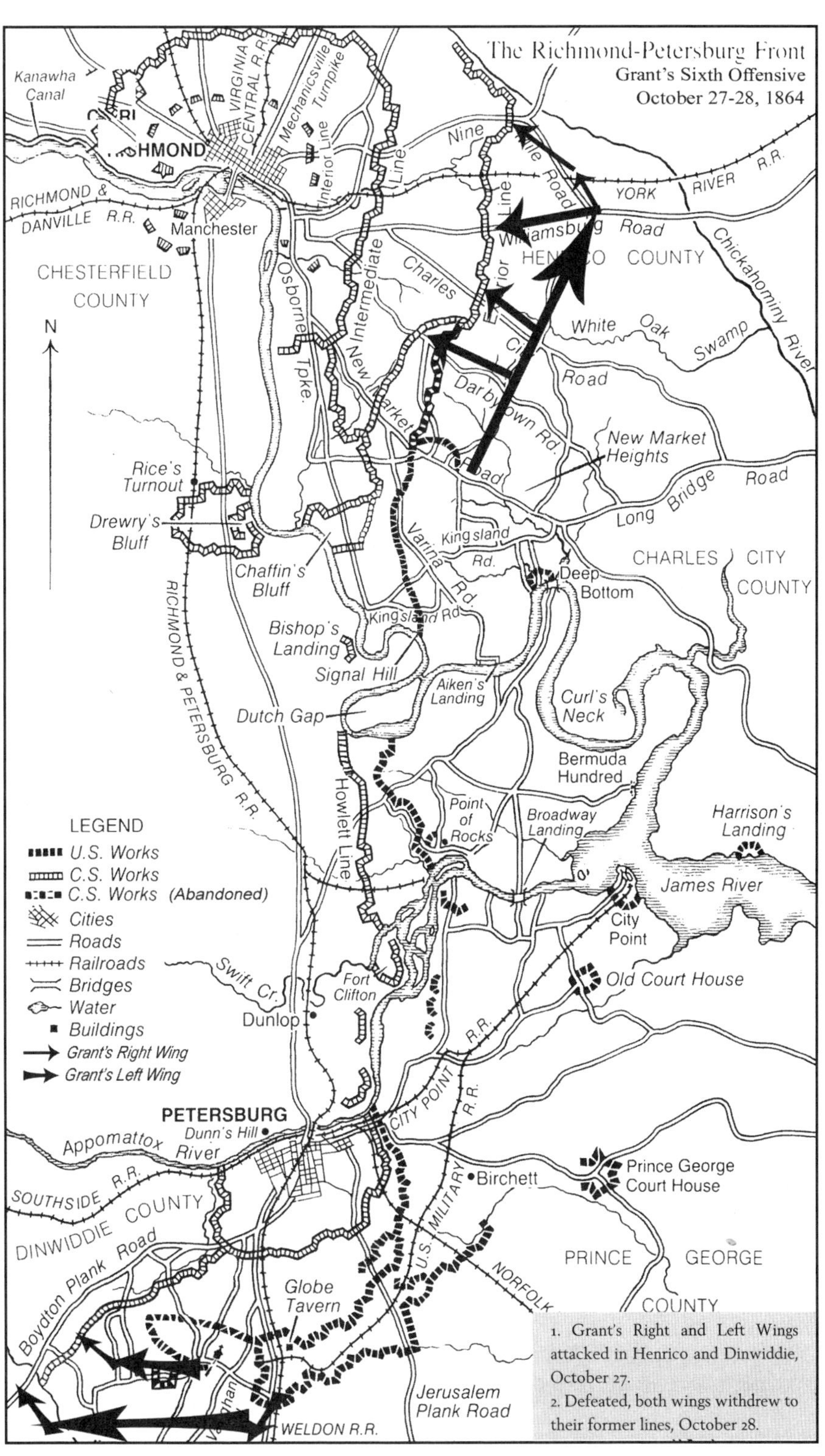
The Richmond-Petersburg Front
Grant's Sixth Offensive
October 27-28, 1864
LEGEND
U.S. Works
C.S. Works
C.S. Works (Abandoned)
Cities
Roads
Railroads
Bridges
Water
Buildings
Grant's Right Wing
Grant's Left Wing
Kanawha Canal
RICHMOND
VIRGINIA CENTRAL R.R.
Mechanicsville Turnpike
Interior Line
Nine Mile Road
YORK RIVER R.R.
RICHMOND & DANVILLE R.R.
Manchester
Williamsburg Road
HENRICO COUNTY
Chickahominy River
CHESTERFIELD COUNTY
Intermediate
Charles City Road
Osborne Tpke.
New Market Road
White Oak Swamp
Darbytown Rd.
New Market Heights
Long Bridge Road
Rice's Turnout
Drewry's Bluff
Chaffin's Bluff
Kingsland Rd.
Varina Rd.
Deep Bottom
CHARLES CITY COUNTY
RICHMOND & PETERSBURG R.R.
Bishop's Landing
Signal Hill
Aiken's Landing
Curl's Neck
Dutch Gap
Bermuda Hundred
Howlett Line
Point of Rocks
Broadway Landing
Harrison's Landing
James River
City Point
Old Court House
Swift Cr.
Fort Clifton
Dunlop
CITY POINT R.R.
PETERSBURG
Dunn's Hill
Appomattox River
SOUTHSIDE R.R.
DINWIDDIE COUNTY
Birchett
Prince George Court House
U.S. MILITARY R.R.
Boydton Plank Road
PRINCE GEORGE COUNTY
NORFOLK
Globe Tavern
Vaughan
Jerusalem Plank Road
WELDON R.R.
1. Grant's Right and Left Wings attacked in Henrico and Dinwiddie, October 27.
2. Defeated, both wings withdrew to their former lines, October 28.

What was different was the timing of the two wings' attacks. The Third Offensive saw sequential strikes. Hancock attacked out of Deep Bottom on July 27 but completely returned to the Petersburg sector before Burnside blew his mine on July 30. In the Fourth Offensive, Hancock again attacked from Deep Bottom on August 14 and had largely finished fighting before Warren struck for Globe Tavern four days later. Even then, the Right Wing remained on the Peninsula until the night of August 20-21, a continuing threat which Richmond's defenders could not ignore. Then in the Fifth Offensive, the Left Wing attacked below Petersburg just one day after the Right Wing struck on the Peninsula; both wings were heavily engaged, September 30-October 2. Finally, in the Sixth Offensive, Butler and Meade struck simultaneously on the Richmond and Petersburg sectors on October 27. Thus, from late July to late October, Grant adjusted the timing of his two-pronged attacks from sequential in the Third Offensive to simultaneous in the Sixth Offensive.

The total failure of the Sixth Offensive led Grant to an even more fundamental change in his operational approach. No longer would he conduct two-pronged attacks on both sides of James River. From now on, his Right Wing would remain quiescent on the Peninsula—still a potential threat to Richmond that could not be disregarded but no longer an attacker. Thereafter, he devoted all efforts to massive first strikes by his Left Wing against supply lines south and west of Petersburg.

The Left Wing's initial such strike came in the Seventh Offensive, December 7-12, as Warren's five divisions tore up the Weldon Railroad well south of Globe Tavern.[20] Even after losing uninterrupted transit on those tracks in mid-August, Confederates still used the railroad as far north as Stony Creek Depot and then trans-shipped supplies by wagon into the Boydton Plank Road and thence to Petersburg. Warren's destructive advance all the way south to the Meherrin River made that supply line much less usable. Even more significant was the Eighth Offensive, February 5-7, whose heavy fighting by the II and V Corps at Armstrong's Mill and Dabney's Mill enabled Meade to extend his left all the way to Hatcher's Run.

20 Warren's strike force contained not only the three divisions of his own V Corps but also the Third Division of the II Corps and the Second Cavalry Division.

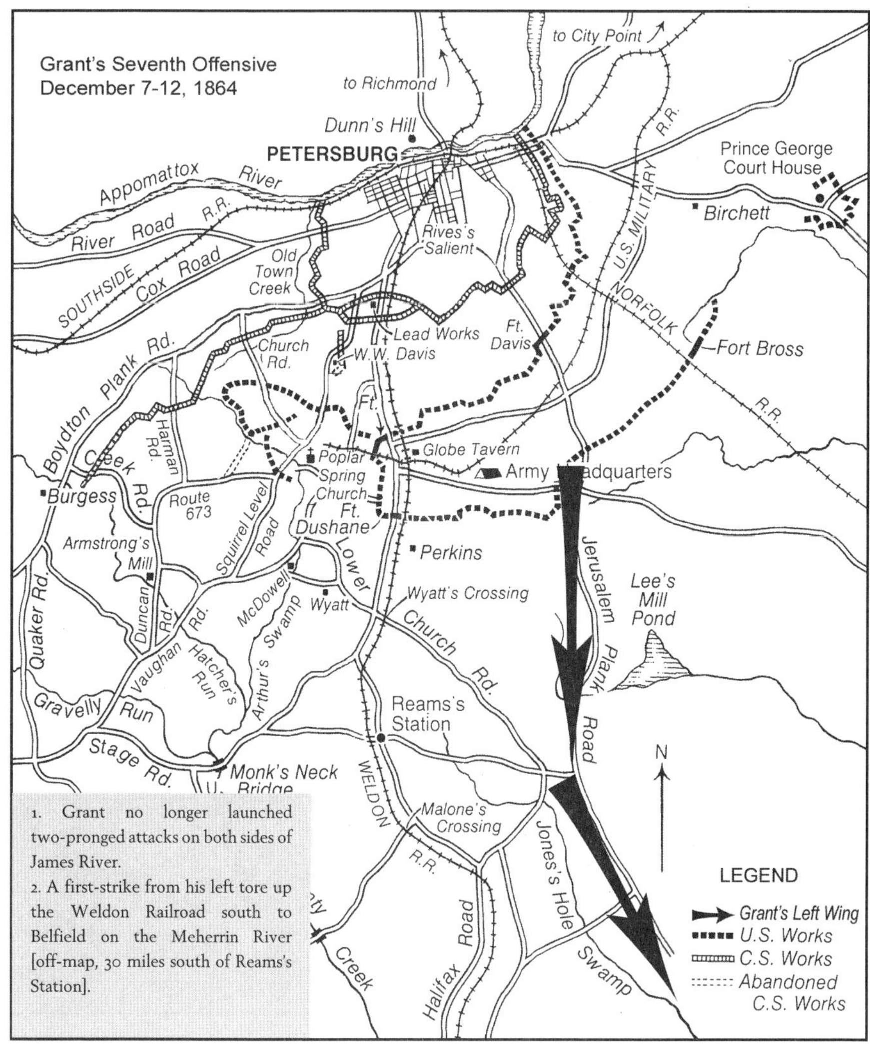

1. Grant no longer launched two-pronged attacks on both sides of James River.
2. A first-strike from his left tore up the Weldon Railroad south to Belfield on the Meherrin River [off-map, 30 miles south of Reams's Station].

Then came the Ninth—and final—Offensive. In a strategic surprise of profound importance, Grant reduced his Right Wing to just three divisions (two on the Richmond sector and one on Bermuda Hundred).[21] Undetected by unwary Graycoats, Major General Edward Ord, who had replaced Butler

21 Major General Godfrey Weitzel, commanding the XXV Corps, had charge of that part of the Army of the James which remained north of the Appomattox River. The three principal forces within his command were the First Division of his corps and the Third Division of the XXIV Corps (both on the Peninsula) and the Bermuda Hundred division on that sector.

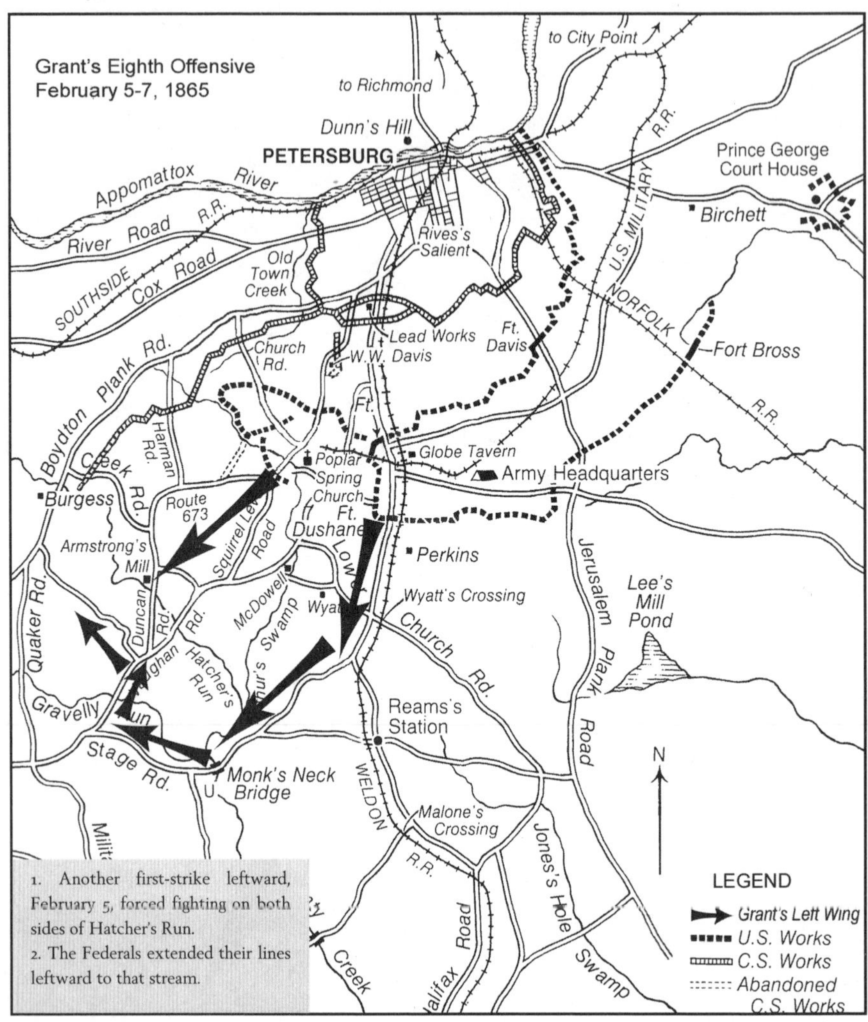

1. Another first-strike leftward, February 5, forced fighting on both sides of Hatcher's Run.
2. The Federals extended their lines leftward to that stream.

commanding the Army of the James, led his remaining four divisions from the Peninsula to the Southside to reinforce the Left Wing below Petersburg.[22] There his cavalry division and Meade's cavalry division joined Sheridan's two cavalry divisions, just returned from the Shenandoah Valley, on the far left. The VI Corps (also back from the Valley since December) and Ord targeted Confederate defenses of the plank road. The II and V Corps

22 Ord's mobile strike force consisted of the First and Independent Divisions of the XXIV Corps plus XXIV Corps headquarters, the Second Division of the XXV Corps, and the Cavalry Division of the Army of the James.

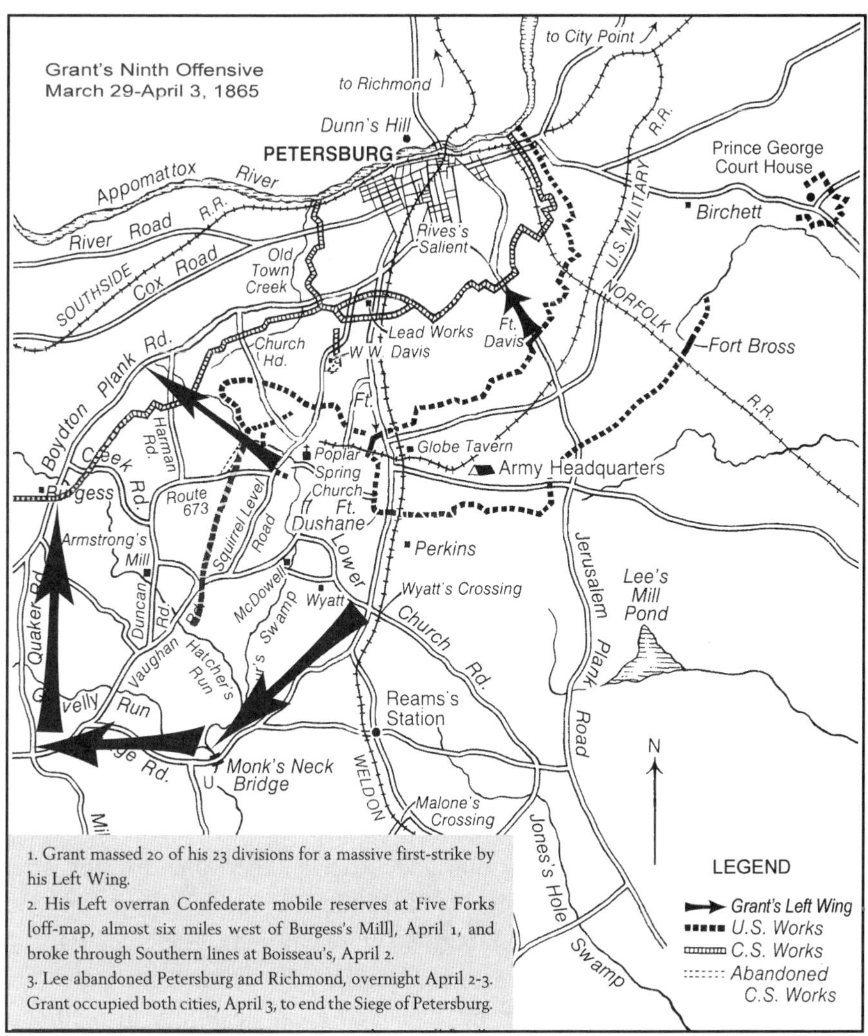

1. Grant massed 20 of his 23 divisions for a massive first-strike by his Left Wing.
2. His Left overran Confederate mobile reserves at Five Forks [off-map, almost six miles west of Burgess's Mill], April 1, and broke through Southern lines at Boisseau's, April 2.
3. Lee abandoned Petersburg and Richmond, overnight April 2-3. Grant occupied both cities, April 3, to end the Siege of Petersburg.

attacked west of Hatcher's Run, and the IX Corps, now occupying the entrenched camp east of Petersburg, stood ready to strike the Cockade City itself.

The Federals went into action west of Hatcher's Run on March 29. As ever throughout the Siege of Petersburg, Lee counterattacked the attackers. Time and again he gained short-term success, but this time the Northerners kept coming. On April 1, Sheridan overran the key crossroads at Five Forks. In an even more significant success the next day, the VI Corps broke through the outer defenses at Boisseau's Farm and cut the plank road and the

Southside Railroad. The Federals then reached the Appomattox River upstream from Petersburg.[23]

Now they closed in on the city from west, south, and east. Even though the IX Corps had failed to storm Petersburg itself on April 2, the city clearly was no longer tenable. Neither was Richmond. Overnight April 2-3, Lee abandoned Petersburg, abandoned his defenses in Chesterfield County, abandoned his positions on the Peninsula, abandoned his capital itself for a last, desperate flight down the Danville Railroad toward North Carolina.

The Bluecoats occupied both Petersburg and Richmond without resistance on Monday, April 3. Grant did not tarry there. That very day, his huge Left Wing, nineteen divisions strong, fresh from its victories at Five Forks and Boisseau's Farm, set off in hot pursuit. One week to the day after the final fighting at Petersburg came Appomattox.

Fighting down that long, bloody road from Culpeper to Appomattox had lasted eleven months. More than nine of those months had been spent besieging Petersburg and, with it, Richmond. That long siege offers insights into the evolving generalship of Ulysses S. Grant.

An obvious quality is his persistence, perseverance, tenacity—call it what one may. He focused his forces on the Army of Northern Virginia and the two cities that it defended and did not relent until he captured all three.

Yet in highlighting this hallmark of his strategy, its key dimensions also must be explored. For one thing, Grant's persistence was far from the futile folly of Burnside in sending one brigade after another, one division after another, to charge Marye's Heights at the Battle of Fredericksburg. June 3 at Cold Harbor and June 18 at Petersburg no more typified Grant's generalship than July 1 at Malvern Hill characterized Lee's. Quite to the contrary, within Grant's great fixity of purpose, he displayed great flexibility of methods. This flexibility came through clearly from July to October as he adjusted the timing of his two-pronged attacks on both sides of James River from sequential to simultaneous. This adaptability is even clearer in the final four months of the siege, when he abandoned two-pronged attacks altogether and relied instead on massive first strikes by his Left Wing.

23 Boisseau's Farm is now on the site of Pamplin Historical Park. Mr. A. Wilson Greene, the long-time, founding Director of that park (now retired), who did such good work there for so many years, has written the foremost study of the Ninth Offensive, *Breaking the Backbone of the Rebellion*.

Tactically, such first strikes brought the Bluecoats' overwhelming force to bear. Operationally, they penetrated less fortified Dinwiddie rather than butt up against the Peninsula's parapets. Strategically, they turned Lee's right and cut him off from the Confederacy rather than turn his left at Richmond and drive him into the Confederacy. Grand strategically, they helped win the war.

These changes flowed from another great quality of Grant's generalship: his ability to recognize, understand, learn from, and apply the lessons of experience. He is renowned for his ability to learn during his operations against Vicksburg in 1862 and 1863. Such a quality continued to characterize his campaign in Virginia in 1864 and 1865. Indeed, that ability to learn from experience explains why he explicitly and repeatedly forbade his subordinates from making frontal attacks against fortified, well defended positions at Petersburg following the disastrous repulse of such a charge there on June 18.[24]

That repulse was but one of many tactical setbacks that befell his forces between May 5, 1864, and April 7, 1865, including many at Petersburg. Such setbacks left Grant undaunted—in part because of his military peace of mind (his quiet confidence in his ability to win the war) and in part because he did not bog down in tactics.[25] Operations, strategy, grand strategy were Grant's domains. In those higher planes, he dominated the war in Virginia in 1864-1865. He controlled the strategic initiative; he wove even a succession of setbacks into successes; and he made things happen.[26]

24 As early as June 21, even before launching the Second Offensive, Grant wrote Meade that, "my desire is that Petersburg be enveloped as far as possible without attacking fortifications. . . ." This determination continued governing the lieutenant general's approach throughout the Siege of Petersburg. As late as February 6, in the midst of the Eighth Offensive, he told his senior subordinate, "I would not recommend making any attack against intrenched lines. . . . " *OR*, v. XL, pt. 2, pp. 268-69, and v. XLVI, pt. 2, p. 417.

25 Grant's quiet confidence in his ability to do the job comes through clearly in his Christmas eve letter to his wife, "I know how much is dependent on me and will prove myself equal to the task. I believe determination can do a great deal to sustain one and I have that quality certainly to its fullest extent." This confidence, so crucial to his conduct of command, is covered more completely in Chapter 5 of this book. The quote is from John Y. Simon, ed., *The Papers of Ulysses S. Grant*, v. XIII, p. 163.

26 The subject of "Success through a Succession of Setbacks" is the theme of Chapter 3 of this book.

"Just do it!" says a more recent Nike than the ancient Greek Goddess of Victory. Grant just did it. Through his flexibility of methods within fixity of purpose, through his ability to learn from experience, through his quiet confidence in his ability to do the job, and through his domination of the strategic and operational initiative, Grant won the Siege of Petersburg, won the great Virginia Campaign of 1864-1865, and won the Civil War. On General-in-Chief Ulysses S. Grant in April of 1865, Winged Victory alighted to bestow her victor's laurels.

Chapter 5

The Generalship of Grant and Lee at Petersburg[1]

The Siege of Petersburg proved the culminating component of the great Virginia Campaign of 1864-65. The contending armies came to that city in mid-June of 1864 because it was worth capturing for the Federals and therefore worth defending for the Confederates. It was the seventh largest city of the Confederacy, and it was the site of the Confederate Lead Works, where bullets were made. Most significantly strategically, it was the communications center for Richmond. From the northeast, southeast, south, and west, four railroads linked Petersburg with Southside Virginia and the rest of the South. Then one railroad connected the Cockade City (as Petersburg was called) with the Confederate capital, twenty-one miles to the north. Protecting Petersburg was essential to protecting Richmond; capturing the communications complex would correspondingly compromise the capital.

The Graycoats beat off initial Union efforts to storm Petersburg on June 18. Less than a week later, Yankee attempts to cut the Weldon Railroad south of the city were routed. By month's end, the mobile warfare of spring,

1 This chapter is based on a presentation that this author first delivered on October 14, 1971, in the "Perspectives in Military History" series at the U.S. Army Military History Research Collection (now the U.S. Army Heritage and Education Center). That was the first talk which this author gave anywhere after coming to Carlisle a year earlier. It became a standard speech, which was subsequently given to Civil War groups and other audiences all across America over the ensuing decades. Their feedback helped it evolve, but always it existed only in outline. This chapter now presents it in full text for the first time.

which had carried the armies from the Rapidan River to the Appomattox River, stagnated into the slowdown of summer, as the Siege of Petersburg began. Over the ensuing nine months, the Federals launched a series of strikes, called "offensives," south of Petersburg and north of James River. The Fourth Offensive in mid-August finally gained a clutch-hold on the Weldon Railroad. The Fifth Offensive in late September nearly netted Petersburg and even Richmond itself—but not quite. The Eighth Offensive in early February extended the Bluecoats' left all the way southwestward to Hatcher's Run. Then the Ninth Offensive, March 29-April 3, finally captured the Cockade City and the capital.[2]

Overnight April 2-3, the Secessionists abandoned Petersburg, abandoned their James River ramparts, abandoned their Peninsula parapets, abandoned their capital itself for a last, desperate flight down the Danville Railroad toward North Carolina. North Carolina proved too far away. The Butternut brigades had been too badly battered during nine months of siege. Federal forces were too advantageously positioned. One week to the day after final fighting at Petersburg came Appomattox.

With that summation of the siege, this chapter will focus on one of its most essential elements, the generalship of the opposing commanders: Lieutenant General Ulysses S. Grant for the North and General Robert E. Lee for the South.[3] The Illinoisan functioned at three levels at this period of the war. He had just become General-in-Chief of the entire Union army on March 10, 1864, and he remained responsible for directing all land operations of the entire Federal war effort. He was also Eastern Theater commander. And he headed the "army group" which operated directly against Lee from the Wilderness through Petersburg to Appomattox.[4]

2 The author's *Richmond Redeemed: The Siege at Petersburg* covers the first phase of the Fifth Offensive, September 29-October 2, 1864. Important studies of other offensives and of the siege itself are cited in Chapters 3 and especially 4 of *Challenges of Command*.

3 The generalship of those two commanders throughout the entire Civil War is analyzed in the first two chapters of *Challenges of Command*.

4 As is pointed out all through *Challenges of Command*, the term "army group" was not in parlance during the Civil War. Yet it accurately describes the force structure which existed during the war at First Corinth, Chattanooga, Atlanta, and Petersburg, so it will unhesitatingly be used. During the siege of the last-named city, Grant's army group consisted of the Army of the Potomac under Major General George G. Meade and the Army of the James under Major Generals Benjamin F. Butler and (as of January 8, 1865) Edward O.C. Ord.

Lee's responsibilities were somewhat less broad in that he did not become Confederate General-in-Chief until February 6, 1865—too late to shape the overall course of the war. However, he too was Eastern Theater commander, and he, in effect, had charge of a small "army group" during the siege.[5] The biggest difference is that Lee continued exercising direct command of the Army of Northern Virginia, as he had done for two years preceding the siege, whereas Grant had not directly commanded a field army since promoted to Western Theater command in October of 1863. The Virginian thus had to attend to administrative details in camp and to operational control in battle, but the lieutenant general at army group level was freed from such duties and could focus on strategy and grand strategy.

As grand strategist, Grant sought to defeat the Confederacy and thus restore the Union. To achieve that goal, he initially strove to defeat Confederate armies, especially the Army of Northern Virginia—if not destroy that army, then cripple it so badly that it could not keep the field against him. Lee thwarted Grant's efforts to win such a battlefield victory in May. By the time that the siege began, Petersburg and Richmond had replaced that army as Grant's targets—not because of some abstract dogma of European strategic theory about strategic sites but because of the inherent importance of those two cities: Petersburg as the communications center and Richmond as the seat of government, center of war industry, and symbol of Southern claims for independence. Capturing those two places, moreover might well also net their defending forces, as had happened when Grant captured Fort Donelson and Vicksburg. At the very least, losing those cities would force the Army of Northern Virginia back into the open field, where it would again become Grant's target.

In targeting that army and those cities, the lieutenant general did not expect to achieve success in one grand Napoleonic victory—one battle in one day that destroyed not only the enemy army but also the enemy will to continue the war. Unlike some Union and Confederate commanders, who fancied themselves modern Napoleons, Grant never succumbed to the allure of the Emperor of the French. But he did understand the advantages of attacking—tactically, operationally, and strategically. Earlier in the war—

5 Lee's army group consisted of his own Army of Northern Virginia and the troops of General P. G. T. Beauregard's Department of North Carolina and Southern Virginia and of Lieutenant General Richard S. Ewell's Department of Richmond.

from Belmont through Fort Donelson and Vicksburg to Missionary Ridge—Grant's attacks had repeatedly delivered devastating defeat to the Southerners in the stronghold, on the battlefield, in the theater. Not surprisingly, the approach which worked so well in the West was what Grant first continued in the East. But the East was not the West; the Army of Northern Virginia was not the garrison of Fort Donelson; and Robert E. Lee was not Braxton Bragg. In a series of bloody repulses from May 5 to June 18, Grant learned that lesson the hard way. But learn it he did. One of his greatest talents was his ability to recognize and apply the lessons of experience.[6]

By late June, as the Siege of Petersburg was beginning, Grant changed from a war of assault to a war of attrition. That latter term is often applied to him but mistakenly, in this author's judgment. He was not a modern Xerxes who sacrificed his own men by the thousands in hopes of killing a few score Secessionists, knowing that replacements were available to him but not to the South. June 3 at Cold Harbor no more typified Grant's generalship than Malvern Hill typified Lee's. Indeed, throughout the Siege of Petersburg, the Illinoisan repeatedly forbade frontal assaults against well fortified and well defended positions. "I would not permit any attack against the enemy, in an entrenched position," Grant directed Meade on July 12, 1864.[7] "I do not want any attack made by you against intrenched and defended positions….," he made clear to Butler on October 24; "let it be distinctly understood by corps commanders that there is to be no attack against defended intrenched positions."[8] As late as March 3, 1865, he told the Army of the Potomac commander that ". . . the object to be gained by attacking intrenchments is not worth the risk to be run."[9]

Grant waged his war of attrition not tactically on the battlefield but operationally in the siege, strategically in the theater, and grand strategically in the entire war effort. Throughout the siege, Grant fixed the Graycoats in place and denied them the strategic initiative. He wore them down physically and psychologically. He simply used the battles that highlighted his

6 This theme is developed more fully in Chapter 3 of this book, "Success through a Succession of Setbacks."

7 *OR*, v. XL, pt. 3, p. 180.

8 Ibid., v. XLII, pt. 3, pp. 331-32.

9 Ibid., v. XLVI, pt. 2, p. 806.

successive offensives as the means for attaining those results and ultimately as the method for pushing the weakened foe over the brink. That brink was almost reached on September 29-30, but Lee fought back and continued the contest for another half year until tactical victory finally became strategic success for Grant on April 2.[10]

Indeed, the Siege of Petersburg had already assumed grand strategic dimensions by late 1864, as Grant explained to Major General William T. Sherman on December 18: "My own opinion is that Lee is averse to going out of Virginia and if the cause of the South is lost, he wants Richmond to be the last place surrendered. If he has such views it may be well to indulge him until we get everything else in our hands."[11] Grant pinning Lee in place at Petersburg, while Major Generals Sherman, Philip H. Sheridan, and George H. Thomas devoured the rest of the Confederacy—that is the essence of a strategic siege.

Yet until that strategic success was achieved, the siege retained its operational dimensions, and battles had their place. These were not, as already explained, Napoleonic grand battles, nor were they the elegant sweeping maneuvers by which Sherman fought and feinted his way through Georgia and the Carolinas. Rather they were a series of short, sharp, two-pronged strikes, the first blow north of James River, the second one at or below Petersburg. The initial strike might well make significant gains of its own. Even if it was blocked, it would likely draw so many Secessionists to the Peninsula as to open up opportunities for the second strike on the Southside. From the Third Offensive in late July to the Sixth Offensive in late October, Grant adjusted the timing of the two strikes from sequential to simultaneous.

The total failure of those simultaneous attacks on October 27, moreover, led him to revise his approach more fundamentally. No longer would he attack on the Richmond sector. Over the next three offensives, he focused on massive first strikes with his left wing. Such an approach carried him down the Weldon Railroad in December, to Hatcher's Run in February, and to victory in April. This evolution of his operations from sequential double-

10 Grant judged the military situation correctly during the Battle of Poplar Spring Church. Lee was prepared to abandon Petersburg on September 30 if necessary to save the capital. Why Lee did not do so, and what happened instead, is covered in *Richmond Redeemed*.

11 *OR*, v. XLIV, pp. 740-41.

strikes in mid-summer to massive first strikes in early spring again illustrates his ability to apply the lessons of experience. They reflect his flexibility of methods within fixity of purpose. They, in sum, typify Grant himself—not brilliant but effective.[12]

In carrying out these evolving operations, Grant felt confident—not boastful like Joe Hooker, not arrogant like Phil Sheridan, not braggadocious like George Custer—but simply calmly, quietly confident in his ability to do the job. This confidence gave him military peace of mind, which freed him from the doubt, fear, anxiety, and torment that vexed so many other Union and Confederate army commanders. Such peace of mind enabled him to focus on winning the siege and winning the war.[13]

Winning at that level is the aim of a strategist. That was what Grant was by this period of the war. As General-in-Chief, as theater commander, even as army group commander, he was responsible for strategy, not tactics. He set objectives, initiated operations, often went to the front to observe, occasionally prodded the pace, but essentially allowed responsible subordinates to exercise the responsibilities of their offices. It was those subordinates who selected strike forces and developed battle plans. The Illinoisan, indeed, often deferred to subordinates in whom he reposed confidence, such as Meade and Sheridan.

As a strategist, moreover, Grant was a commander, not a leader. He did not inspire the devotion of his soldiers the way that the magnetic George B. McClellan, the handsome Winfield Scott Hancock, or the electric Phil Sheridan did. Indeed, soldiers rarely cheered when Grant rode along their marching columns. Yet he remained devoted to them—to sparing their lives from needless sacrifice, to protecting rights of prisoners of war (including U.S. Colored Troops), to avoiding using captives as hostages, and to keeping his men well supplied.[14]

12 Chapter 4 of this book, "Winged Victory," explores more fully Grant's use of two-pronged and single-pronged strikes.

13 Grant articulated this confidence in his Christmas Eve letter to his wife: "I know how much there is dependent on me and will prove myself equal to the task. I believe determination can do a great deal to sustain one, and I have that quality certainly to its fullest extent." John Y. Simon, ed., *Grant Papers*, v. XIII, p. 163.

14 For Grant's discomfort in using prisoners of war as hostages, see Richard J. Sommers, "The Dutch Gap Affair: Military Atrocities and Rights of Negro Soldiers," *Civil War History*, v. XXI, no. 1.

Supplies he had in profusion. Men he had in preponderance. Some critics seem to sneer at him for such superior status—to scorn his success since it stemmed from strength. Such criticism makes no sense. War is not sport between equals. War is strength. It is to Grant's credit that he recognized strength and understood how to use it. Anyone who thinks that his was an easy task should recall that all his predecessors in the East also had enjoyed superiority of manpower and materiel yet had failed to achieve anything better than strategic stalemate, if even that. One of Grant's greatest assets as Commanding General throughout the Siege of Petersburg and the Virginia Campaign of 1864-65 is that he understood how to convert advantages into achievements.

How he did so sheds light on his generalship at Petersburg. For one thing, he concerted his forces—in his army group at Petersburg, in the Eastern Theater, and in the entire war effort. He drew to himself more troops—from backwater areas, from Northern recruiting depots, and from the Shenandoah Valley.[15] Yet in doing so, he was not importunate, as McClellan and William S. Rosecrans had been in their incessant requests for reinforcements. Rather did Grant explain the need and ask—not demand. Indeed, in requesting a call-up of 300,000 more troops in mid-July of 1864, he explicitly made clear to President Abraham Lincoln that "I give this entirely as my views and in no spirit of dictation, always holding myself in readiness to use the material given me to the best advantage I know how." He was accorded such support because he maintained positive relations with

15 Even before the Siege of Petersburg began, Grant heavily reinforced the Army of the Potomac with the IX Corps from Annapolis and with regiments of the VIII and XXII Corps in Maryland and Washington, and he also bolstered the Army of the James with an Ohio National Guard division. He, moreover, transformed the Department of West Virginia and the XVIII Corps from garrison troops into mobile field forces, and he brought the X Corps to Virginia from South Carolina and Florida. Then after the siege was under way, he ordered two more brigades from South Carolina and seven from Louisiana to join him there. Only the Black brigade from South Carolina actually spent the rest of the war in his army group. A few units from Louisiana also reached his front in July but were soon reunited with the main part of their XIX Corps in the Shenandoah Valley, and none of that corps returned to Petersburg. One of the South Carolina brigades also went to the Valley, but it finally reached Grant in late December as part of the transfer of five veteran infantry divisions from the Army of the Shenandoah to Army Group Grant. Two cavalry divisions from the Valley rejoined him in March of 1865. Besides all these veteran forces, the lieutenant general also ordered to Petersburg that year twenty-four white regiments and eight Black regiments that had been created only in mid or late 1864. Four more new USCT units joined him in 1865, two of them just as the siege was ending.

senior civilian leaders. He understood that the enemy capital was Richmond, not Washington, and he did not do battle against his own government. He had already earned Lincoln's trust while serving in the West; he kept that trust at Petersburg. Indeed, the Grant-Lincoln relationship stands as a model for uniformed General-in-Chief and constitutional Commander-in-Chief in wartime.[16]

Other strengths of the lieutenant general also led to victory. For one thing, he showed respect for the Army of the Potomac and did not bring in Western generals to supplant Meade and all other officers who had earned that army's laurels from Dranesville to Rappahannock Bridge. Indeed, Grant was willing to work with and through his available subordinates, not around or despite them.[17] He also kept that army and the Army of the James well supplied with rations, munitions, uniforms, equipment, reinforcements and replacements—and mail from loved ones at home. The North's great numerical superiority of manpower and materiel did little good unless they reached the forces at the front. Grant, the regimental quartermaster from the Mexican War, understood that logistics is the essential undergirding of strategy, operations, and tactics. Throughout the Virginia Campaign and especially at the Siege of Petersburg, he maneuvered so as to remain in full supply up the great tidal rivers of the Old Dominion—at Petersburg via the mighty James River itself. Unlike John Pope and Meade, who earlier in the war had come to grief when Confederates cut their railroad communications, Grant grasped that the Graycoats could never sever James River.[18]

16 The quote from Grant's message of July 19 and President Lincoln's approving and almost bantering reply the following day are in *OR*, v. XL, pt. 3, pp. 333, 344.

17 Other than his own staff, including Chief of Staff Brigadier General John A. Rawlins, the only generals whom Grant brought east were Sheridan and Brigadier General James H. Wilson for the Army of the Potomac and Major Generals William F. Smith and Ord for the Army of the James. Even Wilson, Ord, and Smith, moreover, had served in the East earlier in the war. Smith soon forfeited Grant's esteem and became an enemy. Except for them, the General-in-Chief worked with generals who had long served in the Army of the Potomac. Indeed, in March, 1864, he declined Meade's magnanimous offer to relinquish command to Sherman or some other Western general whom Grant might prefer. Such self-sacrifice for the greater good of winning the war reinforced the Illinoisan's intention to retain Meade in that position.

18 Pope in August of 1862 and Meade in October of 1863 were tied to the Orange and Alexandria Railroad. When Lee cut that supply line in their rear, both Union armies had to retreat to the Heights of Centreville. Grant intentionally avoided that risk by moving leftward throughout the Virginia Campaign. He thereby succeeded not only in freeing

The Illinoisan reached James River and conducted the Siege of Petersburg, moreover, because he dominated the strategic initiative in the Eastern Theater. From the time he left Culpeper County on May 4, 1864, until he reached Appomattox Court House on April 9, 1865—save only for a few weeks in July when the Butternuts threatened Washington—it was Grant, not Lee, who decided when, where, whether, and why to attack. The Virginian was reduced to contesting the operational and tactical initiative. The strategic initiative remained firmly in Grant's control. "Everything is very quiet here," the General-in-Chief wrote a Chicago friend on November 13, "and seems likely to remain so *until I make it otherwise*."[19]

All of these strengths, so well illustrated in the Siege of Petersburg, mark Grant a great general. Yet he was not perfect; no general is, and no person is. He had his faults. Some lay in personal relations with fellow generals. Among those officers, he was true to his friends and bitter to his enemies. Some friends at Petersburg, such as Sheridan and Major General Edward Ord, deserved his respect. Others, such as Brigadier General James H. Wilson, probably did not, at least initially, in the sense that Grant catapulted this promising young staff officer into division command before he was ready for such responsibilities, although Wilson did eventually evolve into a very capable commander.[20] Then, too, while besieging Petersburg, Grant the General-in-Chief continued to give voice to his long-standing dislike of far-distant Rosecrans, Thomas, and Major General Gordon Granger.[21] Much

---

himself from that tenuous and vulnerable rail line but also in opening new lines of communication up Virginia's tidal rivers.

19 Italics have been added to the quotation for emphasis. Simon, op. cit., v. XII, pp. 415-16.

20 Wilson, who graduated from West Point just one year before the Civil War erupted, served on Grant's staff, October, 1862-February, 1864. Although he had never commanded troops at any level in the first three years of the war, Grant elevated him to head the Third Cavalry Division just three weeks before the General-in-Chief launched his Virginia Campaign. Wilson was unquestionably an officer of great promise. He eventually matured into an excellent division and corps commander. In the spring of 1864, however, his inexperience proved problematic for the Yankees.

21 The lieutenant general was downright disturbed over the apparent slowness with which Rosecrans and Thomas, respectively, responded to the Butternut invasion of Missouri in October and Tennessee in December. He nearly removed both officers. His concern about repelling invaders was understandable, but the intensity of his feeling reflected his long-standing dislike of those two generals. His resentment of Granger was relatively more recent, dating only as far back as the relief of Chattanooga and Knoxville, but it too

closer at hand, Grant genuinely respected Meade, whom he called "one of our truest men and ablest officers," yet he failed to recognize how Meade seethed under the surface at what the Pennsylvanian misperceived as disrespectful treatment by the lieutenant general.[22]

Another of Grant's shortcomings was also one of his strengths. His very confidence in ultimate victory at some future time occasionally made him overlook opportunities that were available in current operations. In his Fifth Offensive, for instance, he was convinced that it was over by September 30 or October 1 at the latest. He thereafter devoted himself to gathering reinforcements for his next offensive, whenever he might launch it. Both Meade and Butler wanted to prolong the Fifth Offensive. Out of respect for the Pennsylvanian, Grant allowed him to keep fighting until October 2. When the junior officer, too, saw no further opportunity, Grant readily acceded to his request to end the battle. Butler was not accorded even that latitude but was prohibited from continuing to fight. Hindsight reveals potential opportunities on both sectors that might have been exploited, but Grant remained oblivious to them in his confidence of preparing for victory next time in his upcoming Sixth Offensive.[23]

A third problem also grew from one of Grant's strengths: attenuation and attrition. In forcing the trench lines ever southwestward and attenuating the corresponding Confederate defense lines eventually to the breaking point, Grant attenuated his own lines as well. He had to leave significant portions of his own army group—sometimes over half—to man his earthworks. Such garrison duty drastically reduced troops for his strike forces.[24]

Even worse were the consequences for his comrades of his war of attrition. As he waged it against the Secessionists, that war of attrition was operational, strategic, and grand strategic. But as his own forces suffered

---

manifested itself in his unhappiness that the junior officer was again entrusted with corps command. On the latter point, see Simon, op. cit., v. XIV, pp. 77, 156.

22 Ibid., v. XIII, p. 299.

23 How Grant responded to Butler's and Meade's requests to continue the Fifth Offensive is covered in Chapters 6, 13, and 14 of *Richmond Redeemed*.

24 In the Fifth Offensive, for example, Meade used only thirty-eight per cent of his force in his opening attack on September 30. Even at maximum strength two days later, his strike force included less than half of his army. The rest remained to secure his front and rear lines of trenches and the army group's supply base at City Point.

from it, the attrition was tactical. His army group lost some 55,000 men from the Wilderness through Cold Harbor alone, another 61,500 during the Siege of Petersburg, plus 6,500 more for the Army of the James in the Bermuda Hundred Campaign through June 14—a total of approximately 123,000.[25] Those numbers are staggering quantitatively. They are even worse qualitatively, for the bravest of soldiers in the forefront of fighting—the colonels and captains, the sergeants and stoutest privates—were most likely to fall. Eight Union corps and divisions commanders and thirty-eight brigadiers died during the Virginia Campaign, including twenty at Petersburg.[26] Such losses dulled the fighting edge of famous regiments, even of the vaunted II Corps itself. Bounty men and immigrants fresh off the boat, with little commitment to the cause, could replace those casualties on the rolls but not on the rifle lines. New regiments, though sizable and shiny, were even more raw. Not until such newcomers were seasoned over the winter of 1864-65 did the Army of the Potomac regain some of its combat capability.[27]

25 Approximately 53,500 casualties at Petersburg came from Grant's nine offensives. The other 8,000 losses were inflicted by sharpshooting, shelling, skirmishing, and trench raids that flared almost incessantly during the siege. Besides all those casualties in Grant's and Butler's operations from May 5 to April 2, the Yankees lost approximately 24,000 more men in the Great Valley of the Appalachians, especially in the portion of it called the Shenandoah Valley. Including them raises the grand total of Union casualties to about 147,000. See the author's entry on "Petersburg Campaign" in David and Jeanne Heidler, eds., *Encyclopedia of the American Civil War*, v. III, p. 1504, and his chapter "Land Operations in Virginia in 1864," in William C. Davis, ed., *Virginia at War, 1864*, pp. 10-12.

26 These numbers include eleven generals and twenty-one brevet generals (including ten who were promoted or breveted posthumously) plus fourteen colonels commanding brigades. The cause of death includes combat (forty-one), injury (one), and illness (four). One officer in the last category passed away just twelve days after mustering out from service-related disease. Fourteen officers perished from the Wilderness to Cold Harbor, another one at Bermuda Hundred, eleven in the Valley, and twenty in the Siege of Petersburg. For names and numbers, see the sources in n. 25 plus *Richmond Redeemed*, p. 512 and the accompanying entry on that page in the expanded e-book edition of that work.

27 As already mentioned in n. 15, twenty-four new regiments of white troops and twelve of Black troops reinforced Grant's army group during the Siege of Petersburg. Such units were large, well-armed, and well equipped. With training, seasoning, and experience, many of them became good soldiers by 1865. But outfits that were thrown into action right away in the Sixth Offensive, after having been at the front for less than a month, fared no better than had raw regiments at First Bull Run, South Mountain, and Antietam in the East or at Richmond and Perryville in Kentucky.

Attrition, attenuation, missed opportunities, command personnel problems—besides all these, one more problem beset the Bluecoat commander: he had to wage war against Robert E. Lee and the Army of Northern Virginia.

Throughout the Civil War, Lee's overriding strategic goal was to secure his nation's independence. To achieve that goal, he had to deny victory to the Yankees by defeating their efforts to conquer the Confederacy. Earlier in the contest, he enjoyed considerable success by taking the strategic initiative, disrupting Federal combinations against him, defeating them in detail, and keeping them far from Richmond. Even though his efforts to liberate Maryland in September of 1862 and to carry the war into the North in the early summer of 1863 had come to grief, he still managed to maintain the Rapidan-Rappahannock frontier and to hurl back any Bluecoats who crossed it.

Not so with Ulysses S. Grant, who denied Lee the strategic initiative and drove the frontier from the Rapidan-Rappahannock rivers to the James-Appomattox rivers by mid-June, 1864. The lieutenant general thus confronted Lee with the constricting imperative of the close and immediate defense of Petersburg and Richmond.

Even under such circumstances, the Virginian still sought success through ways that had worked so well earlier in the war. Before the armies reached Petersburg and continuing well into the siege, he again sent forces to the Shenandoah Valley in hopes of reversing Yankee efforts to overrun the Old Dominion, as he had succeeded in doing in 1862. Two years later, his efforts also regained the strategic initiative but only for a few weeks in July. In the longer term, he failed to reverse the course of the campaign and the war. Not only did his forces eventually suffer devastating defeat in the Valley in the autumn, but also Lee's repeated reinforcement of the deteriorating military situation beyond the Blue Ridge seriously jeopardized his own position at Petersburg.[28]

28 Lee sent Major General John C. Breckinridge's Division and Lieutenant General Jubal A. Early's II Corps to Lynchburg and on to the Valley in June, while his army was still at Cold Harbor. Then during the Siege of Petersburg, he dispatched to the Valley the two divisions of Major Generals Joseph B. Kershaw and Fitzhugh Lee in August and Brigadier General Thomas L. Rosser's Cavalry Brigade in September. The absence of their seven brigades seriously weakened Lee's position at Petersburg without achieving offsetting gains beyond the Blue Ridge. Indeed, Lee's decision to recall Kershaw to Richmond in

There at Petersburg, too, Lee continued counterattacking the attackers, as he had done so successfully in the Seven Days and at Second Manassas and Chancellorsville. Now, however, his counterattacks rarely produced spectacular victories that drove the Unionists from the field. More often, his counterattacks succeeded only in slowing the Federal juggernaut and stopping it short of its objective—but not in hurling it back. Follow-up counterattacks, moreover, often incurred higher casualties without corresponding gains.

Yet Lee remained temperamentally disposed to attacking. He continued bold and daring. He frequently masked military weakness with bluff. Most importantly, he did not equate probable disadvantage with certain loss but rather strove to overcome threatening dangers and to redirect the military situation to his advantage. Some other army commanders, when threatened, would fall back. Lee did not fall back; Lee fought back. He thereby often defeated the threat and succeeded in saving his communications complex, his capital, and his country for almost a year.[29]

Like Grant, the Virginian was essentially a strategist for the Eastern Theater and for his army group protecting Richmond and Petersburg. Also like his Federal foeman, Lee relied on his responsible subordinates to execute operations. Capable executive officers—such as P. G. T. Beauregard, A. P. Hill, Wade Hampton, and, later in the siege, James Longstreet and John B. Gordon—proved worthy of his trust.[30] However, more disappointing lieutenant generals, such as Richard H. Anderson and Richard S. Ewell, required closer oversight.[31] Lee sometimes shunted them aside to

mid-September gave Sheridan the opening to win at Winchester and Fisher's Hill. Those battles forced Lee to return Kershaw to Early—too late to undo those defeats and too soon to prevent potential disaster from the Federal breakthrough at Fort Harrison.

29 Contrast Lee's conduct of campaign with General Joseph E. Johnston's in Georgia in 1864. The commander of the Army of Tennessee, whenever threatened by Sherman, would fall back. Lee at Petersburg, whenever threatened by Grant, fought back.

30 Hill was the only one of those five officers who served at Petersburg throughout the entire siege until he was killed on its final day. Even he was frequently ill during those nine months. Of the others, Beauregard and Hampton left for the Western Theater in late September and late January, respectively. Longstreet, who had been severely wounded on May 6, did not return to duty until October 19, and Gordon was not transferred from the Valley to Lee's army group until December 7-9.

31 Because of ill health and poor performance, Ewell was eased out of commanding the II Corps and placed in charge of the Department of Richmond on June 14. Although the II

less responsible positions, but he did not remove them altogether. Better replacements were simply not available. Because of their limitations, Lee had to pay closer attention to their tactical operations than did Grant with his senior subordinates. Also unlike the Illinoisan, the Confederate chieftain could not escape the administrative responsibilities that came with commanding an army. Grant, as army group commander, was spared such tedious duties.

Another major difference between them was that the lieutenant general faced the challenge of converting the North's advantages into achievements, whereas Lee's challenge was quite the opposite: offsetting onslaughts of a far stronger foe. One way that Lee accomplished this was to use all available forces. These included, of course, the veteran, first-class troops of his own army and of Beauregard's and Ewell's departments, including heavy artillery garrisons of Richmond. He also used reserves (youths age seventeen and men ages forty-five to fifty), militia (mostly resident foreign nationals subject to state but not national conscription), and Local Defense Forces (workers in war industry and government offices). In dire emergencies, individual soldiers were drawn from hospitals and military prisons, and civilians were swept up off the streets of Richmond to form provisional regiments. Then, too, the powerful James River Naval Squadron of three ironclads, five gunboats, a school ship, and shore batteries provided strong support.[32]

Such support from the warships, of course, was limited to the range of their guns from the river. Not just that river but all features of the ground Lee used to make his forces more effective. To protect them defensively, he made excellent use of field fortifications. They had long been his forte, and

---

Corps was the more important command, Richmond was no backwater, with Bluecoats so near at hand. The Richmond sector proved an important part of Confederate defense lines throughout the Siege of Petersburg. As to Anderson, he never measured up as Longstreet's temporary successor as I Corps commander after "Old Pete" was wounded in the Wilderness. When the senior officer resumed command on October 19, Anderson was reassigned to head the new IV Corps, formerly Beauregard's two infantry divisions and artillery brigade.

32 An entire brigade of provisionals was improvised in Richmond during the crisis caused by the Federal breakthrough at Fort Harrison on September 29—the day the Northerners came closer to capturing the Confederate capital with a field army than on any other day of the war until they finally occupied the abandoned city without resistance on April 3, 1865. Chapter 4 of *Richmond Redeemed* covers the city's response to that dire danger.

they reached their zenith in the Civil War during the Siege of Petersburg. He also relied on and modified the pre-existing permanent defenses of the Cockade City and the capital. Fortifying key spots turned terrain to his advantage. So did clearing fields of fire, relying on bramble-infested bottomlands as natural abatis, and damming creeks to form impassable moats.[33]

Yet Lee did not use terrain only for defense. He knew the land and its wood trails and byways, and he used such knowledge to launch surprise flank counterattacks on attacking Yankees. Through such surprise, his battalions often beat brigades, and his brigades often turned back corps.

He could make such counterattacks, moreover, because he maintained mobile reserves, almost always south of the Appomattox, occasionally north of James River, too. Such reserves included his cavalry, which from August until late March outnumbered Union cavalry by three to two. Hampton's horsemen thus could not only counter their counterparts in blue but could also man fortifications and even fight Federal foot soldiers defensively and offensively.[34] Such counterattacks, moreover, were not hampered by over-reliance on rigid organizational structure. Often a brigade from one division would be temporarily added to several brigades from another division to strike back at advancing Bluecoats. Only after the danger was defeated would the various brigades rejoin their parent divisions.

Foot soldiers combining to counterattack, horse soldiers fighting Northern infantry, surprise attacks by concealed forces in ravines and forests—all these actions reflect Lee's fundamental philosophy of warfare. He did not sit supinely in his fortifications awaiting Federal attack. When the Unionists moved out to attack him, he moved out to counterattack them.

33 The permanent defenses of both cities, though constructed at leisure when danger was distant, contained serious vulnerabilities—which often revealed themselves only when the Northerners stormed those works in 1864. Lee's use of fortifications to defend the Cockade City and the capital is well addressed in Earl J. Hess's *In the Trenches at Petersburg*.

34 Grant sent three mounted brigades to the Valley at the beginning of August and two more in mid-month. Their departure left his own army group with only four cavalry brigades (eventually reorganized into six). Only two of Lee's cavalry brigades, in contrast, went there in August and one more in late September. The Virginian's six or seven remaining brigades at Petersburg and Richmond thus considerably outnumbered Union horsemen. The Butternuts, moreover, placed their foot dragoons in forward trenches to help block advancing Yankees. Dismounted Northern cavalry, in contrast, remained back on the right bank of James River, where they could help defend Grant's headquarters and central supply depot at City Point but could contribute nothing to his attacks.

Such counterattacks succeeded in prolonging his defense of Petersburg for nine months.

Throughout that period, as throughout the Civil War, Lee enjoyed excellent relations with Jefferson Davis. As with Grant and Lincoln, Lee understood proper relations between General and President. Along with the President's trust came the latitude for Lee to apply his great talents on behalf of his nation.

Yet also as with Grant, the Virginian had handicaps and shortcomings. Many were beyond his control—most obviously the declining quality and quantity of manpower. The capability of Confederate commanders declined markedly from May 5, 1864, to April 2, 1865, as some of Lee's ablest officers and bravest men were killed or wounded. The best modern study of the Overland Campaign places his losses there at 33,500. Beauregard accounted for perhaps another 4,500 in the Bermuda Hundred Campaign, and losses throughout the Siege of Petersburg are estimated at 38,000, including 9,700 during the disastrous Ninth Offensive. Lee's total casualties, May 5-April 2, thus come to about 76,000.[35] Among the dead were two corps commanders, five division commanders, and twenty-six brigadiers, including eleven at Petersburg.[36]

35 This author's earlier research for *Virginia at War, 1864* estimated Southern losses from the Wilderness through Cold Harbor at 28,500. He now defers to the exhaustive research in Alfred Young's invaluable *Lee's Army*, which puts the losses 5,000 higher. Gordon Rhea, the foremost historian of that phase of the war, accepts Alfred Young's figures. The other numbers come from this author's work in *Virginia at War, 1864*, pp. 10-13 and in Heidler and Heidler, *Encyclopedia*, v. III, p. 1504.

36 Two of those commanders died of illness, one of them while a prisoner of war. The other thirty-one were killed or mortally wounded in combat. Twelve perished during the Overland Campaign; ten were killed in the Great Valley of the Appalachians, especially in the Shenandoah portion of it, and the remaining eleven died during the Siege of Petersburg. Nine of the brigade commanders were colonels. The other twenty-four officers were generals, including three major generals and one lieutenant general. These numbers for division commanders include Brigadier General John Hunt Morgan, who had just left Virginia when he was killed at Greeneville, East Tennessee (still part of the Great Valley) two days later. Also included is William H. Harman, who lost his life at the Battle of Waynesborough. As a brigadier general of Virginia militia and a colonel of Virginia reserves, he had led brigades at Harper's Ferry in 1861 and at Piedmont in 1864, respectively. Whether or not he still commanded a brigade of reserves at Waynesborough or simply served there in a personal capacity is not clear. See the sources in n. 35 and also *Richmond Redeemed*, pp. 511-12, especially the expanded e-book edition.

Few units remained to reinforce him after the siege began.[37] Individual replacements did help to fill the ranks that autumn—but not to restore the tone. The problem began when reservists and slaves relieved individual soldiers who had been detailed to duty far in the rear, so that those soldiers could rejoin their regiments at the front. Some of those arriving soldiers served well enough, but others, unhappy at being sent to the war zone, brought disgruntlement, which sometimes became disaffection, which spread corrosively among comrades and often degenerated into desertion.[38]

Making matters worse was the overwhelming repudiation of Northern Peace Democrats in the U.S. election on November 8. The re-election of Abraham Lincoln made unmistakably clear the Northern people's commitment to four more years of unrelenting war. Then one week to the day after the election, Sherman cut loose from Atlanta on his March to the Sea. The devastation he wrought weakened the resolve of even the bravest Southern soldiers at Petersburg. The combination of the destruction of the home front, the re-election of Lincoln, the repudiation of Northern Peace Democrats, and the disaffection among some replacements caused desertion to increase drastically from mid-November onward. Many deserters came into Union lines. Many more literally headed for the hills. The Appalachian hill country teemed with armed gangs of deserters who would fight to keep from being returned to the front.

Desertion worsened the Confederacy's constant shortage of manpower. Lee had long lacked enough men to attack successfully. By early spring of

37 Many Graycoat units came to the Old Dominion from the lower Atlantic coast and East Tennessee in the first six weeks of the Virginia Campaign. Once the Siege of Petersburg began, however, only three first-class foot outfits reinforced Lee's army group: the 9th Georgia Light Artillery Battalion, the 18th Georgia Heavy Artillery Battalion, and the Holcombe Legion of South Carolina, all of which arrived in October. Also, seventeen of Lee's own brigades rejoined him from the Valley, November-March, plus one new cavalry brigade (see nn. 30, 40). Among second-class reinforcements during the siege, at least four Virginia reserve battalions at Richmond and two such battalions at Petersburg helped guard those cities. A different kind of manpower arrived in 1865. As Confederates successively abandoned Savannah, Charleston, and Wilmington, sailors from defunct naval squadrons there were transferred to Richmond to man shore batteries along the right bank of James River between Drewry's Bluff and Bermuda Hundred. When those defenses, in turn, were abandoned overnight, April 2-3, 1865, the crews of those shore batteries were combined into a Naval Brigade, which went down fighting at Sailor's Creek. The crews from the James River Naval Squadron formed another Naval Brigade, which escaped down the railroad to Danville before Sheridan blocked the route.

38 See, for instance, *OR*, v. XLII, pt. 3, pp. 1179-80.

1865, so few soldiers still served in his attenuated lines that he could not even defend successfully. On a sector intended for eight brigades, the four that remained, even within elaborate works, could not stop the VI Corps from storming those defenses. That breakthrough at Boisseau's farm, April 2, doomed not only the lines along the vital Boydton Plank Road but the Cockade City and the capital themselves. The following morning, the Siege of Petersburg finally ended, as Northern soldiers occupied both cities, unopposed.[39]

Nor could Lee retrieve that disaster, because by then he lacked mobile reserves, which had counterattacked all previous Federal offensives. The arrival of Sheridan's six cavalry brigades from the Shenandoah Valley in late March finally over-matched the Southern horsemen, who had been a key component of those mobile reserves.[40] Nor did enough infantry remain mobile. Major General George E. Pickett's Virginia Division, admittedly, initially performed that role during the Ninth Offensive and actually drove the Union cavalry back to Dinwiddie Court House, March 31. But when Pickett forsook his mobility and assumed a defensive posture at Five Forks, only to be crushed there the following day, no other mobile reserves remained to retrieve his defeat—or Lee's on April 2.[41]

Further complicating Confederate conduct of operations is that these ever-diminishing forces were constrained within an overly complicated force structure. Unlike Grant's army group, which consisted of two combat-

39 The definitive work on this breakthrough is A. Wilson Greene's *Breaking the Backbone of the Rebellion*.

40 Four Confederate cavalry brigades also came from the Valley to Petersburg in 1865, but that year saw Hampton take two mounted brigades to South Carolina to oppose Sherman. Thus, only eight Butternut brigades of cavalry remained to resist the Ninth Offensive. Grant launched that offensive with an overwhelming force that included Sheridan's eleven powerful cavalry brigades, many of them armed with repeating carbines.

41 Brigadier General Nathaniel H. Harris's Brigade, which defended Forts Gregg and Whitworth so valiantly on April 2, and Major General Charles W. Field's Division, which that day entered the rightmost sector of the Dimmock Line west of Petersburg, from Battery #45 to the upper Appomattox, were not part of Lee's mobile reserve when the Ninth Offensive began. They were not pulled out of their own sectors on the Howlett Line and the Peninsula until overnight, April 1-2, and did not reach Petersburg until April 2. By then it was too late to counterattack the massive breakthrough spreading out from Boisseau's. All those reinforcements could do was delay the Union advance (through fighting by Harris and show of force by Field). They could not save Petersburg and Richmond, but they at least bought time for Lee to disengage and withdraw from those cities, overnight, April 2-3.

effective armies—the Army of the Potomac with from ten to seventeen divisions and the Army of the James with from six to nine divisions—Lee's army group had only one real army, his own Army of Northern Virginia with seven to thirteen divisions. Its other two components, the Department of North Carolina and Southern Virginia and the Department of Richmond, had only two infantry divisions and one cavalry brigade for the former and one infantry division and one cavalry brigade for the latter. Yet Lee's orders had to filter through those several intermediate department headquarters to reach very few troops.[42] At least that problem could be ameliorated by absorbing the larger department into the Army of Northern Virginia after Beauregard was transferred to the Western Theater in early autumn and by bringing the front-line Richmond troops under Longstreet's operational control on the Peninsula sector.[43]

42 When the Siege of Petersburg began, the Army of the Potomac contained seventeen divisions and the Army of the James seven. The Fifth Offensive three months later marked a low point for both armies, with ten and six divisions, respectively. Those numbers grew to thirteen and nine by the end of 1864 and to twelve and six going into the final offensive. All earlier dates include horsemen as well as foot soldiers. For March 31, 1865, however, those numbers apply only to infantry. There were also four cavalry divisions under Sheridan for a total of twenty-two divisions. Adding a provisional division of foot soldiers from City Point, which existed for a few hours on April 2, raises the grand total to twenty-three. For the Army of Northern Virginia, the corresponding numbers of divisions for those four dates are nine, seven, thirteen, and thirteen. For both sides, a major reason for the fluctuating numbers was the shifting of troops to and from the Shenandoah Valley. Also, both Grant and Lee each transferred two divisions to the Carolinas permanently, and Meade simply reorganized his V and IX Corps from four divisions each to three apiece. Then, too, the transfer of Beauregard's two former divisions to the Army of Northern Virginia in October nominally raised the numbers for that army—but not for Lee's army group.

43 Beauregard left Petersburg on September 23 to inspect defenses along the lower Atlantic coast. On October 3, he was assigned to command the new Military Division of the West. He never returned to Petersburg. Two days later, his headquarters in that city was discontinued, and his two infantry divisions, one cavalry brigade, and four artillery battalions were transferred to Lee's army. The horsemen had long been under Hampton's operational control; now they officially became part of his corps. The infantry and artillery reported briefly to the I and III Corps and on October 19 were constituted a new IV Corps under Anderson. However, since one of those divisions was, in effect, attached to the I Corps from late September until it left for North Carolina in December, Anderson's span of control was reduced to one infantry division, one artillery brigade, and occasionally a few attached brigades from the III Corps. The I Corps also exercised de facto control over Ewell's infantry division and cavalry brigade on the Peninsula front lines. After the emergency caused by the fall of Fort Harrison subsided and the Richmond sector quieted down over the winter of 1864-65, Ewell returned to his headquarters in the city and left his forces at the front under Longstreet's control. Only when "Old Pete" went to Petersburg on April 2 did Ewell take charge of all forces on the Northside for the final day of the siege.

More than this chain-of-command issue and than the qualitative and quantitative decline of manpower, the third problem besetting Lee was of his own making. To be sure, like some of Grant's problems, it grew out of one of the Virginian's strengths. Lee's willingness to strike back, to counterattack, to fight for what was worth defending explains his operational success in saving Petersburg and Richmond for so long. In any given offensive, his initial counterattack usually inflicted high casualties at low cost to produce good results. Problems arose when he followed up that first fighting with further forays later that day or the next day. Usually by then, the Federals were ready for him and repulsed his efforts. Such repulses incurred needless casualties, reduced the disparity of losses between the two sides, diminished the Southern sense of success, and gave the Yankees something about which to cheer. That Lee sought to exploit success is understandable, even praiseworthy. After all, some critics have denounced him for not following up earlier victories at Fredericksburg on December 13-15, Gettysburg on July 1, and Mine Run on December 2. At Petersburg, however, such follow-up attacks reduced, not increased, the extent of his victory.[44]

And yet to counterattack had been and would always be Lee's style of warfare. Earlier in the Civil War, this approach brought him spectacular success. In the Siege of Petersburg, however, it simply limited the Federals' gains and provided a means—at least temporarily—for offsetting his numerical weakness. Deferring defeat proved only temporary—not because such defeat was inevitable but because Grant finally found the way to accomplish it. The Illinoisan concerted his forces grand strategically, strategically, and operationally. He learned from experience and matured his approaches to warfare. And he waged a war of strategic attrition that converted the North's many advantages into achievements.

The generalship of Grant and Lee at Petersburg thus stands significant in demonstrating how to prolong war and how to win war.

44 Globe Tavern, Poplar Spring Church, Second Hatcher's Run, and even to some extent First Darbytown Road and First Hatcher's Run were battles where Southerners did well initially, but their follow-up attacks incurred higher losses with little or no gain.

11. Ulysses S. Grant. LOC

12. George G. Meade. LOC

13. Benjamin Butler. LOC

14. Edward O. C. Ord. LOC

15. Robert E. Lee. *LOC*

16. P. G. T. Beauregard. *LOC*

17. Ambrose Powell Hill. *LOC*

18. Richard S. Ewell. *LOC*

Part II:
The Generals

19. Jacob D. Cox. *LOC*

20. Daniel E. Sickles. *LOC*

21. David B. Birney. *LOC*

22. Alfred H. Terry. *LOC*

23. George G. Meade. LOC

24. Winfield Scott Hancock. LOC

25. Alfred Pleasonton. LOC

26. Alpheus S. Williams. LOC

Chapter 6

American Cincinnatus: Lincoln's Civilian Corps Commanders[1]

Photographers followed Abraham Lincoln everywhere. They were present when the President visited the Army of the Potomac on October 1-4, 1862, after Antietam. Three iconic photographs come down from that visit. One shows Lincoln and Major General George B. McClellan sitting in the army commander's tent. Another photo features McClellan and many subordinate commanders and staff meeting with the President. Not every senior soldier at Sharpsburg, however, belonged to "Little Mac's" army, as the third photo makes clear. It shows Lincoln with a general from a far distant theater—a tall, strapping fellow from southern Illinois: Major General John A. McClernand. McClernand called on his fellow Illinoisan

1 When the author started his higher education at Carleton College in September of 1960, he bought himself a going-away present: the Thomas Yoseloff reprint of *A Compendium of the War of the Rebellion* by Frederick H. Dyer. "Dyer's Compendium," as it is affectionately known, has been his constant companion ever since then. Also indispensable are Francis Heitman's *Historical Register and Dictionary of the United States Army, 1789-1903* and Ezra Warner's *Generals in Blue*. Besides these three classics, Frank Welcher's two-volume *The Union Army, 1861-1865* is useful. Those four books provide some information on the officers and military formations which this chapter covers. The structure, connections, and analyses in the chapter are, of course, the author's own. They were first given at the Chambersburg Civil War Seminar on September 24, 2017. They thus represent the most recent of the ten analytical essays in this book, but they reflect over sixty years of thinking about Civil War force structure and high command. Chapters 7-9 comparably contain continuing concentration on force structure and command.

and long-time legal and political adversary, Abraham Lincoln, in Washington, September 30, and the President invited him to come along to visit the Army of the Potomac.

The presence of this Westerner, this citizen-soldier, among all those Eastern Generals, those Regulars, underscores the fact that the Civil War was fought in the West as well as in the East and that citizen-soldiers as well as Regulars exercised senior leadership in the Union army. Indeed, forty-three non-professionally educated, non-Regular officers ("citizen-soldiers," they are called) commanded corps in the Federal forces, nineteen permanently and twenty-four temporarily—almost one-third of the 136 Yankee corps commanders. Two-thirds of the forty-eight Northern corps, moreover, were led by non-professionals at some period of the war: nineteen permanently and eleven others temporarily.[2]

Exploring all forty-three generals could fill not just one chapter but this entire book. Adding five other foreign-born corps commanders who had been trained professionally in European armies before coming to the United

2 Federal corps were numbered in respect to the armed might of the United States, not in respect to each army. Thus, there was only one IX Corps, whether it served in the Army of Virginia, Army of the Potomac, Army of the Tennessee, or Army of the Ohio. Even early efforts in the Army of Virginia and the Army of the Ohio to number corps only for that particular army lasted just a few months before those corps were renumbered within the national force structure. Hence the I and II Corps of the Army of Virginia became the XI and XII Corps, and the III Corps of that army resumed its original number: I Corps. Again, within the original Army of the Ohio, its three corps eventually evolved into the XIV, XX, and XXI Corps. Northern corps were numbered I through XXV. The following numbers from corps that were discontinued were reassigned to completely different corps: I, IV, VII, X, XIII, XVI, and XX. For the XVI Corps, moreover, its Left Wing and Vicksburg field detachment functioned as de facto corps distinct from the official headquarters in Memphis (The Right Wing eventually became the reconstituted XVI Corps in 1865 for the Mobile Campaign and so is not counted again here). Also in that campaign, Frederick Steele's column from Pensacola functioned as a corps. So did George Crook's command within the Army of the Shenandoah. Indeed, the latter force is often mistakenly called the VIII Corps. The VIII Corps was actually a separate command at that same time period, headquartered in Baltimore. The proper name for Crook's force was "the Army of West Virginia," but for the purposes of this chapter it may be considered an unnumbered corps in Philip Sheridan's army. Other unnumbered corps include the Reserve Corps/Army of the Cumberland (1863), the Provisional Corps/Army of the Ohio (1865), the Corps D'Afrique (1863-64), and two militia corps in the Antietam (1862) and Gettysburg Campaigns (1863). All these infantry corps total forty-one. Adding seven Cavalry Corps for the Army of the Potomac, Army of the Shenandoah, Army of the Cumberland, Army of the Ohio, District of West Tennessee, Military Division of the Mississippi, and Military Division of West Mississippi raises that number to forty-eight.

States would lengthen it further.[3] Those five will thus be excluded from consideration. Passed over as well are seventeen citizen-soldiers (two foreign-born and fifteen American-born) who had charge of corps only briefly (from a few months to even a few hours) and often in quiet periods.[4] Another excluded category is the four heads of geographic departmental commands—the VII, VIII, and briefly XVIII Corps—and the chiefs of two immobile garrison corps.[5] Rather will this analysis focus on mobile corps

3 Major Generals Peter J. Osterhaus, Franz Sigel, and Julius Stahel, Brigadier General Adolph Von Steinwehr, and Brevet Brigadier General August Mersy entered the Union Army from American civil life. However, they had been professionally trained in European armies before moving to the United States (Osterhaus in Prussia, Sigel and Mersy in Baden, Von Steinwehr in Brunswick, and Stahel in Hungary). For the purposes of this chapter, they are considered professionals and will not be further examined. Their comrade in arms, the Prussian-born Major General Carl Schurz, and Brigadier General Regis DeTrobriand from France were citizen-soldiers, but they are among seventeen temporary commanders who will not be explored. Schurz, Von Steinwehr, Stahel, and Sigel each commanded the XI Corps, the first three temporarily and Sigel permanently. The last-named officer also had charge of the Army of West Virginia. His fellow Badener, Mersy, temporarily headed the Left Wing/XVI Corps for one month in 1863, and Osterhaus served as acting commander of the XV Corps during the March to the Sea. DeTrobriand had the briefest tenure: II Corps, October 12, 1864.

4 The seventeen citizen-soldiers who commanded corps temporarily but who will not be covered in this chapter are: **I Corps**, James S. Wadsworth; **II Corps**, Francis C. Barlow, John C. Caldwell, Regis DeTrobriand, and Gershom Mott; **VIII Corps**, Erastus B. Tyler; **XI Corps**, Carl Schurz; **XIII Corps**, William P. Benton, Robert A. Cameron, Michael K. Lawler, and Fitz-Henry Warren; **XV Corps**, Morgan L. Smith; **XVII Corps**, Mortimer D. Leggett and William W. Belknap; **XVIII and XXV Corps**, Charles A. Heckman; **XXIV Corps**, Charles Devens; and **Cavalry Corps/Army of the Potomac**, William W. Wells. Lawler also briefly led the **XIX Corps**, July 6-7, 1864. Schurz was a Major General when he led the XI Corps at Gettysburg; Barlow and Mott were promoted to that grade as of May 26, 1865, but neither actually held that higher rank during their temporary tenure at II Corps headquarters after Appomattox. The other fourteen officers were Brigadier Generals.

5 The VII and VIII Corps were really the Department of Virginia and the Middle Department. These were large, territorial, essentially garrison commands, covering the southeastern part of the Old Dominion and Delaware, Maryland, and sometimes parts of western Virginia, respectively. The same territorial status defined the XVIII Corps (better known as the Department of Virginia and North Carolina) from August, 1863, to the start of the Bermuda Hundred Campaign. Even though their chiefs were among the best-known citizen-soldier corps commanders of the Civil War—Major Generals John A. Dix of the VII, Robert C. Schenck and Lewis Wallace of the VIII, and Benjamin F. Butler of the XVIII—they will not be covered in this chapter because their corps were not mobile when those officers headed them. The XVIII did take the field in the spring of 1864, as did the Left Wing of the XVI Corps. However, that wing was a static garrison in West Tennessee when Major General Richard Oglesby commanded it, April-July, 1863. Almost

that campaigned as parts of field armies. Thirteen citizen-soldiers were officially assigned to command those mobile corps, and seven more held temporary command for prolonged periods in important operations. The service of those twenty citizen-soldiers will be summarized and then generalizations about those generals will be offered.

Since McClernand has already been mentioned, this chapter will start with him. A prewar Congressman, he was a War Democrat: a political opponent of the new Republican Party but an ardent patriot who would fight for the Union—just the sort of leader whom Lincoln wanted to enfold into the war effort. Appointed Brigadier General of Volunteers as of May 17, 1861, he commanded a brigade under U.S. Grant at Belmont and a division under him at Fort Henry, Fort Donelson, and Shiloh. He had charge of the reserve of Henry Halleck's "army group" during the Siege of Corinth.[6]

By late summer of 1862, McClernand (a major general since March 21) considered himself worthy of an army of his own or at least an independent corps, and his visit to Lincoln in early autumn aimed to further that effort. The President did authorize him to lead three divisions—in effect, a corps—directly against Vicksburg late in 1862. However, Grant and Halleck, both of whom detested the ambitious McClernand, outmaneuvered him by adding William T. Sherman's old division to that force and putting Sherman in charge before McClernand reached the front. Their scheme came to naught because Sherman was repulsed at Chickasaw Bayou on December 27-29. Six days later, McClernand arrived, assumed command, and captured Arkansas Post, January 10-11, 1863.

His quasi-independent command lasted less than a month. Grant shifted his main army from central Mississippi to the Mississippi River and took charge of all forces serving there. McClernand was reduced to commanding the XIII Corps as Grant's senior subordinate. His corps was heavily engaged at Bayou Pierre, Champion Hill, the Big Black Bridge, and the two assaults

---

permanently immobile was the failed experiment of the Corps D'Afrique in Louisiana. It nominally had a corps force structure on paper, but it could actually field only a brigade strike force. Thus, it and its citizen-soldier "corps" commander, Brigadier General Daniel Ullmann, are also outside the purview of this study.

6 The anachronistic term "army group" was not used by Civil War armies. Yet it so accurately describes a frequent formation in that conflict—a group of armies, such as Halleck's at Corinth, Sherman's at Atlanta, and Grant's at Chattanooga and Petersburg—that this author does not hesitate to employ it.

on Vicksburg. He then released to newspapers his congratulatory order claiming great achievements for his corps and diminishing the deeds of the other two corps. This unauthorized release of undue credit gave Grant the needed pretext to relieve McClernand on June 19, 1863, while Vicksburg was still besieged.[7]

The insubordinate subordinate never returned to Grant's army. Not until February, 1864, was McClernand restored to commanding the XIII Corps in Texas. He led a brigade from there to reinforce its two divisions in the Red River Campaign and took charge of the entire corps in Louisiana, April 26. Five days later, he became so sick that he had to relinquish command. That corps was discontinued, June 11, 1864. Left without a command and still ill, McClernand resigned on November 30 of that year. He remained active in Democrat politics postwar until he died on September 20, 1890.[8]

Besides McClernand, seven other citizen-soldiers led corps in the Army of the Tennessee. The next most senior was Stephen A. Hurlbut, who was assigned to command the XVI Corps, December 22, 1862, the same date when McClernand was assigned to the XIII Corps. Hurlbut actually assumed his new command, February 5, 1863. A native South Carolinian but a pro-Unionist living in Illinois, where he was active in prewar Republican politics, he served as Lincoln's personal emissary to South Carolina in the Secession crisis. Appointed Brigadier General of Volunteers as of May 17, 1861, and Major General as of September 17, 1862, he led the Fourth Division at Shiloh, First Corinth, Iuka, and Hatchie Bridge. During the Siege of Vicksburg, he was left in command of West Tennessee, headquartered in Memphis, where he was quite content to stay. He did take the field with the XVI Corps during the Meridian Campaign but returned to more congenial garrison duty later in 1864.[9] His inability to intercept Bedford Forrest's Fort

7 McClernand's bombastic congratulatory order and the responses to it by Grant and the other corps commanders are in *OR*, v. XXIV, pt. 1, pp. 102-04, 158-86.

8 Modern biographies are Richard Kiper's *Politician in Uniform* and Christopher Meyer's *McClernand and the Politics of Command*. See also Heitman, *Register*, v. I, p. 657, and Warner, *Blue*, pp. 293-94.

9 In preparing for the Meridian Expedition, Sherman wrote Grant, January 24, that "the 16th Corps had become so domiciled at Memphis and along the rail road that it is like pulling teeth to get them started. . . ." Four days later, Sherman told his wife that "it was politic to break up the force at Memphis which was too large to lie idle & Hurlbut would not reduce it. I had to bring him away and make a radical change. He ranks McPherson and we

Pillow Raid disgusted both Grant and Sherman. The General-in-Chief asked sarcastically, "Does General Hurlbut think if he moves a part of his force after the only enemy within 200 miles of him that the post will run off with the balance of his force?" Sherman snorted back, "General Hurlbut has full 10,000 men at Memphis, but if he had a million he would be on the defensive."[10] Not surprisingly, they relieved him from command on April 17. Yet someone with his connections could not be ignored. On September 23, he took charge of the Department of the Gulf, by then a military backwater but a promising place to create kickbacks.[11] He was replaced in that position on April 22, 1865, and was mustered out two months later, lucky to escape credible corruption charges.[12] Postwar, he was active in Republican politics, served as first Commander-in-Chief of the Grand Army

---

have not confidence enough in his steadiness to put him [in overall charge] on this expedition. He is too easily stampeded by rumors. . . ." Hurlbut's conduct on the expedition worsened Sherman's opinion of him, though the Ohioan professed friendship. On April 11, the day before Fort Pillow fell, Sherman told Hurlbut frankly that "you have a high order of professional knowledge, but I do not think you naturally inclined to the rough contact of field service. Your orders and instructions are all good, but your execution not so good .... Grant thinks you cling too close to Memphis from a love of ease or other reason.... We must now have men of action. . . ." John Simon, ed., *Grant Papers*, v. X, p. 21; Brooks Simpson, ed., *Sherman's Civil War*, pp. 592-93; *OR*, v. XXXII, pt. 3, pp. 326-27.

10 Sherman told his wife that "Hurlbut is timid, and there is no use in denying it." In his order relieving Hurlbut, the Ohioan used the same word in explicitly rebuking the "marked timidity in the management of affairs since Forrest passed north of Memphis." When the former corps commander demanded a court of inquiry, Grant rejected the request as "not consistent with the interests of the public service.... Whether his course was 'timid' or not, it has been unsatisfactory." *OR*, v. XXXII, pt. 3, pp. 366, 382; Simpson, op. cit., p. 626; Simon, op. cit., v. X, p. 286.

11 En route from Illinois to New Orleans to assume command of the Department of the Gulf, Hurlbut stopped in Memphis. While there, he as well as his successor, C.C. Washburn, were lucky not to be captured by Forrest, who raided right into the city on August 21. Even though he did not snare the two generals, Forrest's daring raid forced the recall of the major Union expedition from Oxford, Mississippi.

12 The War Department ordered Major General William F. Smith to investigate corruption along the Mississippi River, especially in and around New Orleans. Much of it focused on Hurlbut, who was accused of taking kickbacks from cotton smugglers. Per Smith's recommendation, Major General E.R.S. Canby, the theater commander, put Hurlbut under house arrest, April 12, 1865, pending his being sent to Washington for court martial. However, the Illinoisan was soon released and was even allowed to eulogize Abraham Lincoln. He was mustered out on June 20, 1865—thus placing him beyond the reach of military law. With the war won but Lincoln murdered, the authorities seemed anxious to sweep this scandal under the rug rather than prosecute a former friend of the martyred president.

of the Republic, and held various diplomatic posts. He passed away on March 27, 1882, while minister to Peru.[13]

Because nominal corps commander Hurlbut spent most of his time in Memphis, other officers led the XVI's troops in the field. The three divisions of that corps which reinforced Grant in June during the Siege of Vicksburg were under Cadwallader Colden Washburn, a prewar businessman and Congressman and younger brother of Grant's patron, Congressman Elihu B. Washburne. He started the war as Colonel of the 2nd Wisconsin Cavalry on February 6, 1862, and was promoted to One-Star on July 16 and to Two-Star on November 29 of that year. As a general officer in 1863, he commanded the Second and then the First Cavalry Divisions of Grant's army in Arkansas, Mississippi, and West Tennessee, March-June; the Detachment of the XVI Corps in the Siege of Vicksburg, June and July; and briefly the XIII Corps in Louisiana, July-November, 1863, including the Second Teche Campaign.[14] He succeeded Hurlbut in charge of the District of West Tennessee on April 23, 1864, but that headquarters was no longer designated the XVI Corps. He commanded various districts along the Mississippi River for the rest of the war until resigning, May 25, 1865.[15] Postwar, he returned to Congress and served as Governor of Wisconsin. Especially noteworthy was his connection with another "General." He organized the company that is now General Mills. Death came on May 14, 1882.[16]

13 The best book on Hurlbut is Jeffrey Lash's *A Politician Turned General*. See also Heitman, *Register*, v. I, p. 559, and Warner, *Blue*, pp. 244-45.

14 Washburn temporarily commanded the XIII Corps in Louisiana, August 7-September 15, 1863, and again from October 19 into early November. Even though Major General Napoleon Jackson Tecumseh Dana was officially assigned to replace him on October 26, the Wisconsinite remained in charge of the three divisions of the XIII Corps at the front at least through November 7, including the Battle of Grand Coteau. By November 12, he had resumed division command and was en route to the Texas coast, where he operated successfully in December. *OR*, v. XXVI, pt. 1, pp. 356-57, 793, 800.

15 Washburn headed the District of West Tennessee, April 23-November 28, 1864, and March 4-May 29, 1865. Between those two tours, he had charge of the District of Vicksburg. Although his resignation dated from May 25, he remained on duty until his replacement arrived four days later. Ibid., v. XLIX, pt. 2, pp. 925-29; Welcher, *Union Army*, v. II, pp. 25-26, 79-80, 151-52.

16 The classic biography of the three Washburn brothers (including Israel, who served as Governor of Maine, 1861-63) is Gaillard Hunt's *Israel, Elihu, and Cadwallader Washburn*. (Elihu added the letter "e" to the end of his family name.) See also Heitman, *Register*, v. I, p. 1004, and Warner, *Blue*, pp. 542-43.

Throughout 1864, while Hurlbut and Washburn themselves remained in Memphis, combat troops of the XVI Corps operated in two wings in separate theaters. Professional soldiers Andrew J. Smith and Joseph A. Mower commanded the Right Wing. Both commanders of the mobile Left Wing were citizen-soldiers: Grenville M. Dodge and Thomas E.G. Ransom.[17] Like Washburn, Dodge is best known for postwar achievements. A railroad surveyor and engineer before 1861, he started the war as colonel of the 4th Iowa. He led a brigade at Pea Ridge so well that he was promoted to One-Star grade as of March 21, 1862, and he headed the Second Division/Army of the Tennessee, November, 1862-August, 1863. Though not promoted to Major General until June 7, 1864, he had charge of the Left Wing/XVI Corps from October 15, 1863, and throughout the Atlanta Campaign from Resaca until he was severely wounded, August 19. By the time he returned to duty, the Left Wing had been discontinued, so he was put in charge of the Department of the Missouri on December 9, 1864. There he fought hostile Indians all across the Great Plains in 1865. He resigned, May 30, 1866. He is best remembered as the Chief Engineer who completed the Union Pacific portion of the transcontinental railroad in 1869. He continued railroading and played a key role in recommending major military reforms to modernize the U.S. Army after the Spanish-American War. When he passed away on January 3,1916, he was the last of all forty-three citizen-soldier corps commanders.[18]

He was succeeded in charge of the Left Wing/XVI Corps by his Norwich classmate Ransom, yet another citizen-soldier from the Prairie State. A prewar engineer like Dodge, Ransom rose from Captain to Colonel of the

17 For most of 1863, as previously noted, the Left Wing of the XVI Corps served as a large garrison force in West Tennessee. Its immobile status puts it and its early commanders—professionals Charles S. Hamilton and Eugene A. Carr, German professional Mersy, and citizen-soldier Oglesby beyond this chapter's purview. In early November, however, the Left Wing under Dodge took the field to secure and extend Sherman's supply lines as he marched eastward to relieve the Siege of Chattanooga. The following April and May, the reinforced Left Wing hastened to the Georgia front. It then operated as a mobile field corps within the Army of the Tennessee throughout the Atlanta Campaign until discontinued on September 22.

18 Many of Dodge's writings are drawn together in his *The Battle of Atlanta and Other Campaigns*. Among biographies, James P. Morgan's new *Grenville Mellen Dodge in the Civil War* joins Stanley Hirshson's long standard *Grenville M. Dodge*. See also Heitman, *Register*, v. I, p. 376, and Warner, *Blue*, pp. 27-28.

11th Illinois by early 1862.[19] He later earned promotion to Brigadier General as of November 29, 1862, as well as brigade and division command. From March 15, 1864, he served as acting commander of the XIII Corps' field force during the Red River Campaign of 1864. Being acting commander did not spare him a bullet at Sabine Cross Roads, April 8. He returned to duty in Georgia, August 2. Seventeen days later, he was elevated to head the Left Wing/XVI Corps, which he led through the capture of Atlanta. When that wing was discontinued, September 22, he was transferred to temporary command of the XVII Corps, which he headed during the Allatoona Campaign until severe illness forced him to relinquish command, October 20. Nine days later, he died of dysentery near Rome, Georgia[20]—one of three citizen-soldier corps commanders to pass away in the war.[21]

By the time of Ransom's death—indeed, throughout the Atlanta Campaign—the other two corps commanders in the Army of the Tennessee were also citizen-soldiers. Like McClernand, John A. Logan was a prewar Congressman and War Democrat from southern Illinois. He entered service as Colonel of the 31st Illinois, led his regiment at Belmont and Forts Henry and Donelson; and commanded a brigade at First Corinth and a division throughout the Vicksburg Campaign. His fighting ability earned him one star as of March 21, 1862, a second star as of that November, and command of the XV Corps on December 11, 1863.[22] Likely because he feared at least in part that the XVII Corps, to which his former division belonged, would be left in backwater garrisons along the Mississippi River, he successfully

19 Ransom rose from Captain through Major to Lieutenant Colonel by July 30, 1861. His commission as Colonel was backdated to February 15, 1862, to recognize his valorous service at Fort Donelson. He, however, was still wearing silver oak leaves when wounded while commanding the 11th Illinois at Shiloh.

20 See Jim Huffstodt's *Hard Dying Men* and Jack Welsh's *Medical Histories of Union Generals* as well as Heitman, *Register*, v. I, p. 816, and Warner, *Blue*, pp. 390-91.

21 Eleven days before Ransom died, David Birney passed away, also from disease. He is covered later. The third citizen-soldier corps commander to give his life was Wadsworth, who was mortally wounded at the Wilderness, May 6, 1864, and died in Confederate care two days later. Although he had temporarily led the I Corps, January 2-4 and March 1-9, 1863, his tenure was too brief to be covered in this chapter.

22 On October 26, 1863, Grant recommended promoting Logan from a division in the XVII Corps to succeed Sherman in charge of the XV Corps. The War Department made that assignment the following day. However, the junior officer did not actually assume command until December 11, after the XV returned from the relief of Knoxville. James Pickett Jones, *Black Jack*, pp. 184-86.

resisted efforts to transfer him to command the XVII and insisted on remaining in charge of the XV. He led the latter formation throughout the Atlanta and Carolinas Campaigns.[23] He temporarily succeeded the slain James B. McPherson in command of the Army of the Tennessee, July 22-27, 1864, but—to his great disgust—was not left in charge of it because he was not a professional soldier. He was finally elevated to command that army on May 19, 1865, but by then the war was over. All he could do was lead it in the Grand Review five days later. He resigned on August 17, 1865. Postwar, he was active in veterans' affairs, especially the early years of the Grand Army of the Republic. He also served as a Radical Republican U.S. Representative and Senator and was the Republican nominee for Vice President in 1884 but was not elected. Two years later, December 26, 1886, he passed away.[24]

Another unsuccessful Vice-Presidential nominee was the fellow corps commander of Logan, Dodge, and Ransom: Francis P. Blair, Jr., scion of a family prominent in American politics since Andrew Jackson's administration. In 1861, as Colonel of the 1st Missouri Infantry and the 1st Missouri Artillery, he led the effort to save St. Louis and Missouri for the Union. Thereafter, as a Brigadier General (August 7, 1862) and a Major General (November 29, 1862), he headed a brigade and division against Vicksburg. He had charge of the XV Corps during the Siege of Chattanooga and the XVII Corps during the Atlanta Campaign, the March to the Sea, and the Carolinas Campaign. He resigned from service, November 1, 1865. Postwar, he reverted to the Democrat politics of his forebears and was the Democrat nominee for Vice President in 1868. Running against a ticket headed by Ulysses S. Grant, the Democrats had no chance that year. He was

23 In January, 1864, Logan actually asked to switch places with James B. McPherson as respective commanders of the XV and XVII Corps. Nothing came of that proposal. The Illinoisan's attitude was much different the following March, when Lincoln himself suggested transferring him to command his former XVII Corps and restoring Frank Blair to permanent command of the XV. Logan successfully resisted "this act of injustice to me," ostensibly because he had familiarized himself with the XV but likely also because he knew it would see much action—and earn him much renown—as soon as the Atlanta Campaign began in early May, whereas the XVII would not reach the front until mid-June at the earliest. Indeed, it is possible that Logan wanted to return to the XVII in January not because of old attachments to it but because it was on the verge of moving against Meridian. Ibid., pp. 190-91; Gary Ecelbarger's *Black Jack Logan,* p. 164.

24 The major biographies of Logan are Jones and Ecelbarger. See also Heitman, *Register*, v. I, p. 638, and Warner, *Blue*, pp. 281-83.

elected to a two-year unexpired term in the U.S. Senate in 1871 and passed away four years later (July 8, 1875).[25]

Six other citizen-soldiers served as corps commanders exclusively in the Western Theater. One of them, Benjamin H. Grierson, made his reputation in the Department and Army of the Tennessee, and he led a corps in that department and elsewhere. A prewar music teacher, he served as major and colonel of the 6th Illinois Cavalry and led a brigade on a renowned raid the length of the Magnolia State during the Vicksburg Campaign, for which he was promoted to Brigadier General as of June 3, 1863. The following year, he commanded a division (eventually designated the Fourth Cavalry Division) operating out of Memphis against Forrest. That July 25, he was placed in charge of the Cavalry Corps of the District of West Tennessee, which he commanded until early November, when it was absorbed into James H. Wilson's new Cavalry Corps of the Military Division of the Mississippi.[26] March 2, 1865, Grierson, whom Grant deemed "a most successful cavalry commander," was promoted to command the new Cavalry Corps of the Military Division of West Mississippi.[27] The war ended, however, before the disparate elements of his corps came together. He himself reached the front at Mobile the day that city surrendered. In the war's few remaining weeks, his horsemen operated in Alabama as a division, not a corps. Already breveted a Major General as of February 10, 1865, he was promoted to that full grade fifteen weeks later. He was mustered out of

25 General Blair and his famous family are covered in William E. Smith's *The Francis Preston Blair Family in Politics* and in Virginia Laas's, ed., *Wartime Washington*. See also Heitman, *Register*, v. I, p. 222, and Warner, *Blue*, pp. 35-37.

26 Wilson assumed command of his new corps, October 24, 1864, and began issuing orders to Grierson two days later. November 6, the date when the superior officer officially designated Grierson's force "the Fourth Cavalry Division," effectively marks the end of the Cavalry Corps of the District of West Tennessee. *OR*, v. XXXIX, pt. 3, pp. 414, 416, 459-60, 661-62.

27 Grierson bridled at being subordinated to Wilson. Their relations deteriorated so badly that the corps commander relieved Grierson from command of the Fourth Cavalry Division on December 13. Rather than leave, however, Grierson conducted another highly successful raid against the Mobile and Ohio Railroad at the end of the month. Only after the strategic situation in the West settled down in January did the junior officer actually depart. On learning that he was available, Grant met with him in Washington and selected him to command the cavalry of Canby's army. Grierson was officially assigned to duty on February 12; he actually took charge of the new cavalry command, March 2, 1865. Simon, op. cit., v. XIII, pp. 396-98; *OR*, v. XLVIII, pt. 1, pp. 786, 823, 1056-57, and v. XLIX, pt. 1, pp. 617, 679.

his volunteer commission, April 30, 1866—but not out of the Army. He was one of five citizen-soldier chiefs of corps to continue in Regular service postwar. He was the first colonel of the new all-Black 10th U.S. Cavalry (the "Buffalo Soldiers") from 1866 to 1890, when he became Brigadier General, U.S. Army, April 5, 1890. He retired three months later and died, September 1, 1911.[28]

Another Western general who stayed in service postwar was Thomas L. Crittenden, who hailed from the prominent Kentucky political family. Unlike his older brother, George, who served in the Old Army and then became a Confederate general, Thomas was a citizen-soldier lawyer who fought for the Union. Commissioned Brigadier General on September 27, 1861, and Major General on July 16, 1862, he commanded the Fifth Division, Army of the Ohio at Shiloh and the equivalent of a corps (eventually numbered the XXI on January 9, 1863) at Perryville, Stone's River, Tullahoma, and Chickamauga. When the Army of the Cumberland was reorganized and the XXI Corps was discontinued on October 9, 1863, he was one of five senior generals to lose a command.[29] He returned to duty on May 11, 1864, commanding the First Division of the IX Corps in Virginia, but he considered division command beneath his stature and resigned that command, June 9. Later that month, at Secretary of War Edwin Stanton's urging, Sherman, who wished the Kentuckian "all honor and success," offered him a division in the Army of the Cumberland in Georgia. This position, too, Crittenden declined as too low for a former corps commander in that army. In disgust, Sherman withdrew the offer. Crittenden held no further command in the Civil War and resigned on December 13, 1864.[30] He served briefly in Kentucky politics in 1866 but longed for army life. Despite his mixed war record, his connections netted him the colonelcy of the new

28 Grierson's memoirs were published in 2008 as *A Just and Righteous Cause*. The classic biography of him is William Leckie's *Unlikely Warriors*. Bruce Dinges' dissertation, "The Making of a Cavalryman," has enduring value. See also Heitman, *Register*, v. I, p. 478, and Warner, *Blue*, pp. 189-90.

29 Besides Crittenden, Major General Alexander M. McCook, commanding the XX Corps, and Brigadier Generals James S. Negley and Horatio P. VanCleve, commanding divisions in the XIV and XXI Corps, respectively, were relieved of those commands. Army of the Cumberland commander, Major General William S. Rosecrans himself, was relieved on October 18.

30 *OR*, v. XXXVIII, pt. 4, pp. 433, 443, 461, 641, and pt. 5, pp. 3-4.

32nd U.S. Infantry in Arizona Territory later that year. When the Regular Army was reduced in 1869, he was transferred to command the 17th U.S. Infantry in Dakota Territory.[31] He retired on May 19, 1881, and passed away October 23, 1893.[32]

A fellow Kentuckian like Crittenden by birth and fellow Illinoisan like McClernand by entry into service, John M. Palmer started the Civil War as colonel of the 14th Illinois. He received his first star on December 20 of that year and his second star as of the following November 29. This prewar Democrat and Republican politician commanded a brigade at Farmington and a division at New Madrid, Stone's River, and Chickamauga. Thereafter, he led the XIV Corps from Missionary Ridge to Utoy Creek. Because in the latter battle he refused to be subordinated to Major General John M. Schofield, his junior in date of rank but his senior in office, he was relieved from corps command on August 6, 1864.[33] The following February, he was placed in charge of the new Department of Kentucky, which he commanded until April of 1866. He was mustered out of Volunteer Service in September of that year. Postwar, he was active in both Republican and Democrat

31 As Colonel of the 32nd U.S., Crittenden commanded the District of Tucson. With the 17th U.S., he initially served on Reconstruction duty in Richmond. From there, his regiment moved to Dakota, where his headquarters were at Fort Rice. The 17th remained in Indian country, but Crittenden himself returned east and served on various boards and courts martial. He commanded the General Recruiting Service in New York City, 1878-80. His final seven months were spent on leave, and he retired May 19, 1881.

32 Crittenden is covered in Damon Eubank's *The John J. Crittenden Family in War and Peace*. See also Heitman, *Register*, v. I, p. 339, and Warner, *Blue*, pp. 100-01.

33 As a Major General to rank continuously from November 29, 1862, Palmer considered himself senior to Major General John M. Schofield, whose initial Two-Star commission as of that date expired the following March, only to have his reappointment to that grade backdated to November 29, one file before Palmer. Irrespective of dates of rank, army commander Schofield took precedence over corps commander Palmer since office trumps grade. The Illinoisan's refusal to take orders from his superior, despite Sherman's efforts, led to his being relieved at his own request, August 6. Palmer's petulance so disgusted Grant that he considered mustering Palmer out of service that fall. Palmer "has rendered good service in the past," wrote Grant, "but unfortunately for his record threw up command of an Army Corps in the presence of the enemy." *OR*, v. XXXVIII, pt. 5, pp. 354-57, 382-85, 391-93, 400, 407; Simon, op. cit., v. XIII, p. 16.

politics, served as Governor of Illinois, and ran for President in 1896 on the Gold Democrat ticket. He died on September 25, 1900.[34]

Another Democrat politician in the Army of the Cumberland was Robert B. Mitchell. He entered the war as Colonel of the 2nd Kansas and fought at Wilson's Creek. A Brigadier General as of April 8, 1862, he commanded the Ninth Division at Perryville and the First Cavalry Division at Tullahoma. When David S. Stanley became ill, Mitchell succeeded to command the Cavalry Corps of the Army of the Cumberland, September 9, 1863, and led it at Chickamauga and the ensuing cavalry operations. By October 27, Mitchell was suffering too severely from his Wilson's Creek wound to remain in the field. After serving on courts martial in 1864, he commanded districts on the Great Plains in 1865, fighting Indians, and was mustered out of service on January 15, 1866, still a One-Star. Postwar he served as Governor of New Mexico Territory. Death came on January 16, 1882.[35]

Yet another Democrat politician never promoted above Brigadier General was Mahlon D. Manson, who commanded the 10th Indiana at Rich Mountain. From Mill Springs through Richmond, Kentucky (where he was captured), to Resaca, he led a brigade. As senior division commander in the XXIII Corps, he succeeded the ailing George L. Hartsuff in charge of that corps, September-December, 1863, during the East Tennessee Campaign, including the Siege of Knoxville. He thereafter reverted to lower commands and was again leading a brigade when he was wounded out at Resaca on May 14, 1864. He resigned on December 21 of that year. Postwar, he held numerous political offices, including Lieutenant Governor of Indiana, before passing away on February 4, 1895.[36]

Besides Manson with the XXIII, the other infantry corps of the Army of the Ohio in the Knoxville/East Tennessee Campaign, the IX, was also temporarily led by a citizen-soldier, Robert B. Potter, a New York City lawyer. He entered the war as Major of the 51st New York, led that regiment as its Colonel across Burnside's Bridge at Antietam, and had charge of a division at Vicksburg and Jackson in 1863 and in Virginia from May, 1864,

34 Palmer wrote his own *Personal Recollections*. His grandson, George T. Palmer, wrote his biography, *A Conscientious Turncoat*. See also Heitman, *Register*, v. I, p. 767, and Warner, *Blue*, pp. 358-59.

35 Heitman, *Register*, v. I, p. 717, and Warner, *Blue*, pp. 328-29.

36 Heitman, *Register*, v. I, p. 688, and Warner, *Blue*, p. 310.

to April, 1865.[37] From August, 1863, to January, 1864, he temporarily commanded the IX Corps during its major operations in East Tennessee. Promoted to Brigadier General as of March 13, 1863, he did not receive his second star until September 29, 1865—the last of the twenty citizen-soldier corps commanders to make that grade. It would prove his last commission. He declined joining in the Regular Army and left service in January of 1866. Unlike many citizen-soldier corps commanders, he did not enter politics postwar but worked briefly for a railroad, then traveled abroad and in the United States and lived as a gentleman of leisure. He died, February 19 1887.[38]

Another lawyer, Jacob D. Cox of Ohio, succeeded Manson at the head of the XXIII Corps after the Siege of Knoxville. Commissioned a Brigadier General in both state and national service at the outbreak of the war, Cox initially commanded a brigade in the Kanawha Valley and then the Kanawha Division itself.[39] He replaced the fallen Jesse Reno in charge of the IX Corps at South Mountain and Antietam. Returned to western Virginia and then the Western Theater, Cox usually led a division but had charge (almost always temporarily) of the XXIII Corps in the East Tennessee, Allatoona, and Raleigh Campaigns, plus most particularly at the Battle of Franklin. Promoted to Major General (for the second time) one week after that battle, he assumed permanent command of that corps, April 2, 1865.[40] He also led the Provisional Corps of the Army of the Ohio, January-March, 1865, including at the Second Battle of Kinston. Postwar, he served as Governor of Ohio, Congressman, and Secretary of the Interior as a Mugwump Republican. He passed away on August 4, 1900.[41]

37 Potter was seriously wounded on the last day of the Siege of Petersburg, April 2, 1865. The wound was first feared mortal, but he soon recovered. His promotion to Major General of Volunteers dated from September 29, 1865. Welsh, *Medical*, pp. 265-66.

38 Heitman, *Register*, v. I, p. 802, and Warner, *Blue*, pp. 382-83.

39 Like McClellan himself, Cox went off to war under state commission as Brigadier General of Ohio Militia, ranking from April 23, 1861. His commission as a One-Star of U.S. Volunteers dated from May 17, 1861.

40 Cox was initially promoted to Major General as of October 6, 1862, but he reverted to One-Star when the U.S. Senate adjourned on March 4, 1863, without confirming him. He was again elevated to that higher grade as of December 7, 1864.

41 Cox wrote extensively on the Civil War. Broadest in scope is his *Military Reminiscences*. The modern biography is Eugene Schmiel's *Citizen General*. That author,

Cox was one of three citizen-soldiers who led a corps in both Eastern and Western theaters. Another was Alpheus S. Williams, a Michigan lawyer, judge, and newspaper publisher. Also like Cox, he entered service in the spring of 1861 under both state and Federal commissions as Brigadier General.[42] For most of the war, he commanded a division from First Winchester to Peach Tree Creek, but he temporarily led a corps on four major occasions: the XII at Antietam and Gettysburg and the XX briefly at Atlanta and entirely on the March to the Sea and the Carolinas Campaign. However, he was never assigned to corps command permanently, and to his great mortification he was replaced at the head of the XX on April 2, 1865.[43] He ended the war as he had begun: a brigadier general commanding a division. He mustered out of service on January 15, 1866. Postwar, he served as a diplomat and a Congressman until he passed away on December 21, 1878.[44]

Williams' superior officer from mid-1861 to mid-1862 was the remaining corps commander in both East and West: Nathaniel P. Banks. The most famous politician corps commander of the Civil War, Banks had served as Speaker of the U.S. House of Representatives, 1856-1857, and as Governor of Massachusetts, 1858-1861. He entered Volunteer Service on May 16, 1861, as a Major General of Volunteers and was one of the five original corps commanders when President Lincoln created that office on March 8, 1862.[45] Because his V Corps was redesignated the territorial Department of the Shenandoah just three weeks later, it will not be covered

---

Christopher Losson, and Jerry Bower wrote dissertations about his Army service. See also Heitman, *Register*, v. I, p. 331; Warner, *Blue*, pp. 97-98.

42 Williams entered service on April 24, 1861, as Brigadier General of Michigan Volunteers. His comparable commission in the U.S. Volunteers dated from twenty-three days later.

43 Williams wrote his daughter, April 15, 1865, that again losing corps command "is one of the curses that I have to bear for not getting my proper rank years ago.... This is about the fortieth time that I have been foisted [hoisted?] up by seniority to be let down by rank!" Milo Quaife, ed., *Cannon's Mouth*, pp. 379-80.

44 Williams' wartime letters were published ibid. A modern dissertation is Jeffrey Charnley's "Neglected Honor." See also Heitman, *Register*, v. I, p. 1039 and Warner, *Blue*, pp. 559-60.

45 Lincoln ordered the creation of the first five corps on March 8. Because the Army of the Potomac was advancing on Manassas then, McClellan secured permission to delay implementing that order for five days.

in depth.[46] Nor will his command of the XIX Corps in Louisiana in 1863 receive attention since it was really a small, independent army: the Army of the Gulf.[47] From June 26 to September 8, 1862, however, he commanded a real corps (as defined in this chapter): the II Corps of the Army of Virginia, the forerunner of the XII Corps. He led this corps to defeat at Cedar Mountain—just as most of his earlier and later operations also ended in defeat. He was not engaged at Second Bull Run because his small corps guarded John Pope's supply wagons at Manassas Junction. On September 8, he took charge of the Defenses of Washington, and command of the corps devolved on Williams; four days later, it was renumbered the XII Corps. Banks was mustered out of service on August 24, 1865. After the war, he served twelve more years in the U.S. House of Representatives. He died on September 1, 1894.[48]

Just as Banks and Williams were closely connected, so were two citizen-soldier corps commanders in the Eastern Theater: Daniel E. Sickles and David B. Birney. A lawyer, Tammany Hall politician, and U.S. Congressman prewar, Sickles was the first commander of the Excelsior

46 Banks' V Corps was distinct from the more famous formation of that number, created on the Peninsula on May 18, 1862, and commanded by seven distinguished Major Generals from Fitz John Porter to Charles Griffin (including Daniel Butterfield, who is covered later in this chapter). Banks' command was successively styled the V Corps, the Department of the Shenandoah, and the II Corps of the Army of Virginia. Four days after he was promoted to command the Defenses of Washington in September of 1862, his former corps was renumbered the XII, the name under which it served from Antietam until discontinued in April of 1864.

47 In autumn, 1862, the Union high command assigned single corps numbers to departments, even armies. Thus, the Department of the South became the X Corps, the Department of North Carolina the XVIII Corps, the large Army of the Cumberland the XIV Corps, the even larger Army of the Tennessee the XIII Corps, and Banks' Department of the Gulf the XIX Corps. Those two armies soon split into four or five corps each. However, Banks' XIX Corps remained its own little army from December, 1862, through the capture of Port Hudson and the later LaFourche operations. Only after the XIII Corps reached Louisiana did the Army of the Gulf contain more than one corps. From then onward, Banks kept serving as army commander, and professional soldier William B. Franklin took charge of the XIX Corps. Thus, the Bay Stater's tenure as "XIX Corps Commander" really represents leading a small army, not heading a distinct corps within a field army.

48 The classic biography of Banks is Fred Harrington's *Fighting Politician*. Recent works are Raymond Banks' *King of Louisiana* and James Hollandsworth's *Pretense of Glory*. See also Heitman, *Register*, v. I, p. 189, and Warner, *Blue*, pp. 17-18.

Brigade in the Civil War.[49] Promoted to Major General as of November 29, 1862, he succeeded his friend and comrade, Major General Joseph Hooker, in charge of the White Diamond Division, which he led at Fredericksburg, and he commanded the III Corps itself at Chancellorsville and Gettysburg.[50] His grievous wound on July 2 in the latter battle handicapped him for further field service, and the adamant opposition of Major General George G. Meade, whom Sickles persuaded the Joint Committee on the Conduct of the War to investigate concerning Gettysburg, prevented his return to the Army of the Potomac. He did serve postwar as military governor of South Carolina under Congressional Reconstruction. When he was finally mustered out as Major General of Volunteers on January 1, 1868, he was the next to last citizen-soldier general still in the Volunteer Service.[51] He nominally continued serving as Colonel of the 42nd U.S. Infantry (an invalid regiment) from 1866 until it was disbanded in 1869—whereupon he was placed on the retired list as a Major General in the Regular Army![52] He subsequently served as ambassador to Spain and figured actively in efforts to commemorate the Battle of Gettysburg. He went to his grave on May 3, 1914, at age 94 and a half—the oldest of the twenty citizen-soldier corps commanders.[53]

49 Sickles entered service as colonel of the 70th New York, June 20, 1861. He received his star on September 3, 1861.

50 Sickles led the III Corps, February 5-July 2, 1863.

51 When Sickles retired, just two generals still served under their Volunteer commissions: One-Star Robert K. Scott, a citizen-soldier, and Two-Star Oliver Howard, a Regular. Scott had only become a general on April 21, 1865, backdated to January 12 of that year. Thus, he served at flag rank for only thirty-nine months, all of them postwar. Sickles, in contrast, was a general for twice as long. Howard was the most long-serving General of Volunteers at eighty-eight months. Scott resigned, July 6, 1868, to become Carpetbagger Governor of South Carolina. Howard continued under that higher commission until January 1, 1869.

52 When the U.S. Army went on its postwar footing in 1866, it included four regiments of invalids: the 42nd through 45th U.S., descended from the wartime Veteran Reserve Corps. All four of their colonels and three lieutenant colonels had been Civil War generals who had been grievously wounded, four of them losing a limb: Sickles and John B. McIntosh of the 42nd, John C. Robinson and Joseph B. Kiddoo of the 43rd, Thomas G. Pitcher and Alexander S. Webb of the 44th, and Wager Swayne of the 45th. The peacetime force of sixty regiments proved larger than America chose to afford and the Army was reduced to forty regiments in 1869. All four units of invalids were consolidated with surviving outfits.

53 W. A. Swanberg's *Sickles the Incredible* and Edgcumb Pinchon's *Yankee King of Spain* have long been the standard biographies of the general. Recent works include James

Another citizen-soldier, David B. Birney, temporarily succeeded Sickles in charge of the III Corps, July 2-9, 1863. This Philadelphia lawyer and son of former Presidential candidate James G. Birney entered the Civil War as colonel of the 23rd Pennsylvania Zouaves. He received his first star as of February 17, 1862, and his second star, May 20, 1863. At those grades he led a brigade on the Peninsula and at Second Bull Run and the Red Diamond Division from September, 1862, to July, 1864.[54] He temporarily took over the II Corps from the ill Winfield Scott Hancock, June 18-27, 1864, and suffered ignominious defeats with it in the Grand Assault at Petersburg on June 18 and at First Weldon Railroad. Despite such setbacks, he was given permanent command of the X Corps, July 23, 1864, and commanded it at First and Second Deep Bottom and Chaffin's Bluff. His great victory at First Darbytown Road saved the Army of the James from potential disaster. Such success cost Birney his life. The strain drained the strength from his disease-riven body, and on October 18—back home in Philadelphia but too late—he died: the highest-ranking Union general to lose his life in the entire Siege of Petersburg and one of only three citizen-soldier corps commanders to die during the war.[55]

Birney was succeeded in X Corps command by Alfred H. Terry. This Yale-educated lawyer entered service as Colonel of the 2nd Connecticut and then the 7th Connecticut. He quickly rose to brigade command (commissioned Brigadier General as of April 25, 1862) and led a division from the Siege of Charleston to the Siege of Petersburg. He had temporary charge of the X Corps at Clay's Farm, Second Darbytown Road, and Second

---

Hessler's *Sickles at Gettysburg*, Thomas Keneally's *American Scoundrel*, and Richard Sauers' *Meade-Sickles Controversy*. William Styple's *Generals in Bronze* and Robert Broadwater's *Gettysburg as the Generals Remembered It* are useful, too. See also Heitman, *Register*, v. I, p. 886, and Warner, *Blue*, pp. 446-47.

54 The "Red Diamond Division" (First Division of the III Corps) ceased to exist in March, 1864, when that corps was discontinued. Its veterans, however, still served in Birney's Third Division of the II Corps. All other former III Corps soldiers in the II Corps were transferred into his division seven weeks later. These veterans remained deeply attached to the III Corps, especially to the Red Diamond Division that introduced distinctive unit patches into the American military. They continued wearing III Corps patches even in the II Corps.

55 The other two generals were Ransom, who also died of disease, and Wadsworth, mortally wounded in the Wilderness. Birney's friend Oliver P. Davis wrote the only biography in 1867: *Life of David Bell Birney*. Welsh, *Medical*, pp. 29-30, concludes he died of typhoid fever. Heitman, *Register*, v. I, p. 220, and Warner, *Blue*, pp. 34-35.

Fair Oaks. He also led a Provisional Corps which captured Fort Fisher, January 15, 1865. That great success in closing access to blockade runners' prime port of Wilmington earned him not only permanent command of his force, which was redesignated the reconstituted X Corps, but also promotion to Major General of Volunteers and Brigadier General of Regulars.[56] He thus held the highest rank of any citizen-soldier in the active Regular Army when it went on its postwar footing in 1866. By that year's end, the U. S. Regular Army included twenty-six generals; only two were citizen-soldiers: Alfred H. Terry and Grant's Chief-of-Staff, John A. Rawlins.[57] Terry served actively in the Indian Wars, especially in Sioux country. He was promoted to Major General of Regulars in 1886 and retired two years later. He died on December 16, 1890.[58]

The final officer to be considered, Daniel Butterfield, also served in the postwar Regulars but under commissions issued early in the Civil War: as Lieutenant-Colonel of the 12th U.S. (May 14, 1861) and Colonel of the 5th U.S. (July 1, 1863). However, he was a citizen-soldier, a prewar businessman who entered service as Colonel of the 12th New York Militia at Arlington Heights and Martinsburg. Commissioned a Brigadier General as of September 7, 1861, he commanded a brigade of Robert Patterson's army in the Valley Campaign of 1861, a brigade of the V Corps on the Peninsula, two brigades of that corps at Second Bull Run, and its entire First Division in McClellan's last campaign. When Joseph Hooker was elevated to command the Center Grand Division on November 16, 1862, Butterfield (the ranking subordinate, though still a One Star) succeeded him in charge of the V Corps, which he led at Fredericksburg. Meade claimed command of that corps later

56 Terry's Regular commission as Brigadier General and provisional Volunteer commission as Major General both dated from his great success on January 15, 1865. That higher grade was formally commissioned on April 20 of that year. The original X Corps in which he had spent most of his military service had been discontinued on December 3, 1864. On March 27, 1865, the Provisional Corps which he had commanded since January was made official and renumbered the reconstituted X Corps.

57 Terry ranked fifteenth among the seventeen Regular generals of the line. He was eighth among the ten One-Stars, ranking ahead of former army commanders Edward Ord and Canby. Among the nine generals of staff, the only citizen-soldier was Rawlins, whose Regular commission dated from March 3, 1865—seven weeks junior to Terry.

58 Much has been written about Terry in the Indian Wars, but little focuses on his Civil War service. The best available work is Carl Marino's dissertation, "Soldier from Connecticut." See also Heitman, *Register*, v. I, p. 951, and Warner, *Blue*, pp. 497-98.

that month by virtue of seniority.[59] When Hooker took over the Army of the Potomac on January 26, 1863, Butterfield became his Chief of Staff for Chancellorsville.

Meade retained him in that office through Gettysburg, but the wounded Butterfield ceased serving there on July 5.[60] He again became Chief of Staff for the four divisions which Hooker took to Tennessee that fall. When Hooker's forces were reorganized as the reconstituted XX Corps the following April, Butterfield took charge of its Third Division for the Atlanta Campaign. Because of continuing ill health, he left the field for good on June 29, 1864. On August 20, as the Atlanta Campaign neared its climax, he wrote Sherman from New York City to ask if he would be given the IV, XIV, or XX Corps, whose permanent command had been vacated. The next day Sherman replied that other officers had received those assignments. In his characteristically pointed way, Sherman summarized, "We must have corps commanders present."[61] Butterfield would not be present with that army group ever again. He mustered out of Volunteer Service on August 24, 1865, but continued serving under his Regular commission until 1870,[62] primarily in New York City in charge of the General Recruiting Service.[63] Even before

59 Both Meade and Butterfield ranked as Major Generals from November 29, 1862 — the Pennsylvanian five files higher than Butterfield. More significantly, Meade had already been commissioned as a Two-Star before Fredericksburg, but Butterfield had not been, so Meade unquestionably had the seniority to claim corps command.

60 Butterfield had been badly bruised by a shell fragment on July 3, but he returned to duty the next day. On July 5, he took it on himself to issue an order which Meade had drafted but not yet promulgated for the Army of the Potomac to move through Maryland in order to intercept the Confederate retreat. When Meade sought to send two corps to reinforce the VI Corps pursuing the Butternuts directly, he was astonished to find his troops already moving to Maryland without his authorization. He made clear his displeasure to Butterfield, who ceased functioning as Chief of Staff that night. The New Yorker left the army ostensibly to recover from his wound but more likely because Meade relieved him as Chief of Staff.

61 *OR*, v. XXXVIII, pt. 5, pp. 614-27.

62 Consolidating the Army in 1869 cost him his commission as Colonel of the 5th U.S. He was thereafter "unassigned" until he resigned on March 14, 1870.

63 In 1866, Butterfield led the effort among wealthy friends in New York City to raise money to pay off the mortgage for General-in-Chief Grant's house in Washington, D.C. Three years later, as Grant prepared to move into the White House, the junior officer again raised money to purchase Grant's residence and give it to incoming General-in-Chief Sherman. The Lieutenant General confided to his brother John on February 21, 1869, that "Dan Butterfield claims to have been largely instrumental in [raising money], but I should much prefer that he not be the chief party. He did the same for Grant some four years ago,

leaving the Regular Army, he was detailed as Assistant Secretary of the Treasury in 1869 but resigned that October due to tangential taint of the "Black Friday" scandal to corner the Gold Market. Despite that scandal, Butterfield—a gentleman of wealth, leisure, and influence—remained active in many veterans, business, and social undertakings until his death on July 17, 1901.[64]

Butterfield had just turned 31 when he took charge of the V Corps, but he was not the youngest of those twenty generals. Ransom, at age 29, holds that distinction. Among permanent corps commanders, Dodge was youngest at 32. All three officers were well below the average age of 40 for the twenty generals. That average increases to 41 for the thirteen permanent commanders and to 42 for the six who started with permanent command (actually, 44 for the first four permanent commanders in 1862).[65] The seven who were only temporary averaged 39.[66] Even that number was skewed upwards by Williams, who at 52 was oldest of all twenty. Hurlbut at 47 was oldest permanent commander.

In overall lifespan, all twenty generals averaged 68.5 years of age. Deducting the two who died during the war raises that figure to 72+. Tough old one-legged Dan Sickles was the most long-lived at 94.5. The last survivor was Dodge, who passed away on January 3, 1916, not quite 85. The youngest to die postwar was the paralyzed Blair at 54 in 1875. The youngest of all was Ransom, who perished in October, 1864, one month short of his 30th birthday. A Vermonter by birth, Ransom entered military service from Illinois. Five other officers also hailed from the Prairie State, and another five came from elsewhere in the Midwest.[67] One entered from Kansas and

---

and Grant has left him at New York all this time on Recruiting duty, when he should have been with his Regiment on the Plains [fighting Indians in Kansas and Colorado]." Simon, op. cit., v. XVI, pp. 74-75, and v. XIX, pp. 128-29.

64 His widow, Julia, compiled *A Biographical Memorial of General Daniel Butterfield*. See Broadwater, op. cit.; Heitman, *Register*, v. I, p. 270-71; Warner, *Blue*, pp. 62-63.

65 The four permanent commanders in 1862 were Banks, Crittenden, McClernand, and Hurlbut. The much younger Grierson and Terry were the first commanders of their respective corps later in the war.

66 The temporary commanders were Butterfield, Manson, Mitchell, Potter, Ransom, Washburn, and Williams.

67 Besides Ransom, the Illinoisans were Grierson, Hurlbut, Logan, McClernand, and Palmer. The other Midwesterners were Cox, Dodge, Manson, Washburn, and Williams.

two from border states.[68] Four more came from the Middle Atlantic region, and the remaining two were New Englanders.[69]

One of the latter, Banks, served as U.S. Speaker of the House and Governor of Massachusetts prewar. Five other future generals were also Congressmen prewar, and five more held state or territorial offices.[70] Six of those eleven were Democrats; three were Republicans; and Banks and Palmer began as Democrats but became Republicans (actually, the Bay Stater belonged to the American Party when he was elected Speaker.).[71] Other prewar occupations include five lawyers, two engineers, two businessmen, one newspaper publisher, and one music teacher. Three of the twenty served in Indian Wars in the 1830s, and five were officers in the Mexican War, two of them as lieutenant-colonels of state regiments.[72]

Banks entered service in 1861 as a major-general. Five others started as One-Stars.[73] Ten began as colonels of their own regiments.[74] Grierson and Potter were initially majors within regiments, and Manson and Ransom were first commissioned as captains of companies. Sixteen of the officers eventually became major-generals, and Ransom and Williams were breveted

68 Mitchell was the Kansan, Blair the Missourian, and Crittenden the Kentuckian.

69 Birney was a Pennsylvanian; Butterfield, Potter, and Sickles hailed from New York. Banks was a Bay Stater; Terry entered from Connecticut.

70 The Congressmen were Banks, Blair, Logan, McClernand, Sickles, and Washburn. The other office-holders were Hurlbut and Palmer in Illinois, Manson in Indiana, Williams in Michigan, and Mitchell in Kansas Territory.

71 The Democrats were Logan, Manson, McClernand, Mitchell, Sickles, and Williams. The Republicans were Blair, Cox, and Hurlbut.

72 Crittenden and McClernand served as privates in the Kentucky Militia in the Second Creek War and in the Illinois Militia in the Black Hawk War, respectively. Hurlbut served as adjutant of a South Carolina regiment in the Second Seminole War. During the Mexican War, Crittenden and Williams were the Lieutenant Colonels of the 3rd Kentucky and the 1st Michigan, respectively. Also in that conflict, Logan, Manson, and Mitchell, respectively, served as company officers in the 1st Illinois, 5th Indiana, and 5th Ohio. Before being commissioned in October of 1847, Crittenden (still a civilian) was volunteer aide to his second cousin Major General Zachary Taylor at Buena Vista.

73 Cox, Crittenden, Hurlbut, McClernand, and Williams entered service as Brigadier Generals.

74 The coming corps commanders who commenced as colonels were Birney, Blair, Butterfield, Dodge, Logan, Mitchell, Palmer, Sickles, Terry, and Washburn.

to that grade. Only Manson and Mitchell finished the war as brigadier-generals.

Banks was one of the five original corps commanders as early as March of 1862, and Crittenden, McClernand, Hurlbut, Grierson, and (in one sense) Terry were also the first commanders of their respective corps. Thirteen officers eventually held permanent command, whereas seven were only temporary. Five of the permanents had previously been temporaries.[75] The average duration of temporary, permanent, and combined command were three months, nearly nine months, and ten months, respectively. The most long-serving permanent corps commander was Logan at over seventeen months (though he was on leave for three and a half of those months).[76] His contemporary, Blair, was longest for time actually on duty: fifteen months out of a total of over sixteen months assigned to corps command. The shortest tour for a permanent commander was Banks' fourteen weeks.[77] For a temporary commander, Mitchell served most briefly at seven weeks. Poor Williams was the longest-serving temporary commander: six tours totaling almost eight months.[78]

Williams led corps in both Eastern and Western Theaters. His long-time senior, Banks, led corps in the East and Gulf.[79] Three other generals served

75 Generals who led corps briefly before receiving permanent command were Blair, Birney, Cox, Palmer, and Terry. Cox led both the IX and XXIII Corps temporarily before being officially assigned to the latter. The other four officers briefly had charge of different corps than the ones they later led permanently.

76 Logan went on leave September 23, 1864, to help campaign for President Lincoln and Republicans in the autumn elections. Before the general could return to the front, Sherman cut loose from Atlanta to march to the sea. The junior officer did not resume command until January 8, 1865, just before the XV Corps left Savannah for Beaufort, South Carolina.

77 Those fourteen weeks represent his command of the II Corps of the Army of Virginia from June 26 to September 8, 1862, and his earlier command of the initial V Corps, March 13-April 4, 1862. Those two names cover essentially the same troops, through their corps headquarters, First Divisions and attached cavalry; only their Second Divisions were different. His subsequent command of the XIX Corps, December 16, 1862-August 20, 1863, is not counted since it was really a small army.

78 Williams led the XII Corps, September 8-12 and September 17-October 20, 1862, and July 1-4 and August 31-September 13, 1863—over eight weeks. Then he had charge of the reconstituted XX Corps, July 28-August 27, 1864, and November 11, 1864-April 2, 1865—virtually twenty-five weeks. Those six tours total almost eight months—all of them as only a temporary commander.

79 This chapter does not focus on Banks' command of the XIX Corps in the Gulf.

entirely in the East: Birney, Butterfield, and Sickles. Terry and Cox each served in three theaters: East, West, and lower Atlantic coast. Four others served in the West and Gulf.[80] The largest number, nine, commanded corps entirely in the West.[81] Thus, sixteen generals spent all or part of their corps command in the West, whereas only seven performed all or part of such duties in the East and only five entirely or partially in the Gulf. Eight of those sixteen belonged to the Department/Army of the Tennessee.[82] That army's wartime commanders were four Regulars—three of them among the greatest generals of the entire Federal Army: Grant, Sherman, and McPherson.[83] Its senior subordinates, in contrast, were overwhelmingly citizen-soldier volunteers. Those citizen-soldiers led corps in that army 63% of the time. Removing Sherman and McPherson from the equation raises the proportion for the remaining corps-command time to 80%.[84]

That army included one citizen-soldier cavalry corps commander, as did the Army of the Cumberland.[85] The other eighteen officers headed infantry corps. Almost all corps were discontinued in June, July, and early August,

80 Those four generals were Grierson, McClernand, Ransom, and Washburn.

81 Blair, Crittenden, Dodge, Hurlbut, Logan, Manson, Mitchell, Palmer, and Potter commanded corps only in the Western Theater.

82 Blair, Dodge, Hurlbut, Logan, McClernand, Ransom, and Washburn led corps in the Army of the Tennessee. Grierson headed a brigade and division in that army and a corps in its parent Department of the Tennessee.

83 The fourth Regular who had charge of the Army of the Tennessee was Oliver Otis Howard. One citizen-soldier, Logan, also commanded it for six days in wartime and for two and a half months postwar.

84 Sherman and McPherson commanded corps in the Army of the Tennessee for nine and sixteen months, respectively. The only other Regular who led a corps there for a considerable period was A.J. Smith, who headed the Right Wing of the XVI Corps (and its successors) for sixteen months. During six of those months, it served in Sherman's Military Division. Other Regulars who briefly led corps in that command were: XIII Corps, George W. Morgan (four weeks) and Ord (six weeks); XV Corps, Frederick Steele (five weeks) and William B. Hazen (ten weeks); XVI Corps, Hamilton (four weeks) and Dana (three weeks); Left Wing/XVI Corps, Carr (six weeks); and XVII Corps, Mower (one week). Command time for all eight generals, combined, comes to thirty-nine weeks (nine months).

85 Grierson led the Cavalry Corps of the District of West Tennessee and of the Military Division of West Mississippi. The comparable corps of the Army of the Cumberland was temporarily under Mitchell at Chickamauga.

1865.[86] By war's end, only four of the twenty generals still headed corps: Terry of the X, Blair of the XVII, Cox of the XXIII, and Grierson of the West Mississippi Cavalry Corps. Of the others, Logan had been promoted to army command; Banks, Dodge, Mitchell, Palmer, and Washburn had been reassigned to command departments or districts (where the only threats came from guerrillas or Indians); Potter and Williams had reverted to division command; and Butterfield, Sickles, and Hurlbut were awaiting orders—the last-named on the verge of being court-martialed for corruption. Crittenden, Manson, and McClernand had resigned in 1864. Disease had claimed Birney and Ransom. Of the fifteen who were still in Volunteer Service in the spring of 1865, three resigned and three others were mustered out that year; two more resigned the following year, and an additional six were mustered out in 1866.[87] Sickles continued serving under his Volunteer commission until finally mustered out, January 1, 1868.

Even then, Sickles remained in uniform as a Regular officer, as did Butterfield, Crittenden, Grierson, and Terry—the latter three for many years. Washburn, Potter, and eventually Butterfield went back into business, and Dodge resumed railroading. Even most of them spent a little time in government. Politics, after all, had been the principal profession of most of those citizen-soldiers prewar. It involved even more of them after the Civil War. Cox, Palmer, and Washburn served as state governors, Manson as

86 Most Federal corps ceased to exist in 1865. The XIX was discontinued on March 20, while the war still raged. The XX's troops were distributed to other corps in early June; June 1 was its official date of termination. The II, V, and VI Corps ended on the 28th of that month, the XIII and XVI on July 20, and the IX on July 27. Almost all remaining corps were discontinued on August 1: the IV, VII, VIII, X, XIV, XV, XVII, XXIII, and XXIV. The I Veteran Corps, which had never really coalesced, petered out by year's end, although its few regiments continued serving into mid-1866. That later year saw the last two corps come to an end: the XXV on January 8 and the XXII on June 11. For the three cavalry corps, that of the Military Division of the Mississippi was discontinued on June 26, 1865. Its counterpart in the Military Division of West Mississippi did not come together as a corps before the war ended. The long-time Cavalry Corps of the Army of the Potomac, moreover, was, in effect, "broken up," as Frederick Dyer calls it—its regiments sent elsewhere or mustered out. The dates of reassignment of their respective commanding generals—Grierson on June 5, 1865, and George Crook on June 27—may be taken as the effective end of those other two corps.

87 Washburn resigned May 25, 1865, just as the war was ending. Later that year, Blair and Logan resigned, and Banks, Butterfield, and Hurlbut were mustered out. The following year, Cox and Dodge resigned, and Grierson, Mitchell, Palmer, Potter, Terry, and Williams were mustered out.

lieutenant-governor, and Mitchell as territorial governor. That last office was a Presidential appointment. So were Cox's and Butterfield's cabinet and sub-cabinet offices and Hurlbut's, Sickles', and Williams' diplomatic posts. Blair, Logan, and Palmer served as U.S. Senators, and Banks, Cox, Hurlbut, Logan, Manson, Sickles, Williams, and even Dodge and Washburn were elected to Congress. McClernand never again held national office, but he remained active in Democrat politics and chaired the party's national convention in 1876. He was among six of those former generals who were Democrats, and seven were Republicans.[88] The only marked change in party allegiance since 1860 occurred for the two renowned corps commanders in the Army of the Tennessee: Logan joined the GOP, and Blair reverted to Democrat. Palmer, not surprisingly, was both. In the ante-bellum years, he was a Democrat who became active in the new Republican Party. During the Gilded Age, he was first elected as a Republican but by 1896 ran for President as a Democrat.

Ranging across the political spectrum was hardly average for a politician, but this historian rates Palmer just "average" as a corps commander. Distilling an entire military career to only one or two words is unfair—but the effort will be made, anyway. None of the twenty generals who have been considered ranks as "excellent" (an evaluation reserved for, say, Hancock or George H. Thomas), but Logan and Terry were "very good," and Blair, Dodge, Ransom, and Williams were "good." Birney and Cox were "above average," and Grierson, Potter, and Washburn as well as Palmer were "average." (Now, to be sure, Grierson had been a great brigadier and a good division commander. He may well have developed into a good corps commander, but the war ended before he could be tested in that higher position.) Butterfield, Crittenden, Manson, Mitchell, and Sickles were tested and place "below average." Finally, Banks, Hurlbut, and McClernand—with whom this chapter began—proved "poor."

Three of the officers rated as "poor," five more as "below average," and another four as "average"—over half of the twenty generals did not excel. Why were such officers selected in the first place? Surely (one must think) it was obvious they were unfit to command corps! Civil War "Political Generals," after all, have become a byword for military incompetence.

88 Blair, Manson, McClernand, Mitchell, Sickles, and Williams were Democrats. The Republicans included Banks, Butterfield, Cox, Dodge, Hurlbut, Logan, and Washburn.

Please note that, so far, this chapter has not used that epithet "Political Generals." Nor will it be used now. It is a misunderstood, misapplied, and misleading misnomer. For one thing, many West Point-educated, Regular, professional officers benefitted from "political" connections—including Grant and Sherman themselves.[89] "Politician General" would be a better term. Ten of the twenty generals were politicians prewar; fourteen pursued that profession postwar. Yet not all were politicians. Some were engineers, publishers, businessmen, even a music teacher. That breadth of work explains the preference for the term "citizen-soldiers."

There were, moreover, understandable practical, moral, and philosophical reasons for entrusting high command to such officers. For one thing, there were not enough qualified Regular officers to fill every command slot, not even corps. That echelon of command was new to the U.S. Army. McClellan initially declined to appoint any of his division commanders (most of them professionals) to corps command until they proved worthy in battle. Lincoln himself imposed corps structure on the Army of the Potomac in March of 1862 and handpicked the first five commanders: four Regulars plus Banks.[90] The Bay Stater proved poor, as did McClernand, Hurlbut, and to a lesser degree Crittenden when they became the first commanders of other corps late that year. However, many of their successors succeeded—because they earned promotion by leading brigades and divisions well. Logan and Terry highlight this quality, as do Birney, Blair, Cox, Dodge, Grierson, Ransom and Williams. Recognizing and rewarding merit is a great American moral value.

89 At the outbreak of the Civil War, Grant was an obscure and somewhat tarnished ex-Regular recently moved to Galena, Illinois. Fortunately for him and for the Union, local Congressman Elihu Washburne (Cadwallader's older brother) championed him as the "hometown boy" and commended him for promotion to Brigadier General. Sherman, too, benefitted from political sponsorship. Although he enjoyed a good reputation in the Old Army, he in effect missed the Mexican War, which had largely ended by the time his forces reached California. He, also, left the Army in the 1850s and was in civil life when the Civil War erupted. From there, he was plucked to command one of the eleven new regiments of Regulars created for the war. Perhaps he was selected as Colonel of the 13th U.S. because of his great potentiality. Even so, his brother John's position as a U.S. Senator and his father-in-law's status as an elder statesman of the Republican Party did not hurt. This political reality does not diminish the military ability of Grant and Sherman. Rather does it recognize that political sponsorship created their initial opportunity to apply their professional talents.

90 The four Regulars were Major Generals Irvin McDowell, Edwin V. Sumner, Samuel P. Heintzelman, and Erasmus D. Keyes for the I through IV Corps, respectively.

Yet even beyond such moral and practical considerations towered the fundamental philosophy of American government: a republic of Virtuous Citizens. The Founding Fathers consciously modeled the new nation on the ancient Roman Republic, as they understood it. That model depended not on Monarchs and Marshals but on Virtuous Citizenry. The Virtuous Citizen participated in the "Public Things," the "Res Publica"—Latin words which are the root of the word "Republic." In peacetime, the Virtuous Citizen voted, served on juries, held public office. In wartime, the Virtuous Citizen took up arms as a militia to defend the Republic. The popularly chosen leaders of their fellow citizens in peacetime—legislators, governors, magistrates, judges—were considered the rightful, or natural, leaders of their fellow citizens in wartime. Aspirants to such offices, moreover, could establish their credentials for leadership by holding military command. This model was as American as George Washington and Andrew Jackson and as ancient as Julius Caesar—the greatest "Political General" of all time—and Lucius Quintius Cincinnatus, the legendary Roman who in the 5th Century (BC) left his farm to defeat the Aequians, then relinquished his military command, and returned to his farm.[91] His example inspired officers of the Continental Army to name their veterans' organization following the Revolutionary War the Society of the Cincinnati.[92]

That society still exists to this day. However, with the increasing professionalization of the American military and of American life from the late 19th Century to the present, the model of the citizen-soldier in high command has fallen into disfavor (indeed, they are now stigmatized as "Political Generals"). Yet, as has been shown, at the time of the Civil War there remained logical philosophical, moral, and practical reasons for adhering to it. This is why this analysis applies the name "American Cincinnatus" to "Lincoln's Civilian Corps Commanders."

91 Some scholars consider the story of Cincinnatus exaggerated or apocryphal. Even so, his image endures as the quintessential citizen-soldier of a republic.

92 The definitive history of the Society of the Cincinnati is *Liberty without Anarchy* by Minor Myers, Jr.

27. Abraham Lincoln and John McClerand. *LOC*

28. Nathaniel P. Banks. *LOC*

29. Francis P. Blair, Jr. *LOC*

30. Cadwallader C. Washburn. *General Mills*

31. John A. McClernand. *LOC*

32. Stephen A. Hurlbut. *Generals in Blue*

33. John A. Logan. *LOC*

34. John M. Palmer. *LOC*

35. Grenville M. Dodge. *LOC*

36. Robert B. Potter. *LOC*

37. Benjamin Grierson. *LOC*

38. Thomas E. G. Ransom. *LOC*

39. Daniel Butterfield. *LOC*

40. Thomas L. Crittenden. *LOC*

41. Mahlon D. Manson.
Crawfordsville Public Library

42. Robert B. Mitchell. *Wikipedia*

Chapter 7

Mac's Main Men: Federal Wing and Corps Commanders in the Antietam Campaign[1]

The great Napoleon himself conceived the concept: the corps d'armee, or army corps. This was a large, almost self-contained formation of two or more divisions, one level below army command. It allowed the army commander to wield numerous divisions over vast spaces, and it served as the element for strategic maneuver and grand tactical (or operational) control. Corps commanders, moreover, were responsible senior subordinates who were accorded considerable latitude—and who were expected to exercise it. Napoleon's marshals served as the original corps commanders—such military legends as Bernadotte, Marmont, Davout, Soult, Lannes, Ney, and Augereau.[2]

Napoleon's adversaries, too, adopted the concept and divided their own armies into corps. By the mid-19th Century, such command structures were

1 This chapter is adapted from a presentation originally given at the Chambersburg Civil War Seminar, July 29, 2012, commemorating the 150th anniversary year of the Antietam Campaign. As in the next two chapters of Part Two, it covers the entire military careers of the eleven wing and corps commanders and does not confine itself only to their service in this one campaign. The chapter benefits from Frederick H. Dyer's *A Compendium of the War of the Rebellion*, Francis B. Heitman's *Historical Register and Biographical Dictionary of the United States Army, 1789-1903*, and Ezra J. Warner's *Generals in Blue*.

2 In 1805, prior to launching his most brilliant campaign, Austerlitz, Napoleon divided his army into seven corps. Six were commanded by officers who had been elevated to marshal the preceding year. Auguste Marmont, who had charge of the II Corps, received his baton in 1808.

common among European powers. Prior to 1861, in contrast, American armies were too small to be broken down into corps. Winfield Scott's army that captured Mexico City in 1847, for instance, contained only nine brigades, grouped into four divisions. His span of control could encompass those four infantry divisions and one mounted brigade. He had no need for the intermediate command echelon of corps.

The Civil War changed that. President Abraham Lincoln's call for 500,000 three-year volunteers led to a large force build-up in all major theaters in the latter part of 1861 and on into the following year. Just in the Eastern Theater, arriving regiments were formed into sixteen divisions along the Potomac from Budd's Ferry upriver to Harper's Ferry and Williamsport, especially in the greater Washington area.[3] The creation of still more divisions was in prospect.[4] Such a huge force was far more than any one army commander could control—even Major General George B. McClellan, General-in-Chief of the entire Union Army and commanding general of the Army of the Potomac.[5] Lincoln repeatedly urged him to group these divisions into corps. "Little Mac" demurred, on the grounds that only two of his subordinates had led even a division or higher formation in combat.[6] Until officers proved themselves in battle as division commanders, he did not want to elevate them to corps command. Whatever the theoretical merits

3 These front-line divisions along the upper, middle, and lower Potomac were under Major General Nathaniel P. Banks and Brigadier Generals Irvin McDowell, Samuel P. Heintzelman, Fitz John Porter, William B. Franklin, Charles P. Stone (later John Sedgwick), Don Carlos Buell (later Erasmus D. Keyes, then Darius N. Couch), George A. McCall, Joseph Hooker, William F. Smith, Louis Blenker, Edwin V. Sumner, Silas Casey, Frederick Lander (later James Shields), George Sykes, and George Stoneman. Stoneman commanded cavalry. All the other divisions were infantry.

4 Two new divisions were created in the spring of 1862: Brigadier General Edward Ord's on May 16 and Major General Franz Sigel's on June 4. Of their twenty-three regiments, sixteen were drawn from the defenses of Washington or Baltimore; six were in existing brigades; and the remaining one was a newly mobilized New York National Guard unit.

5 McClellan became General-in-Chief, November 1, 1861. His tenure there was nearing an end as corps were being organized. Orders creating them were issued, March 8, 1862, but were not announced until March 13. In between then, McClellan was relieved as General-in-Chief, March 11. He kept command of the Army of the Potomac, within which the first five corps were formed, until November 9, 1862.

6 McDowell commanded the Union army at First Bull Run. Heintzelman led one of the five divisions there.

of such reasoning, the reality was that McClellan intended to launch his great spring offensive with an unwieldy army far larger than he could control.

That made no sense to Lincoln. On March 8, 1862, through General War Order Number 2, the President took it on himself to order the Army of the Potomac divided into five corps. He personally selected which division commanders would lead them. They were not McClellan's choices, but—like them or not—he would now have to work with and through them.[7]

Over the ensuing six months—in the Peninsula Campaign, the Second Manassas Campaign, and various operations in the West—Federal army commanders (including "Little Mac") increasingly came to understand how useful corps were for controlling large numbers of troops in maneuver and battle. On May 18, McClellan even created two provisional corps of his own, the new V and VI (later made permanent), led by officers he trusted: Brigadier Generals Fitz-John Porter and William B. Franklin.[8] By September, the entire Union Army included, in effect, sixteen corps of volunteers and Regulars and one corps of militia. Five more corps were created later that year, and another four were added early in 1863.[9]

7 The President appointed McDowell, Sumner, Heintzelman, Keyes, and Banks to command the I, II, III, IV, and V Corps, respectively. Their promotions caused their former divisions to devolve on or be reassigned to Brigadier Generals Rufus King, Israel B. Richardson, Charles S. Hamilton, Darius N. Couch, and Alpheus S. Williams, respectively. On April 4, the original V Corps was discontinued, and Banks' command was renamed the Department of the Shenandoah.

8 Since the original V Corps had been discontinued in April, its number was given to a new corps consisting of Porter's division from the III Corps and Sykes' division, the army reserve. Franklin's division from the I Corps and Smith's division from the IV Corps formed the VI Corps. Brigadier Generals George Morell and Henry W. Slocum took over Porter's and Franklin's former divisions, respectively. Since Franklin's VI Corps and Porter's new V Corps were created by McClellan, they were initially termed "Provisional Corps." The U.S. War Department made them permanent on July 22, 1862.

9 The thirteen corps in the Eastern Theater will be covered later in this chapter. The four corps outside that theater in September of 1862 were the X along the lower Atlantic coast (created on September 3) and the three corps of the Army of the Ohio (formed on September 29). The latter three formations were initially called the I, II, and III Corps of that army. On October 24, the Army of the Ohio was renamed the Army of the Cumberland, also known as the XIV Corps. That huge corps/army was divided into three wings (really de facto corps). On January 9, 1863, those three wings were redesignated the XIV, XX, and XXI Corps. On October 24, 1862, the Army of the Tennessee was numbered the XIII Corps. As with the Army of the Cumberland/XIV Corps, this huge XIII Corps/army was initially divided into wings. On December 18, the more formal numbers of XIII, XV, XVI, and XVII Corps were applied to the major components within that army. Six days later, Union troops in North

The focus of this chapter is on corps and corps commanders in the Maryland Campaign. Of the seventeen Federal corps in September of 1862, thirteen operated in the Eastern Theater. Two of them, however, were far from the field of Antietam: the IV Corps under Major General Erasmus D. Keyes, headquartered at Yorktown, and the VII Corps under Major General John A. Dix, headquartered at Fort Monroe. Now, to be sure, the First Division/IV Corps did reach Alexandria at the end of the Second Bull Run Campaign; it would participate in the Antietam Campaign.[10] Indeed, so severe seemed the situation that McClellan even ordered the mistrusted Second Division/IV Corps to rejoin him, but General-in-Chief Henry W. Halleck vetoed that move, and that division plus IV Corps headquarters remained on the Peninsula.[11] One brigade from the VII Corps, moreover, was transferred to the II Corps in time to fight at Antietam, but Dix's corps

---

Carolina were designated the XVIII Corps. On January 25, 1863, Federal troops in Louisiana were numbered the XIX Corps. Eighteen days later, the Cavalry Corps of the Army of the Potomac was created. The mounted troops of the Army of the Cumberland were structured as a Cavalry Corps in March of that year. The following month, the XXIII Corps was created in Kentucky. Ere then, the name XXII Corps was officially applied to the garrison of Washington, D.C., February 2. This chapter, however, considers that garrison a de facto corps at the time of Antietam, as explained infra.

10 Couch's First Division of the IV Corps arrived at that city at the end of August. During the Maryland Campaign, it operated as part of Franklin's Left Wing of McClellan's army. On September 26, Couch's command was officially transferred to Franklin's VI Corps as its Third Division.

11 McClellan blamed the Second Division of the IV Corps and its commander, Casey, for being surprised at Seven Pines, May 31, 1862. Such criticism was unfair and unfounded, but it governed McClellan's treatment of the division and its commander. Casey was replaced by Brigadier General John J. Peck on June 23. Even under the new leader, the division was not committed to heavy fighting during the Seven Days. Then as the Army of the Potomac pulled out from the Peninsula in August, Peck's division stayed there. Yet so dire was the danger in Maryland by September 9 that McClellan ordered even that division to join him. However, Dix repeatedly protested that losing so many veteran troops would prove fatal to his mission of defending Union footholds in eastern Virginia. As late as September 19, Halleck remained committed to returning Peck to McClellan. With Antietam fought and the crisis of the campaign past, however, Halleck reconsidered where to place the division. On September 24, he authorized Dix to retain Peck. Two days later, Peck and two of his brigades were officially transferred to the VII Corps. As late as October 7, McClellan still asked for Peck's division but without avail. *OR*, v. XVIII, pp. 385, 395-99, 401, and v. XIX, pt. 1, pp. 11-12, 70-71, and pt. 2, pp. 238, 253, 387, 393, and v. LI, pt. 1, pp. 803, 814.

itself continued garrisoning southeastern Virginia rather than joining McClellan.[12]

Also remaining away from the Army of the Potomac were two veteran corps, the III under Major General Samuel P. Heintzelman and the XI under Major General Franz Sigel, which were kept within the defenses of Washington, along with Major General Nathaniel P. Banks' large garrison of that city, which would soon be designated the XXII Corps.[13] Students of the Maryland Campaign should never lose sight of the fact that while six Northern corps battled so desperately on the field of Antietam, three more Union corps languished within Washington's fortifications—a measure of President Lincoln's continuing concern for the capital.

Also in garrison in the Middle Department was Major General John Wool's VIII Corps, headquartered in Baltimore. Although some of its troops were lost in the Harper's Ferry debacle, it did not operate in the field as a corps.[14] Finally, there was the corps of Pennsylvania militia under Brigadier

12 Nine regiments of the VII Corps came forward from rear areas in eastern Virginia to reinforce the Army of the Potomac after Seven Pines and before the Seven Days. However, in the period between the Peninsula Campaign and Antietam, the three regiments of Brigadier General Max Weber's brigade from Suffolk were the only VII Corps troops to join McClellan. Dix retained the rest of his corps plus Peck's division of the IV Corps in his own Department of Virginia. Dyer, *Compendium*, pp. 330-31.

13 On September 8, Banks assumed command of the Military District of Washington, also called the "Defenses of Washington." Among his forces were the III Corps and initially two divisions of the V Corps of the Army of the Potomac plus the XI Corps (the former I Corps/Army of Virginia). The two V Corps divisions left him, September 12 and 14, to reinforce McClellan. The other two corps remained with him throughout the Antietam Campaign. In addition to those three corps, Banks had 26,500 more troops in garrisons, city guards, and training camps on September 10 and 31,500 such forces ten days later. These additional troops included not only heavy artillery regiments and light artillery batteries but also organized regiments, brigades, and divisions of infantry, and a cavalry brigade. Such a strong additional force was the equivalent of another corps, although it would not be formally numbered the XXII Corps until February 2, 1863.

14 Four infantry brigades of the VIII Corps were captured in Harper's Ferry on September 15. Their surrender cost the Yankees heavy loss of men, materiel, and munitions. Yet their presence at the ferry proved a tempting target that caused Robert E. Lee to divide his army to trap them—a risky move, when disclosed through "Lost Order 191," which gave McClellan tremendous opportunity to destroy the separated Southerners. Overnight September 14-15, a small cavalry brigade did escape disaster at the ferry and reach Federal lines, capturing a Confederate ordnance wagon train en route. Then in the immediate aftermath of Antietam, Brigadier General John R. Kenly's Maryland brigade came forward from Baltimore to Hagerstown on September 18-19 and on the next two days confronted Confederate cavalry which had recrossed the Potomac into Maryland at Williamsport. Even after the Graycoats

General John F. Reynolds, which Governor Andrew G. Curtin assembled in the Chambersburg-Greencastle area in the southern end of the Cumberland Valley to try to head off the apprehended invasion of the Commonwealth.[15]

These seven corps—the III, IV, VII, VIII, XI, "XXII," and Pennsylvania Militia—will be considered no further. Yet these corps were major pieces upon the chessboard of war in the Eastern Theater in September, 1862, whose potential or actual activity or inactivity affected the campaign. They were a possible strength or vulnerability for the Yankees. And they were a force in being which Southern invaders could not ignore.

This chapter will instead focus on Federal forces that fought at Antietam: the I, II, V, VI, IX, and XII Corps and the Cavalry Division of the

---

withdrew, Kenly continued guarding that key city where the great Valley Pike crossed that river.

15 Imminent Confederate invasion caused Pennsylvania Governor Andrew G. Curtin to raise state militia. With increasing urgency, he issued calls for them on September 4, 10, and 11. One regiment was formed as early as September 6. Twenty more regiments were raised before Antietam; two others mustered on the day of the battle; and three more were organized over the following four days. Two new three-year Volunteer units, the 15th Pennsylvania Cavalry at Carlisle Barracks and the 145th Pennsylvania, just raised in Erie, were also available. Those twenty-eight regiments were the equivalent of a corps. Curtin expressly requested that Reynolds be reassigned from commanding the Pennsylvania Reserve Division in the I Corps to lead the militia. President Lincoln acceded to his request. The general left his division on September 12 and took charge of the militia two days later. Fellow Volunteer Brigadier Generals Andrew Porter and James Cooper and Regular Major (promoted to Volunteer Brigadier General as of November 29) Israel Vogdes were assigned to help him with the militia. Reynolds soon moved his headquarters from Harrisburg to Chambersburg. He concentrated his forces near the latter city and farther south in Greencastle to head off the Secessionists. His mounted patrols from the 15th Cavalry, which left Carlisle Barracks from September 9 to 16, and the 145th ventured into Maryland and reoccupied Hagerstown, September 15. Two days later, as the Battle of Antietam raged, those two regiments marched to the sound of the guns and actually joined McClellan while the battle was under way. Also on September 17, Reynolds himself reached Hagerstown. He ordered his militia to join him overnight, but many refused to leave Pennsylvania. Even the militia who did come to Hagerstown refused to accompany Reynolds to the battlefield of Antietam on the night of September 17-18. More of them responded to his effort to place a blocking force west of that city against Butternut cavalry who occupied Williamsport on September 19. They participated in light skirmishing on September 20-21, after which the Secessionists withdrew across the Potomac. Their departure marked the end of the Confederate invasion. Such Pennsylvania militia as had entered Maryland returned to the Keystone State on September 21. Curtin disbanded the militia four days later, and most troops were mustered out by the end of the month, although six of the forty-two independent companies did not leave service until October. The last regiment to be discharged was the 25th on September 30-October 1. It had guarded the DuPont Gunpowder Works in Delaware. Reynolds himself was relieved on the 26th and returned to the Army of the Potomac, where he took charge of the I Corps on September 29.

Army of the Potomac—which was equivalent to a corps in many ways. Most of those corps were much stronger during the Maryland Campaign than they had been from late spring through mid-summer. Not only did individual regiments—raised under the calls for 300,000 three-year and nine-month Volunteers—replenish their reduced ranks, but entire divisions were also added to them.[16] The I, II, V, and VI Corps were restored to three divisions each; the IX Corps received a fourth division; and only the XII continued operating with just two divisions.[17] The mounted arm, too,

16 Seventeen new regiments served as part of the six veteran corps at Antietam. Six were nine-month units: the 124th, 125th, 128th, 130th, 132nd, and 137th Pennsylvania. Another Keystone outfit, the 118th, had enlisted for three years, as had the 14th and 16th Connecticut, 20th Maine, 35th Massachusetts, 17th Michigan, 9th New Hampshire, 13th New Jersey, and 107th, 108th, and 121st New York. Right while the battle was under way on the 17th, as already mentioned, two more new three-year regiments from the Keystone State, the 145th Infantry and the 15th Cavalry, arrived from Hagerstown and operated on McClellan's right flank. The horsemen remained with him only until September 21 and then returned to Carlisle Barracks to finish organizing, but the 145th was assigned to the II Corps of his army. Then on the morning after Antietam, Couch's division (including two new three-year units, the 122nd New York and 139th Pennsylvania) reached that battlefield. Also that morning, Brigadier General Andrew A. Humphreys' division of eight Pennsylvania regiments reinforced McClellan. Of them, the 91st had been in service since December, 1861, but had never seen combat. The other outfits were raw: the 123rd, 126th, 129th, 131st, 133rd, 134th, and 155th. Indeed, the 155th did not leave Pittsburgh until September 3 or arrive in Washington until September 6; twelve days later it reached the front. That unit and the 91st enlisted for three years. The other six regiments were just beginning nine-month tours. Two more three-year outfits, the 36th Massachusetts and 20th Michigan, reached Sharpsburg, September 21-22, and were assigned to the IX Corps. Then on September 29, Banks sent twenty more new regiments to the Army of the Potomac. The 21st, 23rd, and 26th New Jersey and 136th Pennsylvania were nine-month units. The others had signed up for three years: the 20th and 21st Connecticut, 19th Maine, 37th Massachusetts, 24th Michigan, 10th and 11th New Hampshire, 15th New Jersey, 123rd, 137th, 140th, 145th, and 149th New York; 121st and 142nd Pennsylvania, and 7th Rhode Island. Sixteen of those twenty regiments left their home states in early or even mid-September, 1862. By month's end, they were assigned to McClellan. Finally, in mid-October, another three-year unit, the 119th Pennsylvania, reached that army from Washington's defenses. All fifty-two new regiments (including cavalry) represented a great infusion of fresh manpower—numerically strong but as yet qualitatively weak because they were inexperienced and untrained. For the first seventeen of them to arrive, their lack of training proved costly as they were sent into battle right away on September 14 and 17.

17 When corps were created in March of 1862, the I through the IV had three divisions apiece. During the spring, however, as Blenker's division was transferred to the Mountain Department and other divisions were reshuffled to create the V and VI Corps, almost all corps were reduced to two divisions each. As the Maryland Campaign began, only the I Corps had been restored to three divisions. On September 12, Weber's brigade from the VII Corps, Brigadier General Nathan Kimball's crack brigade from Banks's original V Corps, and a brigade of three new regiments were united to create a new Third Division of the II

received more regiments but remained just one division.[18] Eleven officers commanded those corps at some point between September 7-17, 1862. This chapter will briefly examine those eleven generals and then generalize about them.

The I Corps' first commander, Major General Irvin McDowell, no longer had charge of it. As of September 7, 1862, Major General Joseph Hooker of Massachusetts (West Point Class of 1837) led it. As a division commander from Yorktown through Second Manassas, he had earned his nickname, "Fighting Joe."[19] A hard-fighting, ambitious officer, Hooker gave promise of willingness, even eagerness, to pitch in to the enemy. After all, the more he accomplished, the higher he would rise—and the more both he and the Union would benefit.[20]

Corps. On that same date, Humphreys' new division was assigned to Porter's V corps as its Third Division. The need to rearm his raw regiments with usable weapons as well as orders to guard the approaches to Frederick understandably delayed Humphreys, so he did not rejoin Porter until the morning after Antietam. Also arriving late that morning was Couch's division of the IV Corps. As already explained, it served as part of Franklin's Left Wing for the first part of the Antietam Campaign; on September 26, it permanently joined the VI Corps as its Third Division. Among the newer corps, only two divisions of the IX Corps fought at Second Bull Run. They were reunited with its Third Division from Fredericksburg about September 5. The following day, the Kanawha Division from western Virginia was appended to the IX Corps as its Fourth Division. Even with four divisions, the IX contained only eight brigades. The V Corps (including Humphreys) also had eight brigades. The II and VI Corps (including Couch) had nine brigades apiece, and the I Corps contained ten. The XII Corps remained the smallest formation, with just five brigades grouped into two divisions.

18 The 1st Massachusetts Cavalry from South Carolina, the 3rd Indiana Cavalry from the I Corps, the 12th Pennsylvania Cavalry from DC, and at least the 8th New York Cavalry from Harper's Ferry reinforced McClellan for Antietam. The other mounted regiment, battalion, and two squadrons from the ferry and the 15th Pennsylvania Cavalry from Reynolds were also at his disposal. Receiving more units led his cavalry chief to restructure his division from two decent-sized brigades to five small ones but not to transform his command into a corps. Not until February, 1863, would the mounted arm of the Army of the Potomac become a Cavalry Corps.

19 Hooker's nickname originated as a newspaper typographical error. A journalist, writing about the general's first battle at Williamsburg, began his story "Fighting—Joe Hooker...." The editor or typesetter misread the dash as a hyphen and rendered the lead "Fighting-Joe Hooker...." With or without a hyphen, the nickname stuck because it captured this commander's combativeness.

20 Walter Hebert wrote the standard *Fighting Joe Hooker*; Heitman, *Register*, v. I, p. 540, Warner, *Blue*, pp. 233-35.

Increased success and reputation did come his way at Antietam. So did a disabling foot wound. To succeed him, McClellan hand-picked not the senior division commander in the I Corps but the best division commander there: Brigadier General George G. Meade of Pennsylvania (West Point Class of 1835).[21] More prudent and more acerbic than Hooker, Meade nevertheless shared his predecessor's penchant for punching. New even to division command, he had taken over the Pennsylvania Reserve Division only on September 12, when Reynolds was transferred to command the Pennsylvania militia. Even so, Meade's service at South Mountain, Sharpsburg, and subsequently Fredericksburg proved spectacular. If he had been killed on December 13, 1862, he would still be remembered as one of the great fighting division commanders of the Northern Army. But, of course, he survived Fredericksburg—and he is remembered for even greater contributions to winning the war.[22]

The II Corps hardly had a newcomer at its head. Major General Edwin V. Sumner of Massachusetts was the only original corps commander from March of 1862 who still led a corps at Antietam. Not a West Pointer but a career officer in the Regular Army since 1819, he had earned a distinguished record in the Mexican and Indian Wars. It is commonplace to claim that at age 65 Sumner was too old for Civil War service, too ossified in Old Army organization to rise to the responsibilities of corps command. Such criticism is discredited by the fact that already in 1862, months before Antietam, Sumner had saved the Army of the Potomac from the two worst perils of destruction it faced in the entire Civil War: at Seven Pines and Glendale.

21 Meade's One-Star commission as of August 31, 1861, was six weeks junior to that of his brother-in-law, James B. Ricketts, who commanded the Second Division of the I Corps at Antietam. Meade initially offered the command to Ricketts, but McClellan repeatedly insisted the junior officer take over the corps. Why "Little Mac" preferred Meade to Ricketts is not clear—perhaps, because Meade had served under him on the Peninsula, whereas Ricketts technically became part of the Army of the Potomac only in early September.

22 The general's grandson published Meade's *Life and Letters*. The classic biography is Freeman Cleaves' *Meade of Gettysburg*. More recent works are Tom Huntington's *Searching for Meade*, Ethan Rafuse's *Meade and the War in the East*, and Richard Sauers' *Victor of Gettysburg*. Also, Heitman, *Register*, v. I, p. 700; Warner, *Blue*, pp. 315-17.

Much he had already accomplished before and during the war. Much more was expected of him.[23]

Sumner had earned a great combat record before the Civil War. Two other corps commanders, Porter and Franklin (both of them now Two-Stars) also enjoyed high prewar reputation, based not only on Mexican War service but also on staff work and West Point class standing. They were McClellan's favorites, to whom he entrusted the new V and VI Corps, May 18, 1862. New Hampshire native Porter (West Point Class of 1845) wielded his corps skillfully at Hanover Court House, Beaver Dam Creek, Gaines' Mill, and Malvern Hill and more controversially at Second Manassas. He was the officer on whose performance and judgment McClellan most relied. He rose with McClellan—and fell with him. Just days after McClellan was relieved of command in November, 1862, Porter was not only removed but arrested and court-martialed. On January 21, 1863, he was cashiered and would not be restored to rank until August, 1886.[24]

The Pennsylvanian Franklin's service was less controversial than Porter's—and less conspicuous. His VI Corps saw less action on the Peninsula than the V Corps, and only one of its brigades arrived in time to fight in the Second Manassas Campaign (where it suffered disaster at Bull Run Bridge). Thus, the VI Corps was relatively large and fresh. McClellan was likely to count on it and its commander for major missions. Yet in the Maryland Campaign and throughout the Civil War, Franklin would repeatedly fail to live up to the high expectations held for him as the first in his Class of 1843 at West Point.[25]

23 Thomas K. Tate recently wrote a biography of Sumner. Two other books on him are by William W. Long and "Francis Stanley" [psued. for Stanley Francis L. Crocchiola]. A modern history of the II Corps at Antietam is Marion Armstrong's *Unfurl Those Colors*. The classic history of that corps comes from the pen of its Assistant Adjutant General, Francis A. Walker. See also Heitman, *Register*, v. I, p. 936, and Warner, *Blue*, pp. 489-90.

24 Otto Eisenschiml wrote the classic *The Celebrated Case of Fitz John Porter*. More recent studies are Curt Anders' *Injustice on Trial*, Donald Jermann's *Scapegoat of Second Manassas*, and Ethan Rafuse's *Fitz John Porter*. William Powell's *History of the Fifth Army Corps* is the standard work on that formation. See also Heitman, *Register*, v. I, p. 799, and Warner, *Blue*, pp. 378-80.

25 The modern biography of Franklin is Mark Snell's *From First to Last*. The classic histories of his corps come from two of his officers, *Following the Greek Cross* by Thomas Hyde and *Three Years in the Sixth Corps* by George Stevens. See also Heitman, *Register*, v. I, p. 434, and Warner, *Blue*, pp. 159-60.

These four corps—I, II, V, and VI—were an inherent part of the Army of the Potomac, and the I and V had also served in Major General John Pope's Army of Virginia in the Second Manassas Campaign. The remaining two corps were new to McClellan's army. The IX Corps just arrived in Virginia in July, 1862, after serving on the lower Atlantic coast: two divisions from North Carolina and one from South Carolina. Then the Kanawha Division from western Virginia was appended to that corps on September 6.[26]

Three officers led that corps during these operations. The one most associated with it was its original commander, Major General Ambrose E. Burnside of Rhode Island (West Point Class of 1847). With its predecessor, a large division, he had gained important victories in eastern North Carolina from February to April of 1862. He had, however, never led a corps in battle—let alone a wing of two corps. A magnetic personality beloved by his IX Corps soldiers, he was conscious of his own limitations—more conscious, indeed, than were his military and civilian superiors.[27]

With Burnside heading the Right Wing of the I and IX Corps, his own IX Corps itself entered the Maryland Campaign under Major General Jesse L. Reno of Pennsylvania (West Point Class of 1846), who had also led it at Second Manassas. Earlier he had commanded a brigade and division under Burnside in North Carolina. A promising officer, he might have proved a

26 In January, 1862, Ambrose E. Burnside's huge division of fifteen regiments, grouped into three brigades, joined the 9th New York Zouaves and 48th Pennsylvania at Hatteras Inlet and proceeded to capture Roanoke Island, New Bern, and Fort Macon by the end of April. Ere then, on April 2, his force (now built up to twenty regiments) was restructured into six brigades, paired into three divisions. It was, in effect, a corps but as yet unnumbered. That July, Burnside left his First Division to garrison his conquests and sailed with his other two divisions to Newport News. There he was joined by a division from South Carolina, which became his new First Division. His force was designated the IX Corps on July 22. The Kanawha Division, which had arrived in the main war zone during the final phase of the Second Manassas Campaign, was attached to the IX, September 6.

27 Burnside was appointed to West Point from Indiana. He re-entered the Army in 1861 from Rhode Island and is customarily associated with that state. The standard works on the general and his forces come from 19th Century authors: Ben Perley Poore's *Life and Public Services of Ambrose E. Burnside* and Augustus Woodbury's *Ambrose E. Burnside and the Ninth Army Corps*. The modern biography is William Marvel's *Burnside*. See also Heitman, *Register*, v. I, p. 266, and Warner, *Blue*, pp. 57-58.

great corps commander—had he lived. He did not. For General Reno, the war and life itself ended in Fox's Gap on September 14.[28]

He was succeeded by his ranking division commander, the Ohioan Brigadier General Jacob D. Cox, who led the IX Corps at Antietam. The youngest of the eleven corps commanders, not quite 34 years old, he was also the only one with no prewar military experience as Regular, Volunteer, or even militiaman. He had led a quasi-independent brigade and division in western Virginia since the summer of 1861 but had arrived in the main war zone only in late August, 1862. Fighting little battles against a weak foe in the mountains was far different from fighting a big battle against the Army of Northern Virginia. Before the war ended, Cox would prove an above average corps commander. How to become one he began learning the hard way, September 17.[29]

Another citizen-soldier, of sorts, was Brigadier General Alpheus S. Williams of the XII Corps. He, however, had been Lieutenant Colonel of the 1st Michigan Volunteers in the Mexican War and a general of Michigan Militia prewar. He had, moreover, seen extensive combat as a division commander under Banks from May through August of 1862. As the senior subordinate, he was acting commander of the XII Corps until September 15 and again for most of the Battle of Antietam. Later in the Civil War, he served as acting corps commander at Gettysburg, part of the Atlanta Campaign, the March to the Sea, and the Carolinas Campaign—but he would never receive permanent corps command or promotion to major general.[30]

Williams' brief displacement, September 15-17, was due to the arrival of Brigadier General Joseph K. F. Mansfield of Connecticut (West Point Class of 1822). A prominent engineer officer in the Mexican War and one of two prewar Inspectors General of the U.S. Army, Mansfield received his first star in the Regular Army as of May 14, 1861. He expected to play a big role in the Civil War. Yet he always seemed to miss out—at Washington

28 Born in Wheeling, (West) Virginia, Reno grew up in Pennsylvania and entered West Point from there, so it is rightly his state. W. F. McConnell, *Remember Reno*; Heitman, *Register*, v. I, pp. 823-24; Warner, *Blue*, pp. 394-95.

29 For sources on Cox, see Chapter 6, n. 41.

30 Williams was breveted Major General on January 12, 1865. Sources on him are given ibid., n. 44.

while fighting raged at First Bull Run, at Norfolk and Suffolk during the Peninsula Campaign. Some of his troops from the Southside joined McClellan's army. He came, too, and now he had charge of a corps—even though he had never commanded troops in battle at any level. His first battle would prove his last. Mortally wounded just as his corps reached the field on September 17, he died the following day. On March 12, 1863, he was promoted to Major General posthumously.[31]

Finally, there is the cavalry commander, Brigadier General Alfred Pleasonton, a native of the District of Columbia (West Point Class of 1844). He led a cavalry brigade during the post-Malvern Hill phase of the Peninsula Campaign. The Cavalry Division/Army of the Potomac had been broken up when its commander, Brigadier General George Stoneman, left that army on August 22. The division was evidently reconstituted about September 2. As senior brigadier, Pleasonton took charge of it. A driving, ambitious officer, he remained to be tested at this higher level of command.[32]

These, then, are brief vignettes of the eleven corps commanders at Antietam individually. Collectively, what generalizations may be offered about them? As to experience, Sumner was an original corps commander. Burnside, Porter, Franklin, and Reno also had long tenure in that position. The other six were new to corps command, though five of them had commanded divisions or at least brigades in battle. Only Mansfield lacked any command experience in combat.[33]

Nine of them were Regulars, including eight West Pointers plus Sumner, who entered the Army from civil life in 1819. Those nine Regulars averaged almost twenty-one years of service in the Old Army; if Burnside's brief tour of six years is excluded, the average for the other eight rises nearly to twenty-three years. Adding the thirty-two+ years that eight of them spent as West Point cadets increases the average to twenty-four and a half years.

31 Mansfield's posthumous promotion was backdated to July 18, 1862. A memorial volume on him was published the year of his death. One of his officers, John M. Gould, later penned *A Narrative of Events Connected with His* [Mansfield's] *Mortal Wounding at Antietam*. See also Heitman, *Register*, v. I, p. 688, and Warner, *Blue*, pp. 309-10.

32 William Styple, *Generals in Bronze*; Heitman, *Register*, v. I, p. 795, and Warner, *Blue*, pp. 373-74 relate to Pleasonton. His command is covered in the first two volumes of Stephen Z. Starr's *The Union Cavalry in the Civil War*.

33 Hooker and Williams had previously led divisions in battle, and Pleasonton had headed a brigade in combat. Meade and Cox had commanded at both levels.

Williams, moreover, had served in the volunteers and militia prewar. Only Cox had no military experience before 1861.

Cox also was the youngest corps commander, not quite 34, and Sumner was the oldest at almost 66. The average age for all eleven was 45 years-5.5 months.

Five were born in New England, one in Pennsylvania, one in Indiana, one in D.C., one in (West) Virginia, and two in foreign lands (to American parents).[34] Three each entered military service from New England, the Middle Atlantic, and the Midwest, one from D.C., and one "at large."[35]

In the months and years of the Civil War following Antietam, Pleasonton rose to command a real cavalry corps; Cox received permanent command of the XXIII Corps; Hooker led initially the V and later the XX Corps; Franklin had charge of the XIX Corps; and Williams repeatedly served as acting commander of the XII and XX Corps.[36] Sumner, Hooker, and Franklin each led grand divisions at the Battle of Fredericksburg.[37]

34 Porter from New Hampshire, Hooker and Sumner from Massachusetts, and Mansfield and Williams from Connecticut were the five New Englanders. Franklin, Burnside, and Pleasonton were born in Pennsylvania, Indiana, and the District of Columbia, respectively. Reno was born in Wheeling, (West) Virginia. Cox and Meade were, respectively, born in Canada and Spain to American parents.

35 Franklin, Mansfield, Pleasonton, and Sumner entered service from their states of birth. So did Burnside and Hooker when they were appointed to the U.S. Military Academy. Both of them resigned from the Army in 1853. When they re-entered service in 1861, they were living in Rhode Island and California, respectively. Meade and Reno joined from Pennsylvania, Cox from Ohio, and Williams from Michigan. For Porter, Heitman and the *Army Register* specify New York and the District of Columbia, respectively. Perhaps Cullum comes closest in stating that Porter was appointed "at large," reflecting his father's far-flung U.S. Navy service.

36 Pleasonton headed the Cavalry Corps/Army of the Potomac, May 22, 1863-March 24, 1864. Cox temporarily led the XXIII Corps on four occasions starting December 20, 1863—most notably at Franklin. He permanently headed a Provisional Corps and then the XXIII in North Carolina, February 25-June 17, 1865. Hooker led the V Corps, November 10-16, 1862, and the XX Corps, April 14-July 28, 1864. Williams succeeded Hooker with the XX and led it July 28-August 27, 1864, and November 11, 1864-April 2, 1865. Ere then, he briefly had charge of the XII Corps, September 17-October 20, 1862, and July 1-4 and August 31-September 13, 1863. Finally, Franklin led the XIX Corps, August 20, 1863-May 2, 1864.

37 A Grand Division was a command arrangement encompassing two corps. It was a more formal and supposedly permanent structure than the "wings" into which the Army of the Potomac was occasionally divided during the Antietam and Gettysburg Campaigns. Sumner's Right Grand Division contained his own II Corps plus the IX. Hooker's Center Grand Division had the V Corps (over which he was placed in command after Antietam)

Sumner was en route to take charge of the Department of the Missouri when he passed away on March 21, 1863, and Hooker commanded the Northern Department, 1864-1865.[38] Burnside, Hooker, and Meade were McClellan's successive successors in command of the Army of the Potomac, and Burnside later led the Army of the Ohio in the Knoxville Campaign.[39] Of the survivors, only Porter played no further part in the Civil War after the Loudoun Valley Campaign in the autumn of 1862, because he was dismissed the service two months later.[40]

---

and the III. Franklin's Left Grand Division included his VI Corps plus the I. The following January 10, the XI and XII Corps were grouped into the Reserve Grand Division under Sigel. Promoting those four generals caused their former corps to pass to Darius Couch, Brigadier General Daniel Butterfield (later George Meade), William F. Smith, and Brigadier General Julius Stahel (later Brigadier General Carl Schurz, who declined to assume command), respectively. Burnside created this force structure on November 14, 1862; it lasted only during his tenure commanding the Army of the Potomac. Ten days after Hooker replaced him in charge of that army, the new commander abolished grand divisions. Each corps thereafter resumed reporting directly to army headquarters.

38 The Northern Department, headquartered in Cincinnati, included the states of Michigan and Ohio, almost all of Indiana and Illinois, and the Kentucky defenses for that city. Hooker was responsible for securing major prisoner of war camps in Sandusky, Columbus, Indianapolis, Chicago, and Rock Island (briefly in Cincinnati, too) and also for guarding against Copperhead disturbances. However, the last Confederate combat incursion into that region occurred fourteen months before he took charge on October 1, 1864. He would face no such intrusions during the ensuing nine months before the department was discontinued on June 27, 1865.

39 Burnside led the Army of the Potomac, November 9, 1862-January 26, 1863, during the Fredericksburg Campaign and the Mud March. Next came Hooker, January 26-June 28, 1863, for Chancellorsville and the start of the Gettysburg Campaign. Meade took charge of that army after Hooker and led it through Gettysburg to Appomattox until it was discontinued, June 28, 1865. Burnside also headed the Department/Army of the Ohio, March 25-December 9, 1863.

40 On November 7-8, 1862, McClellan was relieved from command of the Army of the Potomac. Burnside succeeded him on November 9. The next day, Porter was removed from command of the V Corps and ordered to report to the Adjutant General of the Army in Washington. He departed, November 12, and five days later he was arrested and was brought before a court martial, which sat from November 27 to January 10, 1863. On that final date, it found him guilty of disobeying orders and of misbehaving in the face of the enemy in the Second Bull Run Campaign. It sentenced him to be cashiered. President Lincoln approved the verdict on January 21. As a result, Porter was not only dismissed the service but was also "forever disqualified from holding any office of trust or profit under the Government of the United States." He spent the next quarter century trying to reverse that judgment. Finally, on August 5, 1886, he was restored to his Regular commission of Infantry Colonel, backdated to his original appointment, May 14, 1861. Vindicated at last, he retired two days later.

Yet at war's end, just Meade had a major command, the Army of the Potomac, and Cox and (at least through the Battle of Bentonville) Williams—the two citizen-soldiers—led corps.[41] Hooker and Pleasonton served in backwater areas, and Burnside and Franklin were "awaiting orders."[42] Burnside, Cox, Williams, and Franklin all left service between April, 1865, and March, 1866. Pleasonton and Hooker departed the Regular Army in 1868. Only Meade remained in service for the rest of his life until he passed away on November 6, 1872.[43]

Meade had not reached his 57th birthday when he died. Burnside had barely turned 57, and Hooker was 64 at his passing. The average age at death of the eight officers who survived the war was 68 years-8.5 months. Including the three who died during the conflict reduces the average to just under age 65. The youngest was Reno, who was only 39 when he was mortally wounded. The most long-lived was Franklin, who was 80 when he passed away on March 8, 1903. He and Porter, who died in 1901, nearly at age 79, were the only two of the eleven who lived into the 20th Century.[44]

After leaving the Army, Franklin served twenty-two years as General Manager for Colt's Fire Arms in Connecticut. Other significant postwar service includes Burnside as Rhode Island governor and senator, Williams as congressman from Michigan and minister to El Salvador, and Cox as Ohio governor and congressman and Secretary of the Interior under President Ulysses S. Grant.[45]

41 Although Williams had commanded the XX Corps during the March to the Sea and the Carolinas Campaign from Savannah to Goldsborough, he was replaced in that position with Major General Joseph A. Mower before the Raleigh Campaign and entered his final campaign as he had begun his first campaign in the spring of 1862, a brigadier general commanding a division.

42 Pleasonton left the Army of the Potomac, March 25, 1864. For his subsequent service west of the Mississippi River and postwar, see Chapter 8, nn. 52, 55, and 66.

43 Burnside, Cox, and Franklin resigned. Williams mustered out. Hooker retired. Pleasonton mustered out of Volunteer Service in 1866. He resigned his Regular commission in a huff two years later because he received no higher grade than major; he was restored to the retired rolls in 1888—still a major.

44 Cox died on August 4, 1900, just short of the 20th Century, at age 71 years-9 months. Pleasonton was ten months older than Cox at his passing on February 17, 1897.

45 Soon after the Civil War, Burnside and Cox were elected Governors of Rhode Island and Ohio and served 1866-1869 and 1866-1868, respectively. In those same three years, Williams was Minister to El Salvador. All of them also served together in Congress in the

Cox also wrote a two-volume memoir of Civil War service, and Meade's and Williams' wartime letters have been published. *McClellan's Own Story* was published posthumously. "Little Mac" himself, as well as Hooker, Meade, Sumner, Porter, Franklin, Burnside, Reno, and Cox are the subjects of numerous book-length biographies, and Mansfield's Old Army inspections have also been covered in print.

How, then, may the wartime service of these senior subordinates be summarized? Only one was a great general: Meade. Three others were good at corps level—Sumner, Porter, and Hooker—and Cox eventually proved above average. Williams and Pleasonton were competent. Reno and Mansfield remain question marks, the former a promising officer cut down in his prime, the latter completely unknown. Only Burnside and Franklin clearly fell short of expectations. Yet great officers are appreciated—at least in part—because they stand out from the good, the competent, the mediocre, the disappointing. Such a mix is not uncommon among any group of senior officers. Such a mix marked "Mac's Main Men."

following decade, Burnside as a Senator, 1875-1881; Cox as a Representative, 1877-1879; and Williams as a Representative, 1875-1878. Cox also served in Grant's cabinet, 1869-1870. The Michigander was a Democrat; the other two men were Republicans.

43. George B. McClellan. *LOC*

44. Joseph Hooker. *LOC*

45. Edwin V. Sumner, Sr. *LOC*

46. Fitz John Porter. *LOC*

47. William B. Franklin. LOC

48. Ambrose E. Burnside. LOC

49. Jesse L. Reno. LOC

50. Joseph K. F. Mansfield. LOC

Chapter 8

Meade's Main Men: Federal Wing and Corps Commanders in the Gettysburg Campaign[1]

Europeans often call the First World War "the Great War." To Americans, that name may well be applied to the Civil War. The conflict of 1861-1865 was great in its causations, its course, and its consequences. It involved hundreds of thousands, eventually millions, of soldiers, organized into armies far larger than ever before fielded in American history. Such armies were beyond the span of control of any one commander, no matter how talented. Dividing those armies into corps became essential to provide such control. Corps became the elements for strategic maneuver and the echelons for grand tactical (or operational) control. Corps commanders were responsible senior subordinates who were accorded considerable latitude—and who were expected to exercise it. President Abraham Lincoln himself created the first five corps on March 8, 1862. By the time of the Gettysburg Campaign, a year and a half later, they were the standard structure throughout the Union Army.

1 This chapter expands on a presentation given at the Chambersburg Civil War Seminar on July 26, 2013, marking the 150th anniversary of the Gettysburg Campaign. It covers the entire military careers of the seventeen Federal corps commanders in that campaign and does not dwell on their service only in the battle itself. As in Chapters 6, 7, and 9 of this book, this chapter draws on information in Frederick H. Dyer, *A Compendium of the War of the Rebellion*; in Francis B. Heitman, *Historical Register and Biographical Dictionary of the United States Army, 1789-1903*; and in Ezra J. Warner, *Generals in Blue*.

As of June 30, 1863, Federal forces were grouped into twenty-six infantry corps and two cavalry corps. Eleven of those infantry corps and one cavalry corps fought in the Western Theater.[2] Two more corps served along the lower Atlantic coast and Gulf coast.[3] The remaining thirteen infantry corps and one cavalry corps operated within the Eastern Theater, broadly defined as extending from Philadelphia to New Bern and westward to the Appalachians. Six of those eastern corps significantly influenced the overall strategic maneuvers of the campaign and supplied sizable reinforcements to the Army of the Potomac. They, however, did not fight at Gettysburg, so this chapter will simply specify their existence and will not concentrate on their commanders. They are:

- The VIII Corps under Major General Robert C. Schenck, headquartered in Baltimore and including forces in Delaware, Maryland, and the lower Shenandoah Valley.[4]
- The XXII Corps under Major General Samuel P. Heintzelman, headquartered in Washington and including forces in the defenses of the nation's capital.[5]
- The IV Corps under Major General Erasmus D. Keyes, headquartered in Yorktown, and the VII Corps under Major

2 The numbered corps in the West at the end of June, 1863, were: the IX, XIII, XIV, XV, XVI, XVI-Vicksburg, XVII, XX, XXI, and XXIII. The Army of the Cumberland also contained a Reserve Corps and a Cavalry Corps.

3 The X Corps was headquartered in South Carolina. The XIX Corps operated in Louisiana, as did the Corps D'Afrique. The latter had only five regiments as of that date and was not yet organized as a corps, even on paper; it never became a mobile corps in reality. It is counted as a corps in Chapter 6 but not in this chapter.

4 One brigade of the VIII Corps fought with the XII Corps at Gettysburg. Seven more VIII Corps brigades and four of its former brigades, operating in the field, also figured prominently in the campaign before and after the battle. Even its two brigades remaining in Baltimore afforded some protection to that city. These fourteen brigades of the VIII Corps are covered more fully in Chapter 14 of Volume II of this book.

5 Two cavalry brigades and four infantry brigades of the XXII Corps fought at Gettysburg, and three more of its regiments took the field just after the battle. Even its eleven brigades that remained within Washington's defenses were a strategic bulwark which the Confederates could not ignore. All these XXII Corps troops are covered more fully in Chapter 14 of Volume II of this book.

General John A. Dix, headquartered at Fort Monroe, both of which included forces in southeastern Virginia.[6]

- And the XVIII Corps under Major General John G. Foster, headquartered in New Bern and including troops in North Carolina.[7]

Besides those five corps of Volunteers, the equivalent of a corps of New York National Guardsmen and Pennsylvania Militia (plus a few Volunteer units) served in the Department of the Susquehanna under Major General Darius N. Couch, headquartered in Harrisburg and operating in eastern and central Pennsylvania.[8]

These six corps—IV, VII, VIII, XVIII, XXII, and Susquehanna—will be considered no further. Yet they were major pieces upon the strategic chessboard of war in the Eastern Theater in the summer of 1863. For the Union, they were possible sources of strength or vulnerability. For the South, they were forces in being that could not be ignored. Their potential or actual activity or inactivity unquestionably affected the course of the Pennsylvania Campaign.

6 General Dix, commanding the Department of Virginia, used the IV and VII Corps, reinforced by one brigade of the XVIII Corps, to conduct the Peninsula Campaign of 1863 (June 24-July 7): a strike westward from Williamsburg and Yorktown to threaten Richmond and cut the railroads running from the capital to Fredericksburg and Staunton. When that campaign failed, he sent over half his forces to confront the Confederate invasion of the North. Fifteen of his regiments and one battalion reached Meade while the Butternuts were still in western Maryland. Ten more of his regiments arrived too late to encounter Lee and were assigned to the XXII Corps to replace troops it had sent to Meade. All these IV and VII Corps troops are covered more fully in Chapters 14 and 19 of Volume II of this study.

7 The XVIII Corps sent three regiments first to Dix and thence to Meade and five more regiments straight to Meade. They arrived in the latter phases of the Gettysburg Campaign. Foster also made three feeble forays against the railroad from Weldon to Wilmington, July 3-7. All these XVIII Corps troops are covered more fully in Chapter 14 of Volume II of this study.

8 Couch's mission was to head off the Confederate invasion of the Keystone State, protect Harrisburg and Philadelphia, secure the Susquehanna River, and guard the vital Pennsylvania Railroad. During four crucial weeks from mid-June to early July of 1863, his corps served its purpose: confronting the Confederate invaders, denying them the opportunity to advance unimpeded, vexing their supply lines, and buying time for the Army of the Potomac to reach Pennsylvania and create a direr danger for the Southerners. All these Susquehanna Corps troops are covered more fully in Chapter 14 of Volume II of this study.

This chapter instead focuses on Federal forces that fought in the Battle of Gettysburg as part of the Army of the Potomac: the I, II, III, V, VI, XI, XII, and Cavalry Corps. On moving northward from Maryland into Pennsylvania and even during the ensuing battle itself, those corps were sometimes grouped into wings: informal, temporary arrangements that allowed more senior corps commanders to control several such formations. Elevating officers to wing command, in turn, briefly created vacancies at corps level which senior subordinates temporarily filled. Casualties also caused temporary promotions. Altogether, some seventeen officers—permanent and temporary—led those corps and wings at some point between June 28, 1863, when Major General George G. Meade took charge of that army, and August 3, 1863, when the Gettysburg Campaign ended as the exhausted armies finally rested along the headwaters of the Rappahannock River.[9] This chapter will summarize the service of each of those seventeen commanders earlier in the war, touch briefly on their Gettysburg experience, and go on to cover them post-battle and postwar. It will then generalize about those generals.

One of the best officers headed the Left Wing of the Army of the Potomac, consisting of his own I Corps as well as the III and XI Corps and the First Cavalry Division: Major General John F. Reynolds of Pennsylvania. A West Pointer (Class of 1841) and a brigade commander since September 16, 1861, he had been captured at Gaines' Mill. Exchanged right away, he had led the Pennsylvania Reserve Division at Second Bull Run and the Pennsylvania Militia Corps during the Antietam Campaign.[10]

9 It is mistaken to suppose that the Gettysburg Campaign ended when the Butternuts crossed the Potomac on July 14. That very day, Meade moved his forces to or near the river, and two of his cavalry brigades crossed. On July 15, he moved his forces downriver, and the following day, his main army began crossing. It moved southward up the Loudoun Valley to try to prevent Lee from coming over the Blue Ridge into the piedmont. He, however, eluded the Yankees and emerged east of the mountains. Not until early August did the campaign end, as the battered armies found respite along the upper Rappahannock.

10 In September, 1862, Pennsylvania raised twenty-six regiments of militia—the equivalent of a corps—to head off the Confederate invasion of the North if it reached the Keystone State. Governor Andrew G. Curtin expressly requested that Reynolds be reassigned from leading the Pennsylvania Reserve Division to command the militia. President Lincoln acceded to this request. The general turned the division over to his ranking brigadier, Meade, on September 12 and assumed command of the militia two days later. Reynolds' departure afforded Meade the opportunity to excel as a division commander at South Mountain and Antietam.

Since September 29, 1862, he had charge of the I Corps, which he led in heavy fighting at Fredericksburg and in extensive maneuvering at Chancellorsville. Meade's long-time comrade in arms, close friend, former commander, and now trusted subordinate, Reynolds was the longest serving of all seventeen corps commanders. Nine and a half months of such service ended July 1, 1863, when he was killed in action early on the first day at Gettysburg.[11]

With Reynolds commanding the Left Wing, his own I Corps devolved on its senior division commander, Major General Abner Doubleday of New York (West Point Class of 1842). One of the heroes of Fort Sumter, a brigadier early in the war, and a division commander since South Mountain, he handled the I Corps quite skillfully on July 1. However, his accomplishments that day did not earn him permanent command. On July 2, Meade replaced him with Major General John Newton, who had led the Third Division of the VI Corps. An abrasive abolitionist, Doubleday was unpopular with most Regular officers, including Meade. The insubordinate subordinate resented being supplanted in corps command by some officer four months his junior in date of rank. On July 3, after Pickett's charge was repulsed, Doubleday requested a corps of his own. Two days later, he refused to obey Newton's orders. Far from being restored to the higher office, he was supplanted from all command as of that date, while the Gettysburg Campaign was still under way. He left the Army of the Potomac, July 7, and saw no further field service in the Civil War.[12]

His replacement from the VI Corps, Newton, a Virginian who fought for the Union, had led a brigade on the Peninsula and in the Maryland Campaign and a division at Fredericksburg and Chancellorsville. An outstanding Engineer who graduated second in his West Point class of 1842 before his

11 The standard biography of Reynolds is Edward J. Nichols' *Toward Gettysburg*. See also Heitman, *Register*, v. I, p. 825, and Warner, *Blue*, pp. 396-97.

12 Doubleday himself wrote *Chancellorsville and Gettysburg* in the Scribner "Campaigns of the Civil War" series and also *Reminiscences of Forts Sumter and Moultrie*. His originally unpublished prewar recollections were later brought into print as *My Life in the Old Army*. His accounts are also included in Robert P. Broadwater, ed., *Gettysburg as the Generals Remembered It* and in William Styple, ed., *Generals in Bronze*. Modern biographies of him are JoAnn Bartlett's *Looking beyond the Myth* and Thomas Barthel's *A Civil War Biography*. See also Heitman, *Register*, v. I, p. 380, and Warner, *Blue*, pp. 129-30.

nineteenth birthday, he would continue commanding the I Corps until it was discontinued in March of 1864.[13]

Like the I Corps, the II Corps had numerous chiefs in the Gettysburg Campaign. Since late spring of 1863, Major General Winfield Scott Hancock of Pennsylvania (West Point, 1844) had headed it.[14] One of the great combat commanders of the Federal Army, he had proved an outstanding general of brigade and division from Williamsburg through Chancellorsville and had earned the accolade "superb" from Major General George B. McClellan himself. Although untested at corps level, he was the officer whom Meade picked to go forward and take over the Left Wing on July 1 after Reynolds' death. The following day, Hancock had charge of the Center (II and III Corps). On July 3, he was severely wounded while commanding his own corps in repulsing Pickett's Charge—a wound that would afflict him for the rest of the war and the rest of his life.[15]

During Hancock's elevation to wing command on July 1 and again on July 2, command of the II Corps devolved on his senior subordinate, fellow Pennsylvanian Brigadier General John Gibbon (West Point, 1847). Best remembered as the Regular officer who forged the Iron Brigade into men of steel, Gibbon had led the Second Division of the I Corps at Fredericksburg and the Second Division of the II Corps at Chancellorsville. On July 3, he

13 Broadwater, op. cit.; Styple, op. cit.; Heitman, *Register*, v. I, p. 746, and Warner, *Blue*, pp. 344-45.

14 During the sick leave of official corps commander Couch after Chancellorsville, Hancock temporarily commanded the II Corps, May 22-June 6. Couch briefly resumed charge, June 6-10, but then departed for good to take over the new Department of the Susquehanna. Hancock permanently succeeded him on June 10 and was officially assigned to that position two weeks later. For purposes of this chapter, his corps command will be considered to commence on May 22. Albert M. Gambone, *Enigmatic Valor*, pp. 136-37; Dyer, *Compendium*, p. 287; *OR*, v. XXV, pt. 2, p. 576, and v. XXVII, pt. 3, pp. 8, 9, 55, 299, and v. LI, pt. 1, p. 1045; Francis A. Walker, *II Corps*, pp. 253-55.

15 The Assistant Adjutant General of the II Corps, Lieutenant Colonel Francis A. Walker, wrote the history of that corps and also the best of the early biographies of Hancock. Glenn Tucker's *Hancock the Superb* flourished during the Civil War centennial. Recent biographies are David Jordan's *A Soldier's Life*; Perry Jamieson's *Gettysburg Hero*; and Paul Bretzger's *Observing Hancock at Gettysburg*. Lawrence Kreiser's *Defeating Lee* is the modern history of the II Corps. See also Heitman, *Register*, v. I, pp. 496-97, and Warner, *Blue*, pp. 202-04.

was wounded before Hancock and could not again succeed the superior officer.[16]

For a few hours on Friday, corps command passed to the next ranking subordinate, Brigadier General John C. Caldwell. A citizen-soldier from New England, he entered the Civil War as Colonel of the 11th Maine. He had led a brigade in the II Corps since June 4, 1862. Fifty weeks later, he succeeded Hancock in charge of the First Division of that corps. Gettysburg was his first battle as a division commander; before it ended, he had charge of the II Corps itself.[17] At barely 30 years of age, he was the youngest corps commander in that battle—indeed, the second youngest corps commander in the history of the Army of the Potomac and the sixth youngest of all 136 generals ever to lead a corps in the Union Army.[18]

16 Meade's battle report asserts that Gibbon continued leading the II Corps on July 3 because Hancock retained command of the Center. However, both subordinates as well as Gibbon's successor, Brigadier General William Harrow, make clear that Hancock had charge of only the II Corps that day and that Gibbon had resumed command of his division. Indeed, Gibbon specified that the change occurred at 1:00 a.m., July 3. (*OR*, v. XXVII, pt. 1, pp. 117, 375, 417, 421). As to Gibbon himself, he wrote his *Personal Recollections*, and his account of Gettysburg appears in Broadwater, op. cit. Dennis Lavery and Mark Jordan co-authored the modern biography *Iron Brigade General*. See also Heitman, *Register*, v. I, p. 452, and Warner, *Blue*, pp. 171-72.

17 The *Official Records'* order of battle does not show Caldwell commanding the II Corps. However, Hancock's battle report makes clear that "I transferred the command to Brigadier-General Caldwell." A fuller account comes from II Corps staff officer and postwar historian Walker, who wrote that right after the repulse of Pickett's charge, "feeling himself grow faint with loss of blood, [Hancock] sent a message to General Caldwell, requesting him to assume charge of the corps. It seemed best to General Meade, however, to disturb the natural succession according to rank, and by an order of that evening, General Caldwell was superseded by General William Hays…." Thus, the New Englander headed the corps for several hours on the afternoon and evening of July 3. Three times later in the war Caldwell temporarily led the corps for a week or two but never in combat. *OR*, v. XXVII, pt. 1, pp. 157, 375; Walker, *Second Corps*, pp. 300-01; Dyer, *Compendium*, p. 287.

18 Nine Union corps commanders were born later than Caldwell. However, Major Generals Francis C. Barlow (30 years-6 months) and Wesley Merritt (30 years-7 months) and Brevet Major Generals Alfred Torbert (31 years-1 month) and John W. Turner (31 years-9 months) were older than Caldwell's 30 years-3 months when they assumed corps command. The only officer in Meade's army younger than Caldwell when actually commanding a corps was Brigadier General William Wells (27 years-5 months), and he did not take charge of that army's Cavalry Corps until June 1, 1865, a month and a half after Appomattox; during active combat, his largest command was only a brigade. Corps commanders in other Federal armies who were younger than Caldwell included Brevet Major Generals Thomas Ransom (29 years-3 months) and Adelbert Ames (29 years) and Major General Godfrey Weitzel (28 years-11 months). The youngest Yankee corps

His tenure lasted only a few hours. Before the day was over, Meade assigned Southern-born Brigadier General William Hays (West Point, 1840) to head the corps. Hays was an artillery officer who had succeeded Brigadier General Henry J. Hunt in command of the army's Artillery Reserve at Antietam and Fredericksburg. Chancellorsville was his first battle as an infantry brigadier—and his last: he was captured on May 3. Paroled twelve days later and just recently exchanged, he hastened to rejoin the army, arrived on July 3, and was immediately assigned to head its II Corps. He led it for the rest of the campaign but not for long thereafter. He relinquished corps command to Major General Gouverneur K. Warren just thirteen days after the Gettysburg Campaign ended.[19]

Like the I and II Corps, the III experienced high turnover of commanders. Major General Daniel E. Sickles had led it since February 5, 1863. A controversial New York politician, he went off to war as Colonel of the 70th New York, which became part of his Excelsior Brigade. He proved a combative brigade and then division commander in the III Corps. At the head of that corps, he put up a good fight at Chancellorsville but took quite a pummeling. After that, he vowed never again to fight on low ground as he had on May 3, if high ground was near at hand. Quite willing to exercise the initiative expected of corps commanders, he advanced to the Peach Orchard on July 2 without obtaining permission or even notifying army headquarters.

---

commander of all was Major General James Harrison Wilson (27 years-1 month). Three Confederate corps commanders were also younger than Caldwell: Lieutenant General Stephen D. Lee (almost 30) and Major Generals Fitzhugh Lee (29 and a half) and Joseph Wheeler. Although Wheeler was fifty-one weeks older than Wilson, the Alabaman was the youngest corps commander of the Civil War because he was promoted to that position on March 16, 1863, at age 26 and a half, whereas Wilson was almost two months past his 27th birthday when he took charge of a corps on October 24, 1864.

19 Warren served primarily as Chief Engineer and briefly as acting Chief of Staff of the Army of the Potomac during the Gettysburg Campaign. He would lead the II Corps for most of its operations from August of 1863 until Hancock resumed command the following March. However, since the New Yorker remained a staff officer through July and did not take charge of the corps until August 16, he is not covered in this chapter. For Hays' exchange as a prisoner of war and his rush to reach Gettysburg, see *OR*, v. XXVII, pt. 3, p. 503, and s. 2, v. V, pp. 568, 570-71, 599, 618, 625-26; Association of Graduates of the U.S. Military Academy, *Annual Reunion, 1875*, pp. 68-71. See also Heitman, *Register*, v. I, p. 516, and Warner, *Blue*, pp. 224-25.

That move cost him his leg and his command. Meade never forgave him and never permitted him to return to the Army of the Potomac.[20]

Sickles' temporary successor for the remainder of the battle was his senior subordinate, Major General David B. Birney. Also a citizen-soldier, a Philadelphia lawyer by profession, Birney had entered the Union Army as Colonel of the 23rd Pennsylvania Zouaves. He had led a brigade on the Peninsula and at Second Bull Run and succeeded Phil Kearny in command of the Red Diamond Division. By the summer of 1864, he would receive permanent command of a corps (the X) but not in 1863.[21] On July 9, he was replaced by a more senior officer—and a Regular, at that—Major General William H. French (West Point, 1837). French had led a brigade in the II Corps on the Peninsula and a division in that corps at Antietam, Fredericksburg, and Chancellorsville. On June 26, 1863, he was put in command of most of the VIII Corps troops in the piedmont of his native Maryland (the VIII Corps commander himself, Schenck, was not permitted to leave Baltimore[22]). With those troops French reinforced the Army of the Potomac. Most of them were assigned to the III Corps, and he succeeded to its command, July 9.[23]

Ten officers leading three corps in just five weeks constituted a kaleidoscope of command. The V and VI Corps, in contrast, enjoyed much greater stability. When Meade rose to army command on June 28, his senior

20 For sources on Sickles, see Chapter 6, n. 53, and Broadwater, op. cit.

21 For sources on Birney, see Chapter 6, n. 55.

22 On July 6, Schenck pointed out to the War Department that he had sent over 18,000 soldiers of the VIII Corps into the field to serve under Meade "in my own department." He added that "I propose, with your permission, to leave here, to proceed to-day to Frederick, or wherever the troops may be, to assume the command of them, under General Meade. It appears to me my right, and I trust you will approve my doing so." His trust proved misplaced. General-in-Chief Henry W. Halleck replied the same day that "it is deemed proper that your headquarters should remain for the present in Baltimore. All troops in the field are under General Meade's orders, and will be assigned and moved as he may direct." Clearly the authorities in Washington did not want this politician-general of limited competence but very high rank (senior to all of Meade's corps commanders but Slocum and Sedgwick) commanding at the front, when the campaign's outcome remained in doubt. *OR*, v. XXVII, pt. 3, pp. 570-71.

23 French himself replaced Birney in charge of the III Corps on July 9. French's division, however, apparently was not assigned to that corps as its Third Division until the following day. Ibid., p. 799, and pt. 1, p. 489, also pt. 2, p. 249. For French, see Heitman, *Register*, v. I, p. 437, and Warner, *Blue*, pp. 161-62.

subordinate succeeded him at V Corps headquarters: Major General George Sykes of Delaware (West Point, 1842). Sykes had commanded the U.S. Regular Battalion at First Bull Run, the Army of the Potomac's Reserve Division when it was created, and the Second Division of the V Corps for the past fourteen months. Now the V Corps itself was his. Unspectacular, unflamboyant—he was as sturdy and steadfast as the U.S. Regulars who made up much of his former division.[24]

Reliability was also a hallmark of Connecticut-born Major General John Sedgwick (West Point, 1837). A division commander in the II Corps on the Peninsula, he was severely wounded in the West Wood at Antietam. After he returned to duty shortly after Fredericksburg, he briefly took charge of the II and later the IX Corps and then permanently of the VI Corps, which he led at Chancellorsville. He had not exercised much initiative there, but he had done much hard fighting and had displayed much tactical skill in extricating his corps from dire peril. He and his corps could be counted on to put up a good fight.[25]

At almost 50 years of age, Sedgwick was the oldest permanent corps commander at Gettysburg. At 32 years-eight months, Major General Oliver Otis Howard of Maine was the youngest permanent corps commander there (West Point, 1850). In June, 1861, in the mistaken belief that officers could not hold both Regular and Volunteer commissions simultaneously, Howard resigned from the Regulars to become Colonel of the 3rd Maine, which became part of his brigade at First Bull Run. He continued commanding a brigade at Seven Pines (where he lost his right arm) and Antietam and a division at Fredericksburg. On April 6, 1863, he took over the XI Corps. Less than a month later, it suffered disaster at Chancellorsville. That corps' competence for combat had long been questionable. Now his own fitness for high command was in doubt as well. Yet Howard had qualities that his superiors admired, qualities that led them time and again to pass up easy

24 Timothy J. Reese's modern *Sykes' Regular Infantry Division* complements William Powell's classic *The Fifth Army Corps*. See also Heitman, *Register*, v. I, p. 941-42, and Warner, *Blue*, pp. 492-93.

25 Two volumes of the *Correspondence of John Sedgwick* have been published. Two corps histories by veterans are Thomas W. Hyde's *Following the Greek Cross* and George T. Stevens' *Three years in the Sixth Corps*. Richard Winslow wrote the modern study *General John Sedgwick*. See also Heitman, *Register*, v. I, p. 872, and Warner, *Blue*, pp. 430-31.

opportunities to shelve him and instead not only to retain him in high command but to promote him.[26]

On July 1, when Howard temporarily led the Left Wing between Reynolds' death and Hancock's arrival, his XI Corps passed to its senior division commander, Major General Carl Schurz. An immigrant to the United States after the failed 1848 revolutions in Germany, Schurz was a leader of the German-American community. Though residing in Wisconsin, he was initially appointed Colonel of the 1st New York Cavalry but left it after six weeks to become Minister to Spain. By the spring of 1862, he was back in uniform, commanding a largely German division that saw extensive service under Major Generals John Fremont and Franz Sigel in the final days of the Valley Campaign and throughout the Second Bull Run Campaign and then under Howard at Chancellorsville. He had charge of the XI Corps itself for much of July 1, 1863, but reverted to leading its Third Division when Howard resumed direct command.[27]

A formation often paired with the XI Corps, before and after Gettysburg, was the XII Corps. Its chief, Major General Henry W. Slocum, was the senior corps commander at Gettysburg and the second most long serving there, after Reynolds. Indeed, before the campaign ended, he would equal

26 Howard could have been relieved after Chancellorsville or Gettysburg but was not. Meade did consider breaking up the XI Corps in late July, but he proposed returning Howard to the II Corps, which he would command. That plan was not implemented, but the XI Corps (by then in the Army of the Cumberland) was discontinued on April 14, 1864. Eliminating the command offered the perfect opportunity to eliminate the commander. Instead, Howard was put in charge of another corps in that army, the IV. Then in July, following the death of Major General James B. McPherson, Howard was elevated to command the Army of the Tennessee. Retaining him and promoting him despite repeated opportunities to be rid of him suggests that he possessed qualities of generalship which may not be readily recognizable today but which senior officers of the caliber of Meade, Ulysses S. Grant, William T. Sherman, and George H. Thomas discerned in him. Books by and about Howard include his own *Autobiography*, John Carpenter's Civil War centennial biography *Sword and Olive Branch*, and Gerald Weland's more recent *O.O. Howard*. James Pula is writing the modern history of the XI Corps, *Under the Crescent Moon*. See also Broadwater, op. cit.; Styple, op. cit.; Heitman, *Register*, v. I, pp. 546-47, and Warner, *Blue*, pp. 237-39.

27 Schurz wrote *Reminiscences*, and his *Intimate Letters* have been published. The standard biography is Hans Trefousse's *Carl Schurz*. See also Heitman, *Register*, v. I, p. 866, and Warner, *Blue*, pp. 426-28.

Reynolds' longevity in corps command.[28] Four years after graduating from the U.S. Military Academy in 1852, he resigned from the Army just days after his infant daughter died—the only one of the twelve West Pointers covered in this chapter who did not serve continuously in the Old Army from first commissioning to the outbreak of the Civil War.[29] He returned to his native New York to practice law, but he kept active in that state's National Guard. He came back into service as Colonel of the 27th New York at First Bull Run, where he was wounded. He then commanded the First Division of the VI Corps on the Peninsula and at Crampton's Gap and Antietam, and the XII Corps itself since October 20, 1862. He missed Fredericksburg but came forward for the Mud March and fought at Chancellorsville.[30]

At Gettysburg, Slocum led the Right Wing, containing the V and XII Corps. His elevation caused corps command to devolve upon Brigadier General Alpheus S. Williams. Although a citizen-soldier, he had extensive experience in the prewar Michigan militia and had served as the lieutenant-colonel of the 1st Michigan in the Mexican War. He had seen much combat at the division level—from First Winchester to Chancellorsville—and had led the XII Corps for most of the Battle of Antietam. Now he would lead that corps again at Gettysburg. At nearly 53 years of age, he was the oldest corps commander in that battle.[31]

28 At the time of his death, Reynolds had commanded the I Corps for nine months and three days. That exceeded Slocum's total of eight months-thirteen days, as of July 1. The New Yorker's career—and life—did not end on that date. By the time the Gettysburg Campaign subsided on August 3, he had headed the XII Corps for nine months-fifteen days, slightly surpassing Reynolds. However, when the Pennsylvanian's twelve days in charge of the Militia Corps in 1862 are added, the two generals' tenures are exactly equal as of the end of this campaign. Slocum, of course, would continue in corps command long after Gettysburg—until the XII Corps was discontinued on April 14, 1864, and then with the XX Corps from August 27 to November 11, 1864, when he was promoted to Wing ("Army") command. He thus headed a corps for twenty months-eleven days during the entire war—over twice as long as Reynolds.

29 Technically, Howard, too, resigned from the Regulars on June 4, 1861, but he did so in order to become colonel of the 3rd Maine in the Volunteer Service right away. He thus had no break in military service before the war, and the war was already underway when he did resign.

30 Charles Elihu Slocum wrote *The Life and Services of Major General Henry Warner Slocum*. A 300+page *In Memoriam* book was also published. The modern biography is Brian Melton's *Sherman's Forgotten General*. See also Broadwater, op. cit.; Styple, op. cit.; Heitman, *Register*, v. I, p. 892, and Warner, *Blue*, pp. 451-53.

31 For sources on Williams, see Chapter 6, n. 44.

Besides those seven infantry corps, there was the Cavalry Corps under Major General Alfred Pleasonton (West Point, 1844). A native of the District of Columbia, he had led a cavalry brigade on the Peninsula, a cavalry division at Antietam and Fredericksburg, and the cavalry that fought at Chancellorsville while most horsemen were away raiding in the Rebel rear right to Richmond. On May 22, Pleasonton succeeded Major General George Stoneman in command of that corps. He fought it skillfully at Brandy Station and in the Loudoun Valley. Now he led it toward Gettysburg. Unlike infantry corps, which remained together, the Cavalry Corps had divisions on both flanks of the army. Just because his corps was not intact was no reason that this ambitious, officious, self-important officer would not try to make himself useful and prominent when battle erupted.[32]

These, then, are brief vignettes about the seventeen corps commanders in this campaign individually. Collectively, what generalizations may be offered about them?

Twelve were West Pointers. The remaining five were citizen-soldiers, although Williams, to be sure, had much prewar militia and volunteer experience and Schurz, while not a professional soldier, had seen action as a lieutenant in the Liberal Revolutionary forces in Germany in 1849.[33] The twelve Regulars had served an average of seventeen years-five months in the Old Army. Excluding Slocum's four years raises the average for the other eleven officers to eighteen and two-thirds years. This contrasts with the nine Regulars who led corps at Antietam and who had averaged twenty-two years

32 Sources on Pleasonton and his corps are given in Chapter 7, n. 34.

33 As indicated in Chapter 6 of this book, not only Sickles, Birney, and Caldwell but also Williams and Schurz are considered citizen-soldiers. Despite the Michigander's Volunteer service in the Mexican War and the German's military service in the uprisings of 1848, they were not professionally educated as soldiers and were not commissioned into the Regulars. This differentiates Schurz from other Civil War corps commanders who had served in European armies as professional military officers before coming to America: Major Generals Peter J. Osterhaus, Franz Sigel, and Julius Stahel, Brigadier General Adolph Von Steinwehr, and Brevet Brigadier General August Mersy. During the Gettysburg Campaign, Von Steinwehr commanded the Second Division of Howard's XI Corps, and Sigel and Stahel served in Couch's Susquehanna Militia Corps, but none of them led corps during that period of the war.

of prewar service—or twenty-four if Ambrose E. Burnside's six years are not included.[34]

The difference in prewar service is not surprising because the Gettysburg corps commanders were younger than their Antietam counterparts. The twelve Gettysburg Regulars averaged just over forty-one years of age; adding the five generals from civil life reduces the average age to forty and three-quarters years. The Antietam Regulars averaged five years older than their Gettysburg counterparts; all Antietam corps commanders were four and a half years older than all Gettysburg corps commanders. No general of corps at Gettysburg came close to Edwin V. Sumner's 65 years-7 months at Antietam. The oldest permanent corps commander in the later battle was Sedgwick at 49 years-10 months. Including acting corps commander Williams elevated the upper limit for 1863 by three years. No corps commander in September, 1862, was as young as Caldwell, who was only 30 years-3 months old when he briefly took over the II Corps on July 3, 1863. At age 38 years-2 months, Pleasonton was the youngest "corps" commander at Antietam, but he was only the seventh youngest at Gettysburg. Two permanent and four acting corps generals in July of 1863 were younger than the cavalry general. At age 32 years-8 months, Howard was the youngest permanent corps commander there.[35]

Of the Gettysburg generals, four were born in New England, six in the Middle Atlantic region, six in the South (including Delaware, Maryland, and the District of Columbia), and one in Germany.[36] Three of them entered service from New England, six from the Middle Atlantic region, six from the South, and two from the Midwest.[37]

34 For this paragraph of text and the next one, comparative information on Federal corps commanders in the Antietam Campaign appears in Chapter 7 of this book, "Mac's Main Men."

35 Besides Howard, the other permanent corps commander younger than Pleasonton was Slocum. Interim commanders Caldwell, Schurz, Gibbon, and Birney were also younger than the cavalry general.

36 The New Englanders were Caldwell, Howard, Sedgwick, and Williams. Doubleday, Gibbon, Hancock, Reynolds, Sickles, and Slocum hailed from New York and Pennsylvania. Birney was born in Alabama; Hays and Newton were Virginians; and French, Pleasonton, and Sykes came from the border slave region. Schurz was German.

37 The most significant changes between state of birth and state of entry involved Birney (born, Alabama; entered, Pennsylvania), Gibbon (born, Pennsylvania; entered, North Carolina), Schurz (born, Germany; entered, Wisconsin), and Williams (born, Connecticut;

Williams went off to war as a Brigadier General of Michigan militia on April 24, 1861; received comparable grade in the U.S. Volunteers three weeks later—and never reached higher substantive rank.[38] Four other citizen-soldiers entered service in 1861 as Colonels of regiments, as did two former Regulars.[39] Both of those ex-Regulars, Slocum and Howard, plus one Volunteer, Sickles, each received their first star late that year; so did six other Regulars.[40] The remaining three citizen-soldiers and four more Regulars were not elevated to Brigadier General until 1862, most of them early in the year[41] but Pleasonton not until after the Seven Days Battles and Hays not until after Fredericksburg.[42] Prior to such promotions into the Volunteer Service, the eleven U.S. Army officers on duty when war erupted at Fort Sumter continued serving under their Regular commissions, ranging from Howard's eight weeks to Hays' twenty and a half months.

By the time of Gettysburg, six had already led a corps in combat;[43] two had at least directed a fighting division;[44] eight had commanded both a brigade and a division in battle;[45] and only Hays had headed no higher than a

---

entered, Michigan). Four others changed within regions: Caldwell (born, Vermont; entered, Maine), French (born, Maryland; entered, District of Columbia), Hays (born, Virginia; entered, Tennessee), and Sykes (born Delaware; entered, Maryland). The remaining nine officers entered service from the same states where they were born.

38 Williams was breveted Major General of Volunteers as of January 12, 1865.

39 Those six colonels and their regiments were: Birney, 23rd Pennsylvania; Caldwell, 11th Maine; Howard, 3rd Maine; Schurz, 1st New York Cavalry; Sickles, 70th New York; and Slocum, 27th New York.

40 The other six Regulars were, in order of seniority: Reynolds, Sedgwick, Newton, Hancock, Sykes, and French. Slocum preceded all of them. Howard, then Sickles came between Sedgwick and Newton. Heitman, *Register*, v. I, pp. 29-30.

41 The five officers who were promoted before heavy fighting resumed in 1862 were Doubleday, Birney, Schurz, Caldwell, and Gibbon. Ibid., p. 31.

42 Pleasonton and Hays ranked from July 16 and November 29, 1862, respectively. However, the artillerist was not actually commissioned until December 27, so he still served as a staff lieutenant colonel at Fredericksburg. Ibid., pp. 31-32; Warner, *Blue*, p. 225; *OR*, v. XXI, p. 204.

43 Reynolds, Sickles, Sedgwick, Howard, Slocum, and Williams had previously led a corps in battle.

44 Sykes and Schurz each had led a division in combat.

45 Generals who had headed first a brigade and then a division in former fighting were Doubleday, Newton, Hancock, Gibbon, Caldwell, Birney, French, and Pleasonton.

brigade. He and the other two acting II Corps commanders were only brigadier generals, as was Williams. Of the thirteen major generals, Slocum and Sedgwick ranked from July 4, 1862 (the XII Corps commander was the senior of the two by four files). Seven more ranked from November 29, 1862.[46] Schurz and Newton received their second star just before Chancellorsville, and Birney and Pleasonton were made major generals after that battle—the cavalryman as recently as June 22, 1863.[47] The eight permanent corps commanders had held their positions for an average of a little over six months as of July 1, 1863. Their tenures ranged from Reynolds' nine and a half months to Hancock's and Pleasonton's one and a half months each and Sykes' four days. Not counting the V Corps commander raises the average for the other seven officers to seven months.

Reynolds' tenure ended when he was killed at Gettysburg. Sedgwick was slain at Spotsylvania the following May 9, and Birney died of disease on October 18, 1864. Those three officers were permanent corps commanders at the time of their deaths. Newton, French, Sykes, and Pleasonton continued leading the same corps they had headed in the Gettysburg Campaign until the Army of the Potomac was reorganized on March 25, 1864, when all of them were relieved.[48] Williams, on the other hand, reverted to division command right after the Battle of Gettysburg but headed the XX Corps at Atlanta, the March to the Sea, and the Carolinas Campaign—only to lose it to a ranking officer on April 2, 1865, just before the Raleigh Campaign.[49] Of

---

Caldwell's experience at division level came only on July 2, 1863—the day before he succeeded Hancock in charge of the II Corps.

46 In order of seniority, those major generals were Reynolds, Howard, Sickles, Hancock, Sykes, French, and Doubleday. Heitman, *Register*, v. I, pp. 28-29.

47 Schurz and Newton ranked from March 14 and 30, 1863, respectively. Birney received his second star as of May 20 of that year. Ibid., p. 29.

48 Of those four officers, only Newton was immediately reassigned to another major active front. On April 16, he took charge of the Second Division of the IV Corps in the Army of the Cumberland for the upcoming Atlanta Campaign. He led the division through the capture of that city until September 30. Throughout that campaign, he served as a One-Star. His commission as Major General was revoked on April 18, 1864, and he was reappointed a Brigadier General of Volunteers as of that date.

49 Williams had charge of the XX Corps, July 28-August 27, 1864, and November 11, 1864-April 2, 1865. Still a brigadier general that late in the war, he was superseded by Sherman's favorite subordinate, Major General Joseph A. Mower, on April 2. The Michigander then reverted to division command for the final operations in North Carolina.

all seventeen corps commanders in the Gettysburg Campaign, only Gibbon still headed a corps by the end of the war: the XXIV Corps of the Army of the James.[50]

By then, Hancock, Howard, and Slocum had risen to department and/or army command.[51] On the other hand, Caldwell, Schurz, Hays, sometimes Williams, and even Pleasonton led only a division later in the war.[52] War's

50 When Hancock left the II Corps on November 26, 1864, Gibbon was so upset about not succeeding him that he asked to be relieved. Grant, however, called his bluff, and the subordinate backed down. Gibbon's gambit, however, did not cost him the respect of Grant and Meade, and the General-in-Chief soon found a place for him elsewhere in the army group, not in the Army of the Potomac but in the Army of the James. Gibbon had already temporarily led the XVIII Corps in that army, September 4-22, 1864. On January 15, 1865, he received permanent command of the XXIV Corps in that army, which he headed for the duration of the war.

51 Howard took command of the Department and Army of the Tennessee on July 27, 1864. Slocum led the equivalent of an army, the Left Wing of Sherman's army group, consisting of the XIV and XX Corps, from November 11, 1864, through Georgia and the Carolinas to Goldsborough. On March 28, 1865, his force was designated the Army of Georgia. One month earlier, Hancock took charge of the Middle Military Division and the Department of West Virginia. All three generals served there for the rest of the war.

52 As the Battle of Gettysburg ended, Caldwell, Schurz, and Williams resumed commanding their divisions. The Mainer retained that position until Meade's army was reorganized on March 24, 1864. Schurz kept his command until April 14, when the XI Corps was discontinued. Williams' tenure was much longer; he led his division (first in the XII Corps, then in the XX Corps) from July 4, 1863, to July 28, 1864; from August 27 to November 11, 1864; and from April 2 until the XX Corps was discontinued in June, 1865. Hays, in contrast, had no division to which to return. He left the Army of the Potomac when Warren succeeded him in charge of the II Corps and did not return until February 22, 1865, when he took command of the Second Division of that corps. He led it through the final fighting of the Siege of Petersburg but did not make it to Appomattox. When corps commander Andrew A. Humphreys caught Hays sleeping instead of pursuing the battered Butternuts on April 6, he summarily relieved the junior officer from command. (*OR*, v. XLVI, pt. 3, pp. 597-98). In contrast to those four officers, Pleasonton had charge of no regularly organized division after leaving the Army of the Potomac as part of the general reorganization of March 25, 1864. On April 14, he was made second-in-command of the Department of the Missouri. That remained his primary responsibility for the rest of the year, although he briefly commanded the Districts of Central Missouri and of St. Louis. For most of that time, Missouri was a military backwater. Action increased, however, when the Secessionists invaded the state in late September. To meet their threat, he commanded briefly at St. Louis and Jefferson City. Most significantly, he headed a provisional cavalry division, October 19-27, which dealt devastating defeat to the invaders and helped drive them out of Missouri and Kansas in disorder. With the Southerners in full retreat but the campaign still under way, he had to relinquish command on October 27 because of injury and ill health. (Ibid., v. XXXIII, p. 732; and v. XXXIV, pt. 3, p. 154; and v. XLI, pt. 1, pp. 312-15, 336-43, 491-507, and pt. 2, p. 373, and pt. 3, pp. 48, 302, 378, 405, 508, 539, 708, 729.)

end found Williams still heading a division;[53] Hays back in charge of the Artillery Reserve of the Army of the Potomac;[54] Schurz, Pleasonton, and French in senior staff positions;[55] and Newton and Sykes serving in backwater districts in Florida and Kansas (Sykes not even in command).[56]

53 Williams relinquished command of the XX Corps on April 2, 1865, and then resumed leading its First Division, which he headed until the corps was discontinued in June of that year.

54 After being literally kicked out of division command on April 6, Hays was put in charge of the Artillery Reserve of the Army of the Potomac, a command that he had previously held at Antietam and Fredericksburg. *OR*, v. XLVI, pt. 3, p. 1027.

55 Training troops in Tennessee, campaigning to re-elect President Lincoln, and recruiting veterans for Hancock's I Veteran Corps occupied Schurz for almost a year after the XI Corps was discontinued. All the while, he wanted to return to his own men, some of whom still served in the XX Corps. Neither Sherman nor Slocum wanted him back, especially if he would supplant a veteran division commander. They instead tucked him away as Chief of Staff of the Army of Georgia on April 14—an impressive title but one without command responsibilities. (Ibid., v. XLVII, pt. 3, pp. 75, 112, 121, 212; see also Simon, op. cit., v. XIII, pp. 539-40.) Pleasonton's assignments were more meaningful. After returning to duty following his arduous cavalry operations, he was put back in charge of the District of St. Louis on November 19 and then restored as second-in-command of the department on December 7. His health, however, continued precarious, and he had to return to Philadelphia to convalesce, presumably in the home of his brother, Brigadier General Augustus J. Pleasonton of the Philadelphia Home Guard. He eventually came back to St. Louis and was appointed Chief of Cavalry and Artillery of Major General John Pope's Military Division of the Missouri on March 10, 1865. That, too, was a staff position. Whether or not it would have been converted into command of a cavalry corps remains unknown, since the war ended before Pope could mount an invasion of the Confederate Trans-Mississippi Department. (*OR*, v. XLI, pt. 3, p. 378, and pt. 4, pp. 619, 795-96, and v. XLVIII, pt. 1, pp. 747, 1141; Association of Graduates, *Annual Reunion, 1897*, p. 64). Pleasonton and Schurz at least stayed in the Volunteer Service to the end of the war. French, in contrast, resigned from the Volunteers six weeks after leaving the Army of the Potomac. He thereafter served under his recent Regular promotion to Lieutenant Colonel, 2nd U.S. Artillery. From January to July, 1865, he was Chief of Artillery of the Middle Department. (George W. Cullum, *Biographical Register...of West Point*, v. I, p. 678).

56 Newton left the Army of the Cumberland at the end of September, 1864. On October 15, he was assigned to command the District of Key West and Tortugas. (Ibid., v. XXXIX, pt. 2, pp. 452, 521, and v. XLI, pt. 3, p. 880). At Grant's recommendation, Sykes was sent to the Department of Kansas in April, 1864. The department commander, Major General Samuel R. Curtis, confided to another subordinate that "General Sykes has reported to me for duty, and I hardly know what disposition to make of him. I am better provided with generals than troops." The newcomer was assigned to Fort Leavenworth. On September 1, he was placed in charge of the District of South Kansas, but on October 10—with Confederate invasion well under way—he was removed from that command, to his great chagrin, ostensibly because he was "unable" to take the field. Unlike Pleasonton, Sykes played no role in repelling the invasion. He remained in Kansas for the next eight months. Grant did consider him for division command in the Army of the James in March but did not select him.

Caldwell, Doubleday, and Sickles were no longer in the field. Indeed, the latter two officers had not commanded in the field since Gettysburg.[57]

Yet both Doubleday and Sickles served prominently in the immediate postwar years, as did most of the surviving corps commanders. Only Schurz and Slocum immediately severed all ties with the military by resigning on May 6 and September 28, 1865, respectively.[58] Caldwell and Williams also returned to civil life, but they were not mustered out of Volunteer Service until January 15, 1866. Gibbon, Hays, Pleasonton, and Sykes left Volunteer Service on that date, too; Newton was mustered out from there at the end of that month; and Hancock was mustered out six months later. All six of those officers continued serving in the Regular Army. Also remaining in the Regular Establishment were French and Doubleday, who were mustered out of their Volunteer commissions on May 6, 1864, and August 24, 1865, respectively. Howard, interestingly, continued serving as a Major General of Volunteers until January 1, 1869—the last serving Volunteer general of the entire Civil War. Even after mustering out of Volunteer Service, he reverted to his Regular rank of Brigadier General. Still more remarkable was Sickles, who remained a Major General of Volunteers until January 1, 1868, and then continued as Colonel of the 42nd U.S. (a regiment of invalids) until he retired on April 14, 1869—as a Major General of the United States Regular Army!

Hancock and Howard were already Brigadier Generals of Regulars as of 1864. The Pennsylvanian received his second star when the U.S. Army went on its postwar footing in 1866, and Howard rose to that rank twenty years later. Newton and Gibbon, too, made One-Star in 1884 and 1885, respectively. Also in that postwar establishment of 1866, Gibbon and

---

Finally, on June 7, in response to Grant's authorization of June 2 to "immediately relieve all general and staff officers within your command whose service can be dispensed with," Sykes was relieved from duty in that department and sent home to await orders. (Ibid., v. XXXIII, pp. 722, 730; and v. XXXIV, pt. 3, pp. 199-200; and v. XLI, pt. 3, pp. 12, 763-64, and pt. 4, pp. 242-43, 741-42; and v. XLVI, pt. 2, p. 925; and v. XLVIII, pt. 2, pp. 730, 755; and v. LIII, p. 604).

57 On July 12, 1864, Doubleday was put in charge of one sector of Washington's defenses when the Confederates threatened the capital. When their threat receded, however, he was relieved on July 16. Generally, he presided over boards and courts martial, as did Caldwell. Sickles was on a diplomatic mission to Colombia when the war ended. Ibid., v. XXXVII, pt. 2, pp. 228, 352; Swanberg, op. cit., pp. 259-73.

58 Slocum declined a commission in the postwar Regular Army. Warner, *Blue*, p. 453.

Sickles started as colonels,[59] and Doubleday, Sykes, and French eventually earned their eagles.[60] Hays and Pleasonton, however, remained in their wartime Regular grade of major.[61]

Hancock, Howard, and Sickles were prominent in Reconstruction. The first two of those officers plus Gibbon were Indian fighters. Howard also served as Superintendent of West Point, 1881-82. Newton rose through the Corps of Engineers as lieutenant colonel and colonel to become Brigadier General and Chief of Engineers of the U.S. Army in 1884.[62]

Significant non-military undertakings after the war include serving in Congress (Schurz, Sickles, Slocum, and Williams),[63] serving in a Presidential cabinet (Schurz),[64] and serving in diplomatic posts (Caldwell, Sickles, and Williams).[65] Sickles actively worked to preserve and mark the

59 On mustering out as Major General of Volunteers in January of 1866, former corps commander Gibbon reverted all the way to his Regular grade of Captain of Battery B/4th U.S. Artillery—one of the sharpest drops of any Civil war general. In July of that year, however, he was promoted to Colonel of the 36th U.S. When the Army was reduced from sixty to forty regiments three years later, he became Colonel of the 7th U.S. Sickles did not survive that draw down and retired in 1869. Prior to then, as already mentioned, he was Colonel of the 42nd U.S.

60 When the Civil War ended, Doubleday, Sykes, and French were the Lieutenant Colonels of the 17th and 5th U.S. and 2nd U.S. Artillery, respectively. Doubleday was promoted to Colonel of the 35th U.S. in 1867 and was transferred to the 24th U.S. three years later. Sykes received his eagles in the 20th U.S. in 1868. Not until 1877 did French make Colonel of the 4th U.S. Artillery.

61 Hays and Pleasonton were Majors of the 5th U.S. Artillery and 2nd U.S. Cavalry, respectively.

62 In the Regular Army, Newton was promoted to Major of Engineers in the first summer of the war. That remained his grade when the war ended. He rose to Lieutenant Colonel of Engineers in December of 1865 and to Colonel of Engineers fourteen years later. Becoming the Chief of Engineers in 1884 automatically made him a One-Star until he retired on August 27, 1886.

63 Schurz served as a Republican Senator from Missouri. Sickles, Slocum, and Williams were Democrat Representatives, the first two from New York and the last from Michigan.

64 Schurz served as Secretary of the Interior in the administration of President Rutherford B. Hayes.

65 Schurz served briefly as Minister to Spain in 1861 but held no diplomatic position postwar. Sickles held that posting after the war, and Williams was Minister to El Salvador. Caldwell performed the most extensive diplomatic service as consul in Valparaiso, Chile, and in San Jose, Costa Rica, and as Minister to Uruguay and Paraguay for twenty-seven years cumulatively.

Gettysburg battlefield. Hancock ran unsuccessfully for President in 1880 as the Democrat nominee.

Hays (1875), Sykes (1880), and Hancock (1886) died while still in the Army. Pleasonton, peeved that he had been offered no higher grade than lieutenant-colonel, resigned his Regular commission in 1868. The other six Regulars in due course retired, and Pleasonton too was eventually placed on the retired list in 1888—still a major. He was the first to leave, on January 1, 1868; Howard was the last, on November 8, 1894.[66] The ten Regular officers who survived the war and stayed in uniform served an average of fifteen years after June, 1865. Not counting the short tenures of Pleasonton and Sickles raises the average for the remaining eight to just over eighteen years.

The first of the seventeen corps commanders to die was, of course, Reynolds at age 42 years-9 months. The first to pass away postwar was Hays in 1875 at age 55 years-9 months. The average age for all seventeen officers at their deaths was 66 years-5 months. Excluding the three who died during the war raises the average to 71 years-2 months. Sykes was only 57 at his passing. French, Gibbon, Hancock, Slocum, and Williams were each in their sixties. Caldwell, Doubleday, Howard, Newton, Pleasonton, and Schurz were in their seventies. The youngest to die was Birney at age 39 years-5 months in 1864. The oldest of the entire group was Dan Sickles, who passed away on May 3, 1914, at age 94 years and 7 months.

Sickles was the most controversial of the seventeen generals—undeniably a hard fighter but also an insubordinate subordinate. Hancock towers above all others as the best of the corps commanders—certainly at Gettysburg, probably in the Army of the Potomac, among the best in the entire Union Army. Gibbon, Slocum, and Reynolds were good, solid corps commanders; Birney grew into above average, and Sedgwick was sturdy and reliable. Williams and Pleasonton, too, were competent. Howard must have been better than the surviving sources suggest. Doubleday unquestionably handled his corps skillfully on July 1, but his obnoxious, abrasive personality cost him the opportunity to retain such command. Caldwell, Hays, and Schurz held their positions too briefly to be evaluated. That leaves Newton, Sykes, and French. The commander of the I Corps was brilliant in

66 Besides Pleasonton in 1868 and Howard in 1894, the other five retirees were: Sickles, 1869; Doubleday, 1873; French, 1880; Newton, 1886; and Gibbon, 1891.

thought but indolent certainly in manner and likely in execution.[67] No one ever accused Sykes of brilliance; the nickname he earned was "Tardy George." The worst of the lot was French, who later in 1863 at Wapping Heights on July 23 and again at Payne's Farm on November 27 demonstrated a lack of initiative that singularly unfitted him for corps command. It is no coincidence that when the Army of the Potomac was consolidated from six corps to four in March of 1864, Newton, Sykes, and French lost their jobs. None of them would ever command a corps again.[68]

From great through good to mid-range to mediocre and even to incompetent was quite a span. Yet such was the mix that marked "Meade's Main Men."

67 Colonel Charles S. Wainwright, who commanded the artillery of the I Corps, repeatedly remarked on Newton's indolence. The corps commander "knows enough theoretically at any rate," wrote the brigadier on July 22, 1863, "but is intensely lazy.... being only too glad to leave matters in the hands of anyone who would take all the trouble off his shoulders." Allan Nevins, ed., *A Diary of Battle*, pp. 268-69, also pp. 279-80, 292, 324.

68 As already mentioned, Newton at least commanded a division during the Atlanta Campaign. French and Sykes were sidelined in military backwaters for the rest of the war.

51. John F. Reynolds. *LOC*

52. Abner Doubleday. *LOC*

53. John Newton. *LOC*

54. William H. French. *LOC*

55. John Gibbon. *LOC*

56. John C. Caldwell. *LOC*

57. William Hays. *AHEC*

58. George Sykes. *LOC*

59. John Sedgwick. *LOC*

60. Oliver O. Howard. *LOC*

61. Carl Schurz. *LOC*

62. Henry W. Slocum. *LOC*

Chapter 9

Grant's Main Men: Senior Federal Commanders in the Fifth Offensive at Petersburg[1]

War is violence. So is a riot. What distinguishes a battle from a brawl is that battles are fought by armies. Armies have commanders and command structures that can channel violence toward achieving purposeful objectives in the battle, in the campaign, and in the war. Understanding that structure is central to understanding how armies operate. Understanding the officers who fill senior slots in that structure, moreover, is essential to understanding the ability—or lack thereof—with which those armies operate. This chapter surveys the Northern command structure and senior commanders during part of the Siege of Petersburg. It focuses on such forces on the eve of Grant's Fifth Offensive of the siege,

1 This subject was initially analyzed when introducing the Federal high command to Mr. David A. Ward's "Civil War Tours" group on September 27, 2013, before the author led them over the battlefields of the Fifth Offensive, especially Chaffin's Bluff and Poplar Spring Church. It thus concentrates on the senior generals on the eve of battle much more than on their generalship in the ensuing combat. That focus is preserved in the first part of this chapter. Later pages highlight aspects of the fighting and give much more attention to generalizing about the generals' lives and careers before and after the Fifth Offensive. The author's *Richmond Redeemed: The Siege at Petersburg* is the main source for this chapter. The indispensable guide to Union Army organization continues to be Frederick H. Dyer's *A Compendium of the War of the Rebellion*. Essential, as well, are Francis B. Heitman's *Historical Register and Dictionary of the United States Army, 1789-1903* and Ezra Warner's *Generals in Blue*. Also useful is Frank Welcher's *The Union Army, 1861-1865*, especially Volume I.

September 29-October 19, 1864, and only to a lesser degree follows them through the course of those operations.

It was Grant's offensive, and it should be recognized right up front that his ability to dominate the strategic initiative—whether, when, where, and why to attack—was one of his greatest strengths as a strategist. Thus, it is altogether fitting and proper to begin with Ulysses S. Grant. A native Ohioan who was living in Illinois at the outbreak of the Civil War, Grant was a West Point graduate (Class of 1843) with a sound record in the Mexican War but questionable service in the 1850s, requiring his resignation under a cloud in 1854. He re-entered military service in 1861. Over the next three years, his ability to convert tactical victories into strategic success earned him repeated promotions, not only in the Volunteer Service but also in the Regular Army, all the way to lieutenant-general—the first United States officer to hold that grade since George Washington. As General-in-Chief of the entire Federal Army, he discerned how to convert the North's advantages into achievements as he developed and implemented the grand strategy that eventually won the Civil War. Throughout 1864 and 1865, he remained attentive to his broad responsibilities as General-in-Chief. Yet he did not stay behind a desk in Washington—as his predecessor, Major General Henry W. Halleck, had done—but took the field in Virginia, where he functioned as theater strategist for the East and as army group commander against General Robert E. Lee.[2]

From early May to mid-June, 1864, Army Group Grant (to coin a phrase) did not fare all that well tactically. Strategically, however, Grant secured success through a succession of setbacks as he continued to dominate the initiative and to drive ever more deeply into Virginia.[3] By mid-June, he reached Petersburg. Thereafter the mobile warfare of spring stagnated into the slowdown of summer, as the Siege of Petersburg began

2 The term "army group" is a 20th Century concept not in parlance in the Civil War, yet it is so accurately descriptive—a group of armies, such as Halleck's at First Corinth, Sherman's at Atlanta, and Grant's at Chattanooga and again at Petersburg—that it will unhesitatingly be used. Almost an army group's worth of books has been written by and about Grant. Some of these sources are listed in Chapter 1, n. 8 of *Challenges of Command*. That chapter as well as 3, 4, and 5 of this volume give this historian's perspectives on Grant.

3 This theme of "Success through a Succession of Setbacks" is explored in Chapter 3 of this book.

and Grant pinned down Lee in the constricting imperative of the close and immediate defense of his capital, Richmond, and its rail center, Petersburg.

Five railroads gave Petersburg its strategic importance: one connecting it northward to Richmond and four others running northeast, southeast, south, and west to link those two cities to the rest of Virginia and the rest of the Confederacy. The northeastern and southeastern lines fell to the Federals right away in mid-June. Two months later, the Bluecoats cut the vital Weldon Railroad at Globe Tavern. However, that latter line remained usable for the Butternuts to within eighteen miles of Petersburg, to which they transshipped supplies by wagon. The wagon roads from railhead to rail center, the last remaining railroad into Petersburg from Southside Virginia—and Richmond and Petersburg themselves—were Grant's four targets in his Fifth Offensive. To try to reach them, he used the two armies in Army Group Grant: the Army of the Potomac and the Army of the James.

The Army of the Potomac had been created on July 25, 1861, just after the debacle at First Bull Run.[4] Ever since September 16 of that year, Major General George G. Meade of Pennsylvania, a West Point educated career officer (Class of 1835), had been associated with that army: as a brigade commander through the Seven Days and Second Bull Run, a division commander at South Mountain, Antietam, and Fredericksburg, and V Corps commander at Chancellorsville. On June 28, 1863, he was promoted to lead that army. Within less than a week, he won the greatest tactical victory of the war in the greatest battle of the war: Gettysburg. He remained in charge of that army for the rest of the conflict. However, once Grant took the field to "accompany" that army, Meade ceased to be an independent strategist and became, in effect, Grant's principal executive officer.[5]

The Army of the Potomac was divided into corps. When the corps structure was first imposed on that army on March 8, 1862, it contained five corps. Early in 1863, it had nine corps—at least for a few days.[6] By

4 Right after the Civil War, journalist William Swinton wrote *Campaigns of the Army of the Potomac*. The modern history of that army is Jeffry Wert's *The Sword of Lincoln*. As has been indicated in the Preface to *Challenges of Command*, this historian will forever cherish Bruce Catton's "Army of the Potomac" trilogy.

5 Sources on Meade are listed in Chapter 7, n. 24.

6 During the Mud March in January of 1863, the Army of the Potomac consisted of the I, II, III, V, VI, IX, XI, and XII Corps. The creation of the Cavalry Corps on February 5 nominally raised the number of corps to nine. However, by the time the horsemen actually

September of 1864, however, only three corps remained: the II, V, and IX plus the Second Division of the Cavalry Corps and four independent brigades. This chapter will not cover those brigades but will concentrate on the four larger formations.[7]

The most famous of those forces was Major General Winfield Scott Hancock's II Corps. A West Pointer (Class of 1844) and career officer from Pennsylvania, Hancock had led a battling brigade from Williamsburg through Crampton's Gap and a hard-fighting division from Antietam through Chancellorsville. On May 22, 1863, he took charge of the II Corps, at whose head he contributed significantly to Federal victory at Gettysburg. Grievously wounded there on July 3, he resumed command of the II Corps on March 24, 1864. He led it in heavy fighting from the Wilderness to Second Reams' Station—though temporary convalescence due to a flare-up of his Gettysburg wound spared him the disasters of June 18 and 22. His corps accomplished much from May through August, 1864—but it also suffered much. Even crack troops crack under continuing combat. To help it recuperate, it was allowed to sit out the Fifth Offensive in the demanding but less dangerous duty of holding the Union entrenched camp east of Petersburg, while other forces did the fighting farther west. Only Brevet Major General Gershom Mott's Third Division of Hancock's corps, containing most of the remaining regiments of the discontinued III Corps, engaged in combat during the Fifth Offensive.[8]

---

grouped together a week later, the IX Corps had left for Newport News. It began departing on February 6, and its last elements left four days later. Thus, the Army of the Potomac contained nine corps for less than a week—and even then, only on paper. Welcher, *Union Army*, v. I, pp. 424-25, 500; *OR*, v. XVIII, p. 149.

7 From Chancellorsville through Gettysburg, the Army of the Potomac contained eight corps. In September, 1863, the XI and XII Corps headed west to help relieve Chattanooga. The following March, the I Corps was merged into the V Corps, and the III Corps was divided between the II and VI Corps. The IX Corps did rejoin the army on May 24, but the VI Corps and the First and Third Cavalry Divisions plus Cavalry Corps headquarters were dispatched to Maryland and the Shenandoah Valley in mid-summer. Thus, only the II, V, and IX Corps and the Second Cavalry Division remained with Meade for the Fifth Offensive. He also had four independent brigades: Engineer, Provost, Artillery Reserve, and half the VI Corps Artillery Brigade.

8 Prior to the great reorganization of March, 1864, the First and Second Divisions of the III Corps contained thirty-six infantry regiments. Half a year later, twelve of those regiments had mustered out when their term of service expired, and the 68th and 114th Pennsylvania had been traded to the Provost Brigade for the 93rd New York. The remaining

Mott was attached to Major General John G. Parke's IX Corps. Parke also took his own two white divisions into the field but left his Black division behind to help hold trenches south of Petersburg. Second in his class of 1849 at West Point, Pennsylvanian Parke had served in the Topographical Engineers prewar. His Civil War service was inseparably intertwined with Ambrose E. Burnside: as brigade and division commander in North Carolina and as Chief of Staff at Antietam, Fredericksburg, Knoxville, and the Overland Campaign of 1864. He temporarily commanded the IX Corps at Vicksburg, Jackson, and East Tennessee, and briefly led the Army of the Ohio pursuing James Longstreet right after the Siege of Knoxville. He permanently succeeded Burnside after the Crater fiasco but had not yet led the IX Corps in battle in Virginia. His first fight there would come at Poplar Spring Church on September 30 in the ensuing Fifth Offensive.[9]

Another and considerably younger West Pointer and Topographical Engineer (Class of 1854), Major General Gouverneur K. Warren of New York, led the V Corps, eight of whose nine infantry brigades took part in that battle. Earlier, he commanded the 5th New York Zouaves and then a brigade in that corps and served as Chief Topographical Engineer and Chief Engineer of the Army of the Potomac at Chancellorsville and Gettysburg, respectively. From August 16, 1863, until the wounded Hancock returned to duty in March, 1864, Warren headed the II Corps. On March 24 of that later year, he took charge of the V Corps, which he led from the Wilderness forward. Though a brilliant thinker and an accomplished officer, he suffered from a troubling tendency to insist on having his own way because he was sure that he was always right and anyone who disagreed with him was always wrong. This self-centered arrogance infuriated fellow officers, even

---

twenty-two made up Mott's division of the II Corps, along with the 93rd and the newly arrived 1st Maine Heavy Artillery and 1st Massachusetts Heavy Artillery. This data applies only to the original Red Diamond and White Diamond Divisions. It does not involve the Third Division of the III Corps, which joined the corps only after Gettysburg and which was transferred to the VI Corps in March, 1864. For sources on the II Corps and on Hancock, see Chapter 8, n. 15.

9 Chaplain Augustus Woodbury wrote *Ambrose E. Burnside and the Ninth Army Corps*. For Parke, see Heitman, *Register*, v. I, p. 768, and Warner, *Blue*, pp. 359-60.

his friends. Slowly but surely, he was draining the great reservoir of good will that he had earned at Little Round Top.[10]

Even younger than Warren was the remaining prominent subordinate in the Army of the Potomac: Brevet Major General David M. Gregg, who commanded the Second Cavalry Division. A West Pointer (Class of 1855) like the four other senior officers in that army and a Pennsylvanian like three of them, he commanded the 8th Pennsylvania Cavalry and then a brigade early in the war. Since February 12, 1863, he headed a mounted division, most famously on East Cavalry Field at Gettysburg. With the departure of the First and Third Divisions and Cavalry Corps headquarters for the Shenandoah Valley in July and August, 1864, Gregg became the most senior cavalry officer still with the Army of the Potomac—indeed, with Grant's entire army group.[11]

There was another cavalry division, headed by Brigadier General August V. Kautz. A Badener by birth, an Ohioan by upbringing,[12] he had graduated from West Point in 1852 and had commanded the 2nd Ohio Cavalry and then a brigade earlier in the war. Since its creation on April 28, 1864, he had charge of the Cavalry Division of the Army of the James.[13]

That army was the other major element of Army Group Grant. Unlike the veteran Army of the Potomac, it was a new army, created in the spring of 1864 for the particular purpose of participating in Grant's grand campaign. In addition to Kautz's cavalry division, that army consisted of the X Corps, which Grant had transferred from South Carolina and Florida to Virginia in

10 Brigadier General Joshua Chamberlain planned to write a history of the V Corps right after the Civil War, but being elected Governor of Maine diverted him. The project passed to another officer of that formation, Captain William H. Powell, who wrote *The Fifth Army Corps*. For Warren, his letters were edited by Emerson G. Taylor as *Life and Letters of an American Soldier*. Modern biographies of him are David Jordan's *"Happiness Is Not My Companion"* and Donald Jermann's *Union General Gouverneur Warren*. See also Heitman, *Register*, v. I, p. 1003, and Warner, *Blue*, pp. 541-42.

11 Volume II of Stephen Z. Starr's *The Union Cavalry in the Civil War* covers Gregg's division. The general himself wrote a history of his command at Gettysburg. His modern biography is Milton Burgess's *Pennsylvania Cavalryman*. See also Heitman, *Register*, v. I, p. 476, and Warner, *Blue*, pp. 187-88.

12 Kautz grew up in Grant's hometown of Georgetown, Ohio; they overlapped in the same one-room school there, 1834-36. Cf. the Kautz book in n. 14 and Lloyd Lewis, *Captain Sam Grant*, pp. 23-47.

13 Starr, op. cit., covers this division. For Kautz himself, see *August Valentine Kautz* by Lawrence G. Kautz and also Heitman, *Register*, v. I, p. 586, and Warner, *Blue*, pp. 257-58.

April, and the XVIII Corps, which had been transformed into a mobile field formation from numerous garrisons in southeastern Virginia and North Carolina. The army also had three independent brigades, but they will not be addressed in this chapter.[14]

For the ten weeks prior to the Fifth Offensive, the X Corps had been led by Major General David B. Birney. Like so many other senior officers already mentioned, he hailed from the Keystone State, yet he differed from them in one crucial respect. Unlike all the other permanent corps commanders in Army Group Grant, he was neither a West Pointer nor a professional soldier. Rather was he a citizen-soldier, literally a Philadelphia lawyer and the son of Liberty Party presidential candidate James G. Birney. Earlier in the war he had led the 23rd Pennsylvania Zouaves and then a brigade and division. He briefly succeeded Dan Sickles in charge of the III Corps at Gettysburg, and in Hancock's brief absence he temporarily headed the II Corps during its disastrous defeats on June 18 and 22, 1864. On July 23, 1864, he was reassigned to permanent command of the X Corps in the Army of the James. He led that corps in both battles of Deep Bottom. Now he would again sally from that bridgehead to attack near New Market Heights on September 29.[15]

One day before Birney took charge of the X Corps, a much different officer, Major General Edward Ord of Maryland, assumed command of the XVIII Corps. A West Pointer (Class of 1839) and Old Army veteran, he led a brigade and division in Virginia in 1861 and early 1862 and a corps or wing in Tennessee, Mississippi, and Louisiana in late 1862 and 1863. While in the West, he earned Grant's respect and became a Grant man. This status protected him from the customary consequences of his willful insistence on accepting only assignments that suited his sense of his own importance—usually a career killer when other officers tried to pull that on Grant.[16]

14 The three brigades which will not be explored are the Provisional Brigade, the Naval Brigade, and the First Separate Brigade. Edward G. Longacre wrote the modern study, *Army of Amateurs*.

15 The only biography of Birney was written by his friend Oliver P. Davis in 1867: *Life of David Bell Birney*. See also Heitman, *Register*, v. I, p. 220, and Warner, *Blue*, pp. 34-35.

16 After recovering from his wound at Hatchie Bridge, Ord was assigned to command the forward Federal force at West Point, Virginia, in May of 1863. He considered this as much too small for his stature and arranged to be returned to the Army of the Tennessee. Eleven months later, he rejected being put in charge of raiding forces in West Virginia, even though

Ord would be wounded early on September 29. Command then devolved on his senior subordinate, the Jerseyman Brigadier General Charles A. Heckman. Although he had served as a sergeant in the Voltigeur regiment during the Mexican War, he (like Birney) was essentially a citizen-soldier. His principal prewar job was as a railroad conductor. Earlier in the Civil War, he commanded the 9th New Jersey and then a brigade in battle and briefly (but not in combat) led a division. Along with much of his Star Brigade, he was captured at the Second Battle of Drewry's Bluff, May 16, 1864. Held as a prisoner of war under Federal fire in Charleston that summer, he rejoined the Army of the James only on September 17. His seniority gave him command of the Second Division of the XVIII Corps. Just twelve days later, he was catapulted into corps command on mid-morning of September 29.[17]

Heckman held that office for only the remainder of that day. He was succeeded by Brevet Major General Godfrey Weitzel. Born in Bavaria and raised in Ohio, Weitzel graduated second in his class of 1855 at West Point (six files above David Gregg). His service as Chief Engineer of the Ship Island expedition, which captured New Orleans, cemented his relationship with Major General Benjamin F. Butler. First under Butler and then under Major General Nathaniel P. Banks, he led a brigade and division in Louisiana in 1862 and 1863. Back under Butler by the spring of 1864, he first commanded a division in the XVIII Corps and then served as Chief of Staff and Chief Engineer of the Army of the James. Like Kautz, Brigadier Generals John W. Turner and Adelbert Ames, and Colonel George A. Kensel, Weitzel was a West Point educated, career professional officer who linked his star to Ben Butler. They rose with him—and eventually they fell with him.[18]

Grant hand-picked him for such duty. The General-in-Chief, nevertheless, continued to hold him in high regard and put him in charge of the XVIII Corps, July 21; Ord assumed command the next day. The modern biography of Ord is *Appomattox Commander* by his kinsman, Bernarr Cresap. See also Heitman, *Register*, v. I, p. 759, and Warner, *Blue*, pp. 349-50.

17 Heitman, *Register*, v. I, p. 519, and Warner, *Blue*, pp. 226-27.

18 Weitzel, Kautz, Turner, and Ames each commanded a division in the Army of the James at various periods of the war, but only the Badener was present when the Fifth Offensive erupted. Kensel served as that army's chief of staff during the Fifth and Sixth Offensives. When Turner returned from sick leave, he replaced Kensel in that position, November 20,

In September, 1864, Butler was still in the ascendant. The quintessential "political general" of the Civil War, Butler was an ambitious politician whose career ranged from conservative Democrat through Radical Republican to Greenbacker. Achieving military success was often key to political office in 19th Century America—and, in fairness, that model was quite compatible with the Founding Fathers' vision.[19] As a Massachusetts Militia Brigadier General, Butler in 1861 occupied Annapolis and Baltimore. As a U.S. Volunteer Major General, he secured Fort Monroe and captured Hatteras Inlet that year, occupied New Orleans in 1862, and commanded the Army of the James throughout 1864. His talents as a trial lawyer made him a keen intelligence analyst. His mercurial personality made him a vacillating field commander. With all his strengths and weaknesses, he remained in the field in army command: the ranking subordinate in Army Group Grant—indeed, the ranking Major General of Volunteers in the entire Union Army still serving on an active front.[20]

Within Butler's army, combat casualties led to first Heckman and then Weitzel taking over the XVIII Corps in the first twenty-four hours of

---

1864-March 20, 1865. Ames came back from leave a month before Turner and led the First Division of the X Corps in the final phase of the Fifth Offensive, including the Second Battle of the Darbytown Road. In 1870, Ames married Ben Butler's daughter. The first of the absentees to return, overnight on September 29-30, was Weitzel, who came back from an inspection-reconnoitering tour in North Carolina as Chief Engineer of Butler's department. He was immediately assigned to supersede Heckman commanding the XVIII Corps. Regrettably, this author's friend, the respected historian Dr. Arthur Bergeron, did not complete his biography of Weitzel before his untimely passing in 2010. Five years later, G. William Quatman published *A Young General* on Weitzel. See also Heitman, *Register*, v. I, p. 1015, and Warner, *Blue*, pp. 548-49.

19 This model of citizen-soldiers as senior commanders is articulated in Chapter 6 of this book, "American Cincinnatus."

20 Three Major Generals did rank Butler in the autumn of 1864: George B. McClellan in the Regulars and John A. Dix and Nathaniel P. Banks in the Volunteers. However, "Little Mac" was home "awaiting orders;" Banks was on leave; and Dix commanded the Department of the East, headquartered in New York City. Butler thus was the senior officer in that grade actually serving at the front as of then. The Bay Stater wrote his autobiography, *Butler's Book*, and his grand-daughter, Jessie Ames Marshall, published five volumes of his *Private and Official Correspondence*. Mid-to-late 20th Century biographies of him are Richard Holzman's *Stormy Ben Butler*, Howard Nash's *Stormy Petrel*, Dick Nolan's *The Damnedest Yankee*, Hans Trefousse's *The South Called Him Beast*, Robert Werlich's *"Beast" Butler*, and Richard West's *Lincoln's Scapegoat General*. See also Heitman, *Register*, v. I, p. 268, and Warner, *Blue*, pp. 60-61.

fighting. Three other officers also rose to corps command during the Fifth Offensive but much later in the operation.

One of them, also in the Army of the James, was combat connected, too. Birney had been ill even during initial fighting at New Market Heights and Fort Gilmer. As combat quieted down in early October, he took to his sick bed, but he arose from there to win the First Battle of the Darbytown Road, October 7. Saving the Army of the James from potential disaster drained what little strength remained in his disease-wracked body. On October 10, desperately ill, he left for home in Philadelphia on sick leave.

His senior subordinate, Brevet Major General Alfred H. Terry, succeeded him and commanded the X Corps in the Second Battle of the Darbytown Road three days later. A Connecticut lawyer turned citizen-soldier, Terry entered service in 1861 as Colonel of the 2nd Connecticut and later the 7th Connecticut. He received his first star as of April 25, 1862, and he headed a division from the Siege of Charleston through Bermuda Hundred to the Siege of Petersburg. He temporarily led the X Corps itself at Clay's Farm. Now he commanded it again during the final phase of the Fifth Offensive.[21]

Also in mid-October, the Army of the Potomac received two temporary corps commanders but under much less alarming circumstances—the request to find relief from the relentless combat raging over the past five months. As the initial heavy fighting of the Fifth Offensive subsided on both sides of James River by October 2, ten senior officers of the Army of the Potomac availed themselves of the supposed respite to take leave. First to depart was Warren, October 7.[22]

21 Much has been written about Terry in the Indian Wars, but little focuses on his Civil War service. The best available work is Carl Marino's dissertation, "Soldier from Connecticut." See also Heitman, *Register*, v. I, p. 951, and Warner, *Blue*, pp. 497-98.

22 In just seven days in mid-month, ten of Meade's prominent subordinates went on leave: October 7, Warren; October 8, Major General John Gibbon; October 9, Mott and Brigadier General Edward Ferrero; October 10, Major General Andrew Humphreys; October 11, Colonel James Gwyn and Major James Grindlay; October 12, Colonel Charles H.T. Collis; and October 13, Colonel George H. Sharpe and Major Benjamin F. Fisher. Warren and Mott have already been identified. Gibbon led the Second Division/II Corps. Ferrero headed the Third Division/IX Corps. Gwyn and Grindlay were former V Corps brigadiers who fought at Poplar Spring Church, September 30 and October 1, respectively. The other officers served at army headquarters—Humphreys as Chief of Staff, Collis as commander of the HQ portion of the Provost Brigade, Sharpe as Chief Military Intelligence Officer, and Fisher as Chief Signal Officer.

His temporary replacement was his senior division commander, Brevet Major General Samuel W. Crawford, yet another Pennsylvanian. By then, Crawford had been in the U.S. Army for thirteen and a half years—the first ten of them as an assistant surgeon. Not just any Army doctor, he was the doctor of Fort Sumter during the Secession crisis. All officers who endured that ordeal became instant national heroes. He was commissioned Major of the new 13th U.S. (William T. Sherman's own regiment) as of May 14, 1861, and Brigadier General of Volunteers on April 25, 1862.[23] He led a brigade at Cedar Mountain and a division at Antietam and again from Gettysburg through Globe Tavern. His initial role in the Fifth Offensive was to oversee all V and IX Corps troops remaining in the pre-existing trenches and not accompanying the strike force toward Peebles's farm. On October 7, however, he took charge of the V Corps when Warren left. That very day, the Fifth Offensive flared up again on the Northside. Fighting there caused Grant to order the Army of the Potomac back into action on October 8 in the ensuing Second Battle of the Squirrel Level Road.[24]

That little battle sputtered out in one day.[25] As quiet returned, Hancock temporarily absented himself from corps headquarters on October 12 to visit City Point and the Army of the James. With the four most senior generals of the II Corps gone, its command devolved temporarily on Brigadier General

23 Nine officers served in Fort Sumter when the Civil War began. The following list shows the rank for eight of them in the fort, their first promotion on returning north, and their highest wartime grade and position: Major Robert Anderson (Brigadier General, USA / Bvt. Major General, department commander); Captain John G. Foster (Brigadier General, USV / Major General, department commander); Captain Abner Doubleday (Major, 17th U.S. / Major General, corps commander); Captain Truman Seymour (Captain, 5th U.S. Artillery / Bvt. Major General, division commander); 1st Lt. Jefferson C. Davis (Captain, 1st U.S. Artillery / Bvt. Major General, corps commander); 2nd Lt. Norman J. Hall (Captain, 5th U.S. Artillery / Colonel, brigade commander); 2nd Lt. George W. Snyder (Bvt. Major, 1st U.S. Artillery / died November 17, 1861); Assistant Surgeon Samuel W. Crawford (Major, 13th U.S. / Bvt. Major General, division commander). From among these officers, declining health caused Hall to leave field service right after Gettysburg, and early death cut short the military career of Snyder. The ninth officer, Second Lieutenant Richard Kidder Meade, Jr., forfeited his claim to be a U.S. national hero by resigning from the Army on May 1, 1861. He followed his native Virginia into the Confederacy and died there on July 31, 1862, as a Major in the Southern Army.

24 The modern biography of Crawford is Richard Wagner's *For Honor, Flag, and Family*. See also Heitman, *Register*, v. I, p. 337, and Warner, *Blue*, pp. 99-100.

25 For an overview of the Second Battle of the Squirrel Level Road, see the author's "The Battle No One Wanted," *CWTI*, v. XIV, no. 5.

Philippe Regis Denis DeKeredern DeTrobriand.[26] Born into a French noble family in 1816, he moved to the United States in the 1840s and eventually became editor of a French-language newspaper in New York City. He entered the Union Army in 1861 as Colonel of the 55th New York, transferred to lead the 38th New York the next year, and saw combat with them at Williamsburg, Fredericksburg, and Chancellorsville. At Gettysburg and Second Kelly's Ford, he led a brigade. Annoyed at not being promoted, he was mustered out of service on November 22, 1863. The Army wanted him back, and he re-entered service the following January 5 as a Brigadier General. After initially serving in New York harbor, he was assigned to a brigade in the II Corps on July 13 and headed it at First and Second Deep Bottom and Poplar Spring Church. By seniority, he took over the Third Division when Mott left on October 9 and then the II Corps itself when Hancock was away three days later.[27] Thus, DeTrobriand technically was a corps commander during the Fifth Offensive.[28]

These, then, were the three later replacements, the two early replacements, and the ten original senior soldiers of Grant's Fifth Offensive. Beyond considering them consecutively, conclusions may also be conveyed about them collectively.[29]

Nine of them were West-Point educated military professionals, and Crawford also was a Regular. Grant had resigned his commission under difficult circumstances eleven years after graduating and did not re-enter the army until the Civil War erupted. Meade, too, had left military service

26 Gibbon departed on October 8 to meet his sister from North Carolina, who had a pass through Confederate lines, and escort her to his home in Philadelphia. Mott left the next day. The First Division's official commander, Brevet Major General Francis C. Barlow, had been on prolonged sick leave since August 17, and his replacement, Brigadier General Nelson A. Miles, was junior to DeTrobriand, as were all other brigadiers in the II Corps. Thus, the Frenchman succeeded to corps command by seniority when Hancock took off for a few hours on October 12.

27 *OR*, v. XLII, pt. 3, p. 180.

28 The best sources on DeTrobriand are his memoir, *Four Years with the Army of the Potomac*, and William Styple's edition of *Our Noble Blood*. See also Heitman, *Register*, v. I, p. 370, and Warner, *Blue*, pp. 121-22.

29 DeTrobriand, Terry, and Crawford were the later replacements. Heckman and Weitzel rose to corps command on the first day of the Fifth Offensive. The ten original senior officers were General-in-Chief Grant himself; Meade, Hancock, Warren, Parke, and Gregg in the Army of the Potomac; and Butler, Birney, Ord, and Kautz in the Army of the James.

sixteen months out of the U.S. Military Academy but had been recommissioned in May of 1842. He and the other eight Regulars continued serving in the Old Army right up to the outbreak of the Civil War. From Ord's twenty-two years to Gregg's and Weitzel's six each, those ten officers averaged twelve years apiece in the prewar Army. Adding the four years that nine of them spent at West Point plus Kautz's one year as a private in the 1st Ohio during the Mexican War raises the average to fifteen years and eight months each.

For those ten Regulars as well as the five citizen-soldiers, most had entered military service from the Middle Atlantic region: six from Pennsylvania, two from New York, and one from New Jersey.[30] Three joined from the Midwest: the two Germans and initially Grant from Ohio, the future General-in-Chief returning in 1861 from Illinois. Butler and Terry were New Englanders, and Ord was a semi-Southerner, who entered from the culturally Southern District of Columbia.

Their places of birth were somewhat more widespread. Again, the Mid-Atlantic predominated, with one from New York and five from the Keystone State.[31] Birney as well as Ord were born in slave states. Butler and Terry hailed from New Hampshire and Connecticut, respectively. Grant was the only native Midwesterner, an Ohioan. The remaining four were born overseas—Kautz and Weitzel in Germany, DeTrobriand in France, and Meade in Spain to American parents.

Meade, as well as Hancock, Ord, and Parke, entered Volunteer Service in 1861 as Brigadier Generals.[32] Butler started at that grade in the Massachusetts Militia but soon received Two Stars in the U.S. Volunteers. Birney, DeTrobriand, Terry, and Grant himself began as Colonels of regiments. Warren and Heckman were initially Lieutenant Colonels, and Crawford started one grade below them. The two cavalrymen, Gregg and Kautz, stayed in their Regular rank of Captain throughout 1861 and were

30 Birney, Crawford, Gregg, Hancock, Meade, and Parke entered service from the Keystone State. DeTrobriand and Warren were New Yorkers, and Heckman hailed from New Jersey.

31 Crawford, Gregg, Hancock, Heckman, and Parke were born in Pennsylvania. Warren was native to New York.

32 Technically, all the Regular officers held junior grades in the U.S. Army when the Civil War began and for several weeks or months thereafter. This paragraph covers their first significant promotions in the Volunteers by the late summer and early autumn of 1861.

promoted to Colonels of regiments only in 1862.[33] That latter year saw Weitzel take the biggest single upward bound of any of the fifteen officers. He remained a First Lieutenant of Engineers throughout his service at Ship Island and New Orleans until—under Butler's patronage—he rocketed straight up to Brigadier General as of August 29, 1862.[34]

Weitzel was the youngest of the fifteen when the Fifth Offensive began, not quite 29, and Gregg was 31 and a half. At the other end of the scale, Meade was the oldest: just three months short of his 49th birthday. DeTrobriand was only half a year younger than Meade. The average age for all fifteen was 39 and a half. The three most senior officers averaged over 45 years and 8 months. The ten corps commanders averaged approximately seven years younger than their superiors (The five original corps chiefs averaged 39 and a half; their five replacements averaged sixteen months younger.) Not surprisingly, the two cavalry generals were much younger; they averaged 34.

Only three of the fifteen remained in their positions for the rest of the Civil War: Grant, Meade, and Parke. Weitzel and Terry received comparable commands after the X and XVIII Corps were discontinued on December 3, 1864. The Bavarian headed the new XXV Corps right away. Terry reverted to division command for a month, but in January, 1865, he took charge of a Provisional Corps in North Carolina, which was designated the reconstituted X Corps on March 27. Kautz, too, stayed at the same level, though with less responsibility; in March, 1865, he was reassigned from leading the independent Cavalry Division to heading an infantry division within Weitzel's corps.

The other nine generals went up, down, or out. Ord and Hancock were promoted to command the Army of the James and the Middle Military Division, respectively. Crawford and DeTrobriand reverted to division and brigade command when their official corps chieftains returned. The

33 On May 14, 1861, Gregg was promoted from adjutant of the 1st U.S. Dragoons to captain in the new 3rd U.S. Cavalry (redesignated the 6th U.S. Cavalry in August of that year). He stayed in that position until promoted to Colonel of the 8th Pennsylvania Cavalry, January 24, 1862. Kautz, too, left the 4th U.S. to become a captain in the 3rd [6th] U.S. Cavalry on May 14, 1861, but he remained with that regiment for sixteen months and did not become Colonel of the 2nd Ohio Cavalry until September 2, 1862. Heitman, *Register*, v. I, pp. 476, 586.

34 Ibid., p. 1015.

Frenchman did temporarily succeed the wounded Mott at the head of the Third Division from Sailor's Creek through Appomattox. Crawford, too, again led the V Corps temporarily in January, 1865, but permanent command of it was not entrusted to him when Warren was relieved of command on April 1.[35] Earlier that year, Butler and Heckman had also been relieved.[36] Gregg resigned his Regular and Volunteer commissions as of February 3, 1865.[37] The remaining officer, Birney, did not survive the Fifth Offensive. His sick leave came too late; on October 18, he died of disease.[38]

Two other citizen-soldiers, both relieved from active duty and awaiting orders, resigned their Volunteer commissions in 1865, Heckman on May 25 and Butler on November 30. Nine more officers also left Volunteer Service postwar, Warren by resigning on May 27, 1865, and Crawford, DeTrobriand, Hancock, Kautz, Ord, Parke, Terry, and Weitzel by mustering out between January and September of the following year. Grant and Meade had already vacated their Volunteer commissions during the war, when promoted to senior grades in the permanent establishment.

Nine wartime Regular officers stayed in service postwar under their U.S. Army commissions. Grant, elevated to Four-Star grade in 1866, continued as

35 Warren continued leading the V Corps through the Fifth, Sixth, Seventh, and Eighth Offensives and well into the Ninth. Late on April 1, 1865, after delivering the attack that won the Battle of Five Forks, he was relieved of command by Major General Philip H. Sheridan in one of the worst injustices of the Civil War.

36 Butler remained at the head of the Army of the James through the Sixth Offensive. He also had charge of troops in New York City who made sure that no disruptions occurred on election day, November 8, 1864. The overwhelming re-election of President Abraham Lincoln actually reduced the need to retain troublesome politician-generals in command. Thus, when Butler's attempt to blow up Fort Fisher, North Carolina, with a boat full of gunpowder on December 24, 1864, ended in fiasco, Grant had the long-awaited justification to relieve the Bay Stater from command on January 7, 1865. Heckman lasted only two months longer than Butler. After yielding his brief command of the XVIII Corps to Weitzel, the Jerseyman resumed heading his division in that corps and then a division in the new XXV Corps. Indeed, when Weitzel went on leave, Heckman led the XXV Corps itself, January 1-February 2, 1865. His seniority, far from being an asset, troubled Ord, who was no longer just his corps commander but now his army commander. The Marylander had long since lost confidence in Heckman and relieved him on March 23 because "he . . . is not fit to command." Simon, op. cit., x. XIV, pp. 209-10; *OR*, v. XLVI, pt. 3, pp. 87-88.

37 Although Gregg's resignation took effect on February 3, 1865, he remained in command of his division through the Eighth Offensive, February 5-7, and did not relinquish command until February 9. *OR*, v. XLVI, pt. 2, pp. 499-500.

38 Jack Welsh's *Medical Histories of Union Generals*, pp. 29-30, concludes Birney died of typhoid fever.

General-in-Chief until March 4, 1869, when he became Commander-in-Chief as the Eighteenth President of the United States. Meade and Hancock served as Major Generals of Regulars, and Ord started with One-Star rank. Crawford, who was already Lieutenant Colonel of the 2nd U.S. as of February 17, 1864, rose to colonel of the 16th U.S. five years later and then returned to the 2nd U.S. as its Colonel one month after that. Kautz, too, started as Lieutenant Colonel of the 34th U.S. in 1866, held comparable grade in the 15th U.S. as of 1869, was promoted to Colonel of the 8th U.S. in 1874, and was elevated to Brigadier General on April 20, 1891. Except for Meade, the Engineers—who had rightfully risen in rank in Volunteer Service—fared far less well in the peacetime establishment.[39] Parke, Warren, and Weitzel—formerly Major Generals commanding corps—each reverted to Major in the Corps of Engineers. The Pennsylvanian, despite his good war record, rose only to Colonel before retiring in 1889 with his final tour as Superintendent of the U.S. Military Academy.[40] Warren (blighted by the wrath of Philip H. Sheridan) and Weitzel (tainted as a Ben Butler protégé) languished even lower and were promoted only one grade late in life.

Ironically, the ex-Regular, David Gregg, sought to re-enter service, and Hancock and many other senior generals supported him. However, a bureaucratic bungle led to the Colonelcy of the 8th U.S. Cavalry being offered to his cousin, Brevet Brigadier General J. Irvin Gregg, a citizen-soldier who had headed the 16th Pennsylvania Cavalry and then a brigade but not a division during the war. Rather than disadvantage his cousin, David withdrew from consideration, and the new regiment went to Irvin.

39 Because the highest-ranking graduates of the U.S. Military Academy were commissioned into the Corps of Engineers or the Topographical Engineers, Engineer officers were regarded as the most promising prospects for senior command in the Civil War. Thus, in the Fifth Offensive, Meade, Warren, Parke, and Weitzel were Engineers. So were Major Generals McClellan, William S. Rosecrans, James B. McPherson, and many other prominent Union commanders—as well as such senior Southern soldiers as Generals Robert E. Lee, Joseph E. Johnston, and P.G.T. Beauregard. This subject is elaborated in Chapter 20 of a later volume of this book, "Federal and Confederate Engineers in the Gettysburg Campaign."

40 Parke chose to retire in 1889, four years before the mandatory age, because he was not selected as Chief Engineer of the Army in 1888. U.S. Military Academy Association of Graduates, *Annual Reunion, 1902*, p. 38.

Besides Irvin Gregg, two other citizen-soldiers commissioned into the Regulars were Terry and DeTrobriand. The New Englander's great victory in capturing Fort Fisher, January 15, 1865, earned him Two Stars in the Volunteer Service and One Star in the U.S. Army, ranking from that date. He thus became the highest-ranking citizen-soldier in the entire Union Army to continue in Regular Service postwar.[41] He rose to Major General of Regulars on March 3, 1886. DeTrobriand did not ascend as high, but he was commissioned Colonel of the 31st U.S. in 1866 and held comparable grade in the 13th U.S. when the Regular Army's force structure was reduced three years later.

Terry, DeTrobriand, and the nine prewar Regulars who served after Appomattox remained in uniform an average of seventeen more years. Subtracting Grant's postwar tour of less than four years raises the average to eighteen and a half years. Grant, of course, left to become President. Crawford, DeTrobriand, Ord, Terry, Parke, and finally Kautz retired in 1873, 1879, 1880, 1888, 1889, and 1892, respectively. Meade (1872), Warren (1882), Weitzel (1884), and Hancock (1886) died in service.

Weitzel was barely 48 and Warren only 52 and a half when they passed away, the two youngest of the fourteen postwar survivors. The average age of death for all fifteen was 64 years-five months. Not counting Birney at 39+ raises the average for the others to just over 66. The three most senior officers lived an average of 64 years-nine months. The ten corps commanders averaged 62 (64 years-seven months without Birney). The two cavalrymen averaged 75 years, but that number is skewed upward by Gregg, who lived to age 83 years-four months.[42] When he passed away on August 7, 1916, he was the last of those fifteen generals and the only one to survive into the 20th Century.[43]

41 When the U.S. Army went on its peacetime footing in the latter part of 1866, Terry was one of only two citizen-soldiers among the twenty-six active duty generals. He ranked fifteenth among the seventeen Regular generals of the line. He was eighth among the ten One-Stars, ranking ahead of former army commanders Edward Ord and Edward Canby. Among the nine generals of staff, the only citizen-soldier was Grant's Chief of Staff, John A. Rawlins, whose Regular commission as Brigadier General dated from March 3, 1865—seven weeks junior to Terry.

42 DeTrobriand was next oldest at age 81.

43 Parke passed away on December 16, 1900—just sixteen days before the 20th Century began.

After resigning in February of 1865, Gregg lived for fifty-one and a half years. Adding Butler and Heckman, who also resigned that year, sets an average of thirty-six and a half years that these three men lived in civil life postwar. That figure is almost three and a half times as great as the civil life for the seven officers who retired from Regular Service postwar: just ten years and eight months.

The post-military activities of those ten former generals varied greatly. Grant served as President, 1869-1877. Butler ran for President on the Greenback ticket in 1884 but was corked back in his bottle. The previous year he served as Governor of Massachusetts as a Greenbacker and Democrat. Earlier he was a Radical Republican Congressman for ten years and managed the House of Representative's prosecution of the impeachment trial of President Andrew Johnson. Gregg, too, held office, Auditor General of Pennsylvania. He also farmed in Delaware, served briefly as consul in Prague, and took part in historical preservation and veterans activities, especially the Loyal Legion. Crawford, too, was active in helping preserve the Gettysburg battlefield; he also traveled the world on behalf of the British Royal Geographic Society. DeTrobriand (since 1874 a French count) visited his native land and alternated between New Orleans and New York. Heckman, his nemesis Ord, and Parke were involved in railroading—the last as a director of a DC railroad, the Marylander building a new line in Mexico, the junior officer as a dispatcher in New Jersey. Kautz and Terry simply enjoyed their few remaining years as retirees.

While retired, Grant, Butler, and DeTrobriand composed autobiographies, and Crawford wrote a memoir of Fort Sumter.[44] Gregg wrote about his cavalry at Gettysburg, scene of his greatest service, and was active in preserving the battle's history.[45] Mrs. Hancock penned a memoir of her husband, and descendants published the wartime family letters of Meade, Warren, and DeTrobriand.[46] The modern multi-volume edition of *The*

44 In addition to the already cited *Personal Memoirs of U.S. Grant*, *Butler's Book*, and *Four Years with the Army of the Potomac* may be mentioned Crawford's *The Genesis of the Civil War*.

45 Gregg wrote *The Second Cavalry Division of the Army of the Potomac in the Gettysburg Campaign*.

46 The editions of Butler's, Meade's, Warren's, and DeTrobriand's letters have already been cited. Almira R. Hancock wrote *Reminiscences of Winfield Scott Hancock by His Wife*.

Papers of Ulysses S. Grant, under the magisterial editorship of Professors John Y. Simon and John Marszalek, towers as a monument to historical editing.[47] All these writings are among many sources which contribute to understanding Federal generalship in the Siege of Petersburg during the early autumn of 1864.

These, then, were the senior soldiers who would wage Grant's Fifth Offensive at Petersburg: General-in-Chief Grant himself, his two army commanders, Meade and Butler; the four major subordinates in the Army of the Potomac, Hancock, Warren, Parke, and Gregg; their counterparts in the Army of the James, Birney, Ord, Weitzel, Kautz, and Terry; and their temporary replacements, Crawford, DeTrobriand, and Heckman. Their strengths and shortcomings as commanders contributed significantly to the outcome of the Fifth Offensive—what was accomplished and what was not.

How may their service be summarized in the ensuing Fifth Offensive and in the war?[48] Grant stands pre-eminent, not just in rank and office but in strategic vision and practical sense to understand how to convert advantages into achievements. He came close to capturing Petersburg and even Richmond in this operation. Six months later, he would take those two cities—and Lee's army and, with them, the Confederacy itself.

His best subordinate, Meade, continued to show professional competence in executing Grant's intent, even in prolonging the search for success a day beyond when the General-in-Chief was willing to end the battle. Yet on more fundamental matters of perceiving how vulnerable the Secessionists were on September 29 and again on October 2, the Major General did not even recognize opportunity, let alone seize it. Butler, in contrast, had no difficulty envisioning opportunities, some of them real, others illusory. His problem continued to be his mercurial mood swings that fluctuated between triumphant conquest and dire doom—an infixity of purpose that allowed opportunity to elude him.

Among Meade's corps commanders, the renowned Hancock was not put to the test in the Fifth Offensive. Not until late October would he fight his

47 From 1967 to 2009, the Ulysses S. Grant Association published thirty-one volumes of Grant's papers, edited by the legendary John Y. Simon. His renowned successor, John Marszalek, edited the final, supplemental v. XXXII in 2012.

48 The conclusions and analyses in the rest of this chapter are developed more fully throughout *Richmond Redeemed*, especially in its Chapter 15.

final battle and fulfill his field service with his mastery of minor tactics.[49] Warren, on the other hand, demonstrated his tactical mastery a month earlier: offensively at Peebles's Farm, defensively at Pegram's Farm and First Squirrel Level Road. Yet his technical skill continued clouded by the willfulness and fault-finding that characterized his corps command. Parke's problems proved particularly perplexing. In his first battle as corps commander in the Army of the Potomac, he failed to coordinate his forces and barely fended off disaster on September 30. Nor would he seek opportunity two days later. Eventually he would mature into a competent corps commander, but such success came only in 1865. By then, Gregg would be gone, but in the Fifth Offensive, the cavalryman again demonstrated his skill in securing his army's vulnerable left flank. It was not his fault that the Yankees were unable to advance as far as Grant intended.

More fault can be found with Gregg's counterpart in the Army of the James. Kautz again failed to force the issue on September 29 to try to break through the Intermediate Line into Richmond itself. Even worse disaster befell him eight days later, when he was driven from Johnson's plantation with the loss of all his artillery. Kautz's disaster at First Darbytown Road opened the way for the greatest success of Birney's career in beating off pursuing Butternuts. Birney's earlier operations in the Fifth Offensive were hesitant, just as had happened in the Second and Fourth Offensives. Whether or not he would have eventually fulfilled his potentiality to become more than an above average corps commander is unanswerable. What is clear is that his career ended gloriously on October 7.

Credit for executing Birney's plans that day goes to Terry. In his next test as a corps commander in his own right, the Connecticut man proved hesitant and unsure.[50] He would improve with experience and in the following January would achieve at Fort Fisher one of the greatest successes ever attained by a Federal corps. For the XVIII Corps, its greatest victory came on September 29, when it broke through at Fort Harrison and bade fair to capture the Confederate capital itself. Ord deserves credit for that breakthrough. He also deserves blame for again recklessly exposing himself

49 Hancock's final fight, First Hatcher's Run, was his most masterful. It is covered briefly in the author's "The Battle of the Boydton Plank Road, October 27-28, 1864," *Civil War Magazine*, No. LXVII.

50 The Second Battle of the Darbytown Road, October 13, 1864.

at the front and going down with a wound that cost the Union his services for two months—especially his continuing leadership that day, which might have exploited the initial advantage. His immediate replacement, Heckman, proved grossly incompetent. His piecemeal probes squandered the opportunity Ord had obtained. Weitzel was a more reliable replacement and won solid success against Southern assaults, September 30. Winning defensive battles is not difficult. How Weitzel would fare when he had to attack remained unknown during the Fifth Offensive. The answer would come in the Sixth Offensive—and it would not be favorable to the general and to the Union.[51]

For the remaining two generals, DeTrobriand's tiny tenure at II Corps headquarters on one relatively quiet day offers no insight into his fitness for command higher than the brigade that he led so well. Even Crawford's day in the sun at Second Squirrel Level Road sheds little light on his aptitude for corps command. Neither Meade nor his Confederate counterpart, A.P. Hill, saw any need to fight a battle on October 8, and Crawford operated accordingly.[52]

Crawford and DeTrobriand, unknowable; Butler and Kautz, marginal; Heckman, incompetent; Birney and Weitzel, uncertain; Parke and Terry, unfulfilled; Warren and Ord, good but flawed; Hancock, good but inactive; Meade and Gregg, sound and competent; and Grant, outstanding. Not surprisingly, the best Federal general was Grant himself. After all, this was his Fifth Offensive at Petersburg.

51 The Second Battle of Fair Oaks, October 27, 1864.

52 See the author's "The Battle No One Wanted," *CWTI*, v. XIV, no. 5.

63. Gouverneur K. Warren. LOC

64. John G. Parke. LOC

65. Samuel W. Crawford. LOC

66. David M. Gregg. LOC

67. Charles A. Heckman. LOC

68. Godfrey Weitzel. LOC

69. August V. Kautz. LOC

70. P. Regis DeTrobriand. LOC

Chapter 10

Founding Fathers: Renowned Revolutionary War Relatives of Significant Civil War Soldiers and Statesmen[1]

"Four score and seven years ago our fathers brought forth on this continent a new nation, conceived in liberty and dedicated to the proposition that all men are created equal. Now we are engaged in a great Civil War, testing whether that nation or any nation so conceived and so dedicated can long endure."

Abraham Lincoln's immortal Gettysburg Address is better remembered not for that opening but for its subsequent soaring sentiments such as "these dead shall not have died in vain" and "this nation, under God, shall have a new birth of freedom" and especially "government of the people, by the people, for the people shall not perish from the earth." This chapter, though, lingers on Lincoln's leading line—"our fathers brought forth on this continent a new nation . . . "—particularly on those two words "our fathers." A century and a half later, the words "our fathers," or more commonly "Founding Fathers," are, alas, virtually meaningless—a figure of speech, a political platitude, with no real resonance within the American republic.

1 This chapter is adapted from a presentation first given at the Edwin C. Bearss Military Leadership and Combat Seminar of the Chambersburg Civil War Seminars, April 7, 2017. In this chapter, by way of complementing decades of studying the Civil War, the author found the following websites, when used judiciously, helpful in confirming links among those 19th Century personages and their famous Revolutionary War ancestors: www.ancestry.com, www.en.wikipedia.org, www.findagrave.com, www.geni.com, www.suddenlink.net, and www.wikitree.com.

In the mid-19th Century, in contrast, connections with the "Founding Fathers" were markedly more meaningful. The Battle of Gettysburg, as President Lincoln pointed out, was fought only "four score and seven years" after the Declaration of Independence was signed. The Civil War itself began just eighty-five years after that signing and merely seventy-two years after the Constitution took effect. That short span of time encompassed at most four, often three, occasionally two, even just one generation. The Founding Fathers literally were the great-grandfathers, the grandfathers, sometimes even the fathers of the generation that fought the Civil War.

This chapter highlights a few of the family connections that united the "Greatest Generations" of the 18th and 19th Centuries—the generation that gained American independence and the generation that either preserved the American nation or else fought for Confederate independence. All such ties, at whatever level, meant something to individual family members. A private in the 1860s was undoubtedly proud of his ancestor who was a private in the 1770s. Even more so would an enlisted man in the Civil War cherish his famous forebear among the Founding Fathers. And certainly, Abraham Lincoln knew that his namesake grandfather served as a captain in the Virginia militia during the Revolutionary War and was later killed by Indians in Kentucky.[2] His Confederate counterpart, Jefferson Davis, comparably comprehended that his father, Samuel Davis, fought as a private and captain within the South Carolina and Georgia militia during that war.[3]

Those three levels of connection from 18th to 19th Century—obscure person to obscure person, famous person to obscure person, and obscure person to famous person—though meaningful to particular individuals, fall outside this chapter's purview. Rather does it recount renowned

2 On April 1, 1854, the future U.S. President wrote to a relative about his grandfather that "I am the grandson of your Uncle Abraham; and the story of his death by the Indians, and of Uncle Mordecai, then fourteen years old, killing one of the Indians, is the legend more strongly than all others imprinted upon my mind and memory." The elder Abraham Lincoln was residing in the Kentucky portion of Virginia when he was killed by an Indian in 1786. His son Mordecai then killed the Indian, who was about to abduct Mordecai's brother Thomas Lincoln. Twenty-three years later, Thomas became the father of the Great Emancipator. How history would have unfolded if Thomas had been abducted is unknowable—but troubling to consider. Roy P. Basler, ed., *The Collected Works of Abraham Lincoln*, v. II, pp. 217-18.

3 In an autobiography and memoir that he wrote within weeks of his passing, Jefferson Davis made a point of mentioning his father's service in the Revolutionary War. Haskell Monroe, ed., *The Papers of Jefferson Davis*, v. I, pp. liii, lxvii.

Revolutionary War relatives of significant Civil War soldiers and statesmen. It focuses, moreover, on direct and near-term descent (more or less)—not on fifth cousins, brothers-in-law of brothers-in-law, or some distant kinship in the British Isles eight generations before the ancestors came to North America.

Within those criteria—acclaimed ancestors of distinguished descendants—fifty-nine Founding Fathers have been identified so far, related to ninety-one Civil Warriors. This chapter makes no claim to be comprehensive. There are, undoubtedly, many more kinships, especially through female lines of descent.[4]

With that caveat, this chapter will look at those famous Founding Fathers, whose descendants figured prominently in the Civil War. Lincoln suggests where to begin: "four score and seven" years before Gettysburg, with American Independence.

Patriots from all regions—New England, the Middle Colonies, the South—helped inspire and lead that independence movement. However, it was from the Old Dominion that there came a stirring speech which embodied the movement: "Give me Liberty or give me Death!" Those words, proclaimed on March 23, 1775, at the Second Virginia Convention immortalized Patrick Henry (1736-99) in the pantheon of patriots. Already renowned for his vehement and eloquent opposition to the Stamp Act ten years earlier, Henry served as a delegate to both Continental Congresses and as the first Governor of Virginia after the Declaration of Independence, 1776-1779. Briefly as a soldier, more as a government official, most of all as an orator, he was one of the most famous leaders of the American independence movement.

His great-grandson Colonel William R. Aylett (1833-1900) also fought for independence—Confederate independence. A prewar lawyer, he rose from captain to colonel of the 53rd Virginia. Gettysburg was his first battle as colonel of that regiment. Probably fortunately for himself, he was wounded during the heavy bombardment preceding Pickett's Charge and was unable to accompany his troops during the assault. In the charge, his successor was seriously wounded and captured, and the commanders of the other four regiments in the brigade were killed, as was their brigade

4 If readers know of additional such family ties, this author would welcome learning of them. Please contact me at RichmondRedeemed@aol.com.

commander, Brigadier General Lewis A. Armistead.[5] Aylett recovered from his wound, returned to his regiment, and often commanded the brigade but only as senior colonel. He was never promoted to brigadier general and was still a colonel when captured at Sailor's Creek. He was released on July 25, 1865. By then the war was over. He resumed practicing law. Death finally came long after Gettysburg, August 8, 1900.[6]

Aylett's fighting thus failed to win Southern independence. Nor did his ancestor's addresses by themselves throw off British rule. More practical measures were required for revolution, and they were initiated by the Fifth Virginia Convention, which met May 5-July 6, 1776. Its presiding officer was Edmund Pendleton (1721-1803), who in the absence of the Royal Governor became the de facto Patriot governor of Virginia. A wealthy planter and lawyer, former delegate to the First Continental Congress, and future Chief Justice of Virginia, he presided over the decisive actions of that convention.

Before those actions are considered, Pendleton's kin need to be recognized. Since he had no children from either of his two marriages, his designated heir became his nephew, also an Edmund Pendleton, styled "Junior" (1743-1827). Junior's grandson (hence the great-great-nephew of Chief Justice Pendleton) was Brigadier General William Nelson Pendleton (1809-1883), the original Captain of the First Rockbridge Artillery and the Chief of Artillery of the Army of Northern Virginia. The general's son, in turn, was Colonel Alexander S. ("Sandy") Pendleton (1840-64), who served as Chief of Staff for Lieutenant Generals Thomas J. ("Stonewall") Jackson, Richard S. Ewell, and Jubal A. Early until he was killed at Fisher's Hill, September 22, 1864. The general's daughter, Susan, moreover, married Brigadier General Edwin G. Lee (1836-1870), the third Colonel of the 33rd Virginia of the Stonewall Brigade and later the commander of Virginia Reserves in the Shenandoah Valley.

What made the Fifth Virginia Convention so renowned was not the Pendleton relatives but the Virginia Resolution, which the convention adopted May 15, 1776. The convention instructed its delegation to the

5 Kathy Georg Harrison and John W. Busey, *Nothing but Glory*, pp. 386-474. Armistead's great-uncle, Brevet Brigadier General George Baylor, was one of George Washington's aides-de-camp; see endnote 13.

6 Robert K. Krick, *Lee's Colonels*, p. 40.

Second Continental Congress, meeting in Philadelphia, to present that resolution for Congress's action. On June 7, 1776, the distilled essence of the resolution was introduced. It declared: "Resolved, That these United Colonies are, and of right ought to be, free and independent States, that they are absolved from all allegiance to the British Crown, and that all political connection between them and the State of Great Britain is, and ought to be, totally dissolved."

The delegate who introduced that resolution was Richard Henry Lee (1732-1794). He was a member of the Virginia House of Burgesses and of both Continental Congresses; he served as President of the Twelfth Congress, 1784-85, and as United States Senator, 1789-92. Because he not just introduced the resolution that led to American freedom but also signed the ensuing Declaration of Independence, he became known affectionately to his descendants as "The Old Signer."[7]

Among those descendants, two grandsons figured prominently in the Civil War. Rear Admiral Samuel Phillips Lee (1812-97) served in the U.S. Navy, 1825-79. He captained the U.S.S. *Oneida* at the Battle of New Orleans and headed the North Atlantic Blockading Squadron, September, 1862-October, 1864, and the Mississippi River Naval Squadron, November, 1864, to the end of the war. His brother, Brevet Major John Fitzgerald Lee (1813-84), graduated from West Point in 1834 and served in the U.S. Army until 1862. Although his grade was not high, his office was eminent. From 1849 onwards, he served as the Judge Advocate of the Army, the first officer to hold that highest legal office since 1802.[8] A conservative like his brother's in-laws, the Blairs,[9] Major Lee was uncomfortable using military

7 Virginia Jeans Laas, ed., *Wartime Washington*, pp. 343-44.

8 Various officers served as Judge Advocate General of the Army, 1775-83. The position lapsed after the Revolutionary War but was revived, 1794-1802, under very junior officers. Again from 1814 to 1821, judge advocates were assigned to geographical commands rather than serving Army-wide. Not until 1849 was the office of "Judge Advocate of the Army" created to provide legal services for the entire force. John F. Lee was breveted major, a relatively high grade, and assigned to that office for the next thirteen years. Francis B. Heitman, *Historical Register and Biographical Dictionary of the U.S. Army*, v. I, p. 39.

9 Samuel P. Lee married Elizabeth (Blair) Lee. Her oldest brother, Montgomery, Lincoln's Postmaster General, led the conservative block in his cabinet. Her younger brother, Frank, a Major General in the Union Army, was the Democrat Vice Presidential nominee in 1868. Their father, Francis P. Blair, Sr., a Jacksonian Nationalist from that President's kitchen cabinet, was an elder statesman of the new GOP Party. Their mother,

commissions to try suspects in the North while civil courts were still open. Rather than remove such a well-connected officer, Secretary of War Edwin M. Stanton created the new office of Judge Advocate General and appointed the cooperative Brigadier General Joseph Holt to it, September 3, 1862. Outranked and outflanked, Major Lee resigned the next day. Under Holt's leadership, the government made effective use of military commissions for the rest of the war.

Those mid-19th Century Lees continued looking up to their grandfather and his brother and fellow signer (their great-uncle), Francis Lightfoot Lee.[10] Both Richard Henry Lee and Francis Lightfoot Lee had a Declaration of Independence to sign because the Second Continental Congress responded to the Virginia Resolution by declaring independence. The principal author of the Declaration was Thomas Jefferson (1743-1826). One of the most famous Founding Fathers, Jefferson went on to serve as the second Governor of Virginia, Minister to France, first Secretary of State, second Vice President, and third President of the United States.

In addition to all those contributions, he was also the grandfather of Brigadier General George Wythe Randolph (1818-67). Randolph served in the U.S. Navy, 1831-39, and thereafter practiced law in his native Virginia. He brought his Richmond Howitzers into Confederate service in 1861 and commanded the artillery at one of the South's earliest victories, Big Bethel. Promoted to Brigadier General as of February 12, 1862, he served as the third Confederate Secretary of War from March to November of that year. He resigned on November 15 because of continuing disagreements with President Davis. Ill health prevented him from returning to active duty, and he resigned his military commission two years later.

Jefferson was not the only drafter and signer of the Declaration of Independence with strong Civil War connections. John Adams (1735-1826) also served on the committee that prepared that document. He subsequently held diplomat assignments to France, Holland, and Great Britain in the 1770s and 1780s, and served as the first Vice President and second President

---

Eliza, was a daughter of Colonel Nathaniel Gist (1733-96) and step-daughter of Brevet Major General Charles Scott (1739-1813), both of Revolutionary War renown.

10 Richard Henry's brother Francis Lightfoot Lee (1734-97), a delegate to both Continental Congresses, also signed the Declaration of Independence. Two other brothers (hence great-uncles of the Civil War Lees) William (1739-95) and Arthur (1740-92) were American diplomats during the Revolutionary War.

of the United States. He was also the father of John Quincy Adams (1767-1848). The younger man rose to eminence in the early national period as U.S. minister to various European powers, Senator and Representative from Massachusetts, Secretary of State, and sixth President of the United States. However, John Quincy's service on his father's staff during key diplomatic missions to France and Holland during the Revolutionary War, including the peace negotiations that ended the war, entitle him, too, to be considered a Founding Father.

John Quincy was also the father of Ambassador Charles Francis Adams, Sr. (1807-86). A member of the pre-Civil War Massachusetts legislature and unsuccessful Free-Soil Party candidate for Vice President in 1844, he is best known as U.S. Minister to Great Britain, 1861-68. His son, Brevet Brigadier General Charles Francis Adams, Jr. (1835-1915), moreover, served as a company officer in the 1st Massachusetts Cavalry, 1861-64, and as Colonel of the 5th Massachusetts Cavalry in 1865. He was breveted Brigadier General March 13 of that year. Thus, the general was the grandson of one President and the great-grandson of another. The diplomat, moreover, was the son and grandson of those two statesmen. This is one of several instances of only one generation separating a Founding Father from a Civil War son.

More generations separated Civil War kin from another preeminent Founding Father and drafter of the Declaration, Benjamin Franklin (1706-90). Scientist, author, publisher, genius—Franklin was the most famous person in the Thirteen Colonies before the American Revolution. His subsequent service as diplomat and Signer of both the Declaration of Independence and the U.S. Constitution sealed his status in the American pantheon. Through his common-law marriage with Deborah Read, he became the great-grandfather of Matilda Bache, who married William H. Emory (1811-87). A graduate of West Point in 1831, Emory served with distinction against Mexicans, Mormons, and Indians prewar and was promoted from lieutenant to lieutenant colonel. In May, 1861, he briefly resigned his commission and considered going south, but he stayed with the Union and rose from commanding a brigade and division to heading the XIX Corps and the Department of West Virginia as a Major General. He continued in service postwar until retiring in 1876.[11]

11 General Emory was also related to George Washington's aide-de-camp, Tench Tilghman; see endnote 29.

With Franklin and Adams and Jefferson connected to Civil War leaders, it is altogether fitting and proper to mention George Washington as well. His connection leads back to the Lees, not to Richard Henry, Francis, Arthur, and William but to their second cousin Henry Lee III (1756-1818)—better known as "Light Horse Harry" Lee. Although that officer rose only from captain to lieutenant colonel, his command of light dragoons with the main Continental Army in the Middle States and later in South Carolina made him the most acclaimed American cavalryman in the Revolutionary War. He later became a Major General in the Quasi-War of 1798 and also commanded first the Virginia militia and then all militia in the field during the Whiskey Rebellion in his capacity as Governor of Virginia.

Even with such distinguished service, his greatest legacy was his progeny. He was the father of seven sons, two of whom became prominent in the Civil War; they were literally sons of a Founding Father. The elder of those sons was Captain Sydney Smith Lee (1802-69). He served in the U.S. Navy, 1820-61, including the Mexican War and the expedition to open Japan to the outside world. He was also Commandant of Midshipmen at the U.S. Naval Academy and Commandant of the Philadelphia Navy Yard. Like his more famous brother, he went south with his native Virginia. There he served as Commander and Captain in the Confederate Navy, 1861-65.

Smith Lee's wife was Anna Mason, sister of James M. Mason (1798-1871), a prewar U.S. Senator and the Confederate minister to Great Britain, whose seizure by the U.S. Navy in the Trent Affair nearly provoked war between those two nations. Anna and James M. Mason, in turn, were the grandchildren of George Mason IV (1725-92), the author of the Virginia constitution and the father of the U.S. Bill of Rights. The most prominent son of Smith and Anna (Mason) Lee was Major General Fitzhugh Lee (1835-1905). A West Point graduate, he served in the U.S. Army, 1856-61, and then joined the Confederate Army, where he rose from lieutenant colonel to corps commander. Postwar, he served as Governor of Virginia, and he returned to the U.S. Army as a Major General of Volunteers and Brigadier General of Regulars, 1898-1901, during the Spanish-American War and ensuing occupation of Cuba—part of wise national policy to help reunite the nation by not oppressing former Confederates as perpetual enemies but instead by welcoming them back into the country's cause against a common foe. Fitz Lee thus had a double connection to Founding Fathers: "Light Horse Harry" Lee was his paternal grandfather, and George Mason was his maternal great-grandfather.[12]

Even greater military achievements and even more illustrious kinship highlight another of "Light Horse Harry" Lee's sons, General Robert E. Lee (1807-1870)—the best known of all family ties between prominent personages of the Revolution and Civil War. Prewar Superintendent of the U.S. Military Academy, from which he had graduated in 1829, he earned a brilliant record in the Old Army, especially in the Mexican War. Still more brilliant was his Confederate service as Commanding General of the Army of Northern Virginia and eventually as Confederate General-in-Chief. They mark him as one of the greatest generals in American history.[13]

His two older sons were also prominent in the Civil War. Major General George Washington Custis Lee (1832-1913) graduated at the head of his West Point Class of 1854 and served in the U.S. Army until he went south in 1861. In the Graycoat Army, he served as military aide-de-camp to President Davis, commander of the Richmond Local Defense Brigade, and Commanding General of the infantry division of the Department of Richmond. He was captured at Sailor's Creek. His brother Major General W. H. F. ("Rooney") Lee (1837-1891) had been captured almost two years earlier but was exchanged the following spring and rose to division command in his father's army.

The mother of Custis and "Rooney" Lee and the wife of Robert E. Lee was Mary Custis Lee, the granddaughter of John Parke Custis (1754-1781) and the step-great-granddaughter of General George Washington. Jackie Custis, as John was nicknamed, was Washington's step-son and his civilian aide at the Siege of Yorktown in 1781. Joy over the great American victory there dampened on November 5, just seventeen days after Lord Charles Cornwallis surrendered, when young Custis died of camp fever.

Earlier that year, Jackie's only son was born, and he would become the father of the future Mrs. Robert E. Lee. Her father was named George Washington Parke Custis in honor of his step-grandfather, who adopted him

12 George Mason was also tied to Samuel Cooper, Frank Wheaton, and Don Carlos Buell; see endnote 33.

13 This author's assessment of Robert E. Lee is presented more fully in Chapter 2 of this book.

as his own son. George Washington himself (1732-99) needs no introduction: Victor of the Revolutionary War, President of the Constitutional Convention, first President of the United States—not just a Founding Father but the Father of His Country.[14]

Two of Washington's ablest subordinates were Major Generals Nathanael Greene (1742-86) and Henry Knox (1750-1806). Greene led a division in Washington's army, served as Quartermaster General of the Continental Army, 1778-80, and commanded the Southern Department from 1780 onward. In the latter capacity, he reportedly lost every battle and won every campaign; he thwarted British efforts to regain the southern colonies and confined enemy forces to a few coastal enclaves. Knox, on the other hand, remained with Washington and served as his Chief of Artillery for almost the entire war. His transfer of cannons from Fort Ticonderoga over snowy mountains to Dorchester Heights in 1776 forced the British to evacuate Boston. He succeeded Washington in charge of the Continental Army in 1783-84. He then was Secretary of War, 1785-94 under the Articles of Confederation and the Constitution.

Both Knox and Greene had distinguished descendants. Greene's grandson, Brigadier General George S. Greene (1801-99), graduated from West Point in 1819 and served in the U.S. Army until 1836. He returned to duty in 1861 as Colonel of the 60th New York and later led a brigade and division before mustering out in 1866. George's eldest son, Samuel Dana Greene (1839-84), graduated from the U.S. Naval Academy in 1859. As a Navy lieutenant, he served as executive officer of the U.S.S. *Monitor* in the Battle of Hampton Roads and temporarily commanded that vessel during the final part of the battle after its captain was wounded. Young Greene survived the sinking of the first ironclad on December 31, 1862, and served through the rest of the war. He rose to commander in the postwar Navy and stayed in service until his death in 1884.[15]

14 Biologically and legally, Mary Custis Lee was the step-great-granddaughter of George Washington. But since he had adopted her infant father as his son, she could also be considered the President's granddaughter. The former relationship made Washington the great-grandfather-in-law of R.E. Lee and the great-great-grandfather of G.W.C. and W.H.F. Lee. The adoption, however, made the President the grandfather-in-law of R. E. Lee and the great-grandfather of Lee's sons.

15 Tormented by the inconclusive outcome of the battle and perhaps also by the loss of so many shipmates when the *Monitor* sank, Greene wrote one last account of the combat for

The U.S. Navy was also where Knox's grandson, Henry Knox Thatcher (1806-80), served. He rose from midshipman in 1823 to Acting Rear Admiral in 1865. He served as Commodore of the Mediterranean Squadron in 1863, led a naval division in the two battles of Fort Fisher, and commanded the West Gulf Blockading Squadron in the Siege of Mobile and the occupation of Galveston. He continued serving in the Navy as a full Rear Admiral until 1870.

One more Continental General merits mention, for his own sake and for his son-in-law's. Major General Philip Schuyler (1733-1804) served in the Continental Congress in 1775 and 1779-80 and commanded the Northern Department, 1775-77. Relieved for failing to stop Sir John Burgoyne's invasion of upstate New York, he was vindicated from charges of dereliction of duty but resigned his commission in 1779. He later served two partial terms in the U.S. Senate. Even with all his wealth and military and civic eminence, he is best remembered as the father-in-law of Lieutenant Colonel Alexander Hamilton (1757-1804). Hamilton commanded an artillery battery early in the Revolutionary War and led a light infantry battalion at Yorktown. Most significantly, he served as George Washington's principal aide-de-camp, 1777-81. Postwar, he led efforts to ratify the U.S. Constitution, served as the first Secretary of the Treasury, and returned to military service during the Quasi-War of 1798 as Major General and Inspector General. After George Washington's death, Hamilton became the Senior General of the Army until 1800. Four years later, Hamilton was mortally wounded in a duel with another of Washington's former aides, Aaron Burr.[16]

One of Hamilton's grandsons (hence, Schuyler's great-grandson) was Major General Schuyler Hamilton (1822-1903). A West Pointer, he served in the Army, 1841-55 and 1861-63, including over seven years on General-in-Chief Winfield Scott's staff, 1847-54 and again in 1861. He led a division at New Madrid and Island Number 10 and a wing at the Siege of Corinth. Continuing ill health from a severe wound in the Mexican War caused him to resign in February, 1863. His sister Elizabeth Hamilton (1835-84) (hence,

Century Magazine, then took his own life on December 11, 1884. His article appears in *Battles and Leaders*, v. I, pp. 719-29.

16 Unlike Hamilton, who served on Washington's staff for four years, Burr served only two weeks in 1776 and then returned to more congenial service with combat troops.

Philip Schuyler's great-granddaughter and Alexander Hamilton's granddaughter) married Major General Henry W. Halleck (1815-72) in 1855. Also a West Pointer, Halleck served in the Army, 1839-54 and again 1861-72. He commanded the Department of the Missouri and then the Western Theater and from July, 1862, to March, 1864, served as General-in-Chief of the entire U.S. Army. He served as Army Chief of Staff for the rest of the war and continued in military service until his passing in 1872. Three years after his death, his widow married Brigadier General George W. Cullum (1809-1892), who served, 1833-74. He was Winfield Scott's aide-de-camp, April-November, 1861, and Halleck's Chief of Staff, November, 1861-September, 1864, when he became Superintendent of his alma mater, the U.S. Military Academy. He left that position two years later and retired in 1874. Through marriage, Cullum and Halleck were grandsons-in-law to Hamilton and great-grandsons-in-law to Schuyler.

Alexander Hamilton, Philip Schuyler, Nathanael Greene, Henry Knox, Patrick Henry, Edmund Pendleton, George Mason, Jackie Custis, all those Lees, and of course John Adams and John Quincy Adams, Thomas Jefferson, Benjamin Franklin, and George Washington himself—those eighteen patriots were but some of the Founding Fathers whose descendants served prominently in the Civil War. The following tables list forty more such family connections. Those tables cover Signers of the Declaration of Independence, Continental and Militia generals and senior officers and their staffs in the Revolutionary War, other Revolutionary Patriots, Signers of the U.S. Constitution—and one remarkable family. Summary analyses follow the final table (with table endnotes at the end of this chapter, pp. 214-29).

Table 1.
Signers of the Declaration of Independence[1]

Founding Father	**Relationship**	**Civil War Kin**
Carter Braxton	Grandfather	LTC Carter Braxton, CSA[2]
Charles Carroll of Carrollton	Fourth-Cousin	BG Samuel Carroll, USA[3]
Elbridge Gerry	Grandfather	Bvt MG Edward D. Townsend, USA[4]
Benjamin Harrison V	Great-Grandfather	Bvt BG Benjamin Harrison, USA[5]

Francis Hopkinson	Great-Grandfather-in-Law	MG Abner Doubleday, USA[6]
Arthur Middleton	Grandfather; Great-Uncle; Great-Grandfather-in-Law	BG Arthur M. Manigault, CSA[7]
Lewis Morris III	Grandfather; Great-Grandfather; Great-Grandfather-in-Law	Bvt MG William W. Morris, USA; Col. Lewis O. Morris, USA; Col. Peter A. Porter, USA[8]
Thomas Nelson	Great-Uncle	Col. William Nelson, CSA[9]
Robert Treat Paine	Great-Grandfather	BG Charles J. Paine, USA[10]
Benjamin Rush Richard Stockton	Grandfather; Great-Grandfather	Col. Richard H. Rush, Jr., USA[11]
Edward Rutledge	Great-Uncle, Great-Uncle-in-Law	Col. Benjamin H. Rutledge, CSA; Capt. Duncan Ingraham, CSA[12]

Table 2.
Continental and Militia Generals and Senior Officers and Their Staffs[13]

Founding Father	**Relationship**	**Civil War Kin**
MG Ethan Allen	Grandfather	MG Ethan Allen Hitchcock, USA[14]
Col. Ephraim Blaine	Great-Grandfather	Rep. James G. Blaine, USA[15]
BG George Rogers Clark	Uncle; Step-Uncle	BG Meriwether Lewis Clark, CSA; RADM William Radford, USA[16]
Bvt MG James Clinton; BG George Clinton	Great-Grandfather; Great-Great Uncle	Major De Witt Clinton, USA[17]
BG Persifor Frazer	Step-Great-Grandfather	BG Frank C. Armstrong, CSA[18]
BG Christopher Gadsden	Great-Grandfather	BG Thomas F. Drayton VI, CSA; Capt. Percival Drayton, USA[19]
BG Peter Gansevoort	Grandfather	Bvt BG Henry S. Gansevoort, USA[20]
BG Mordecai Gist	Third-Cousin	Gov. William H. Gist, CSA BG States Rights Gist, CSA[21]
LTC/MG Wade Hampton, Sr.	Grandfather	LTG Wade Hampton III, CSA; LTC Frank Hampton, CSA[22]

BG Isaac Huger; MG Thomas Pinckney	Great-Uncle, Great-Great-Uncle; Grandfather; Grt.-Grandfather	MG Benjamin Huger, CSA; Col. Frank Huger, CSA[23]
LTC John Laurens	Uncle-in-Law	Capt. Duncan Ingraham, CSA[24]
Capt. John Marshall, Col. Thomas Marshall	Grandfather-in-Law, Great-Uncle Third-Cousin; Great-Great-Grandfather, Great-Great-Uncle	Col. Hilary P. Jones, CSA; LTC Charles Marshall, CSA; BG Humphrey Marshall, CSA[25]
BG Hugh Mercer	Grandfather; Great-Grandfather	BG Hugh W. Mercer, CSA; Col. George S. Patton, CSA; Col. Isaac W. Patton, CSA; Col. John M. Patton, Jr., CSA; Col. Waller T. Patton, CSA[26]
BG Andrew Pickens	Grandfather	Gov. Francis W. Pickens, CSA[27]
Col. Isaac Shelby	Third-Cousin	MG Joseph O. Shelby, CSA[28]
LTC Tench Tilghman	Grandfather; Great-Grandfather; Great-Uncle; Great-Great-Uncle; Third-Cousin	MG Tench Tilghman, "CSA;" Col. Tench F. Tilghman, "CSA;" BG Lloyd Tilghman, CSA; MG William H. Emory, USA; Bvt BG Benjamin Tilghman, USA[29]

Table 3. Revolutionary War Patriots[30]

Founding Father	**Relationship**	**Civil War Kin**
William Henry Drayton	Third-Cousin	BG Thomas F. Drayton VI, CSA; Captain Percival Drayton, USA[31]
Henry Laurens	Grandfather-in-Law	Capt. Duncan Ingraham, CSA[32]
George Mason IV	Grandfather; Grandfather-in-Law; Great-Grandfather Great-Grandfather-in-Law	Sen. James M. Mason, CSA; Gen. Samuel Cooper, CSA; Capt. Sydney Smith Lee, CSA; MG Fitzhugh Lee, CSA; MG Frank Wheaton, USA[33]
Angus McDonald	Grandfather	Col. Angus W. McDonald, CSA[34]

Paul Revere	Grandfather	BG Joseph W. Revere, USA; BG Paul J. Revere, USA[35]

Table 4. Signers of the United States Constitution[36]		
Founding Father	**Relationship**	**Civil War Kin**
Daniel of St. Thomas Jenifer	Great-Uncle	Col. Walter H. Jenifer, CSA[37]
Rufus King	Grandfather; Great-Uncle-in-Law	BG Rufus King, USA; BG Archibald Gracie, CSA[38]
Charles Cotesworth Pinckney	Great-Uncle, Great-Great Uncle	MG Benjamin Huger, CSA; Col. Frank Huger, CSA[39]
John Rutledge	Great-Uncle; Grandfather-in-Law	Col. Benjamin H. Rutledge, CSA; Capt. Duncan Ingraham, CSA[40]

Table 5. Frontier Patriot: 1. William C. Preston [WCP][41]		
Founding Father	Relationship of his sister & his children[42]	Civil War Kin
WCP's sister: 2. Letitia (Preston) Breckinridge	Grandmother; Great-Grandmother	Rev. Robert J. Breckinridge, Sr., USA; Col. Robert J. Breckinridge, Jr., CSA; Col. W.C.P. Breckinridge, CSA; Lt. Joseph C. Breckinridge, USA; MG John C. Breckinridge, CSA; BG John B. Grayson, CSA; Col. Peter A. Porter, USA[43]
WCP's daughter: 1a. Letitia (Preston) Floyd	Mother	BG John B. Floyd, CSA[44]
WCP's son: 1b. James Patton Preston	Father	Sen. William B. Preston, CSA; Col. Robert T. Preston, CSA[45]
WCP's son: 1c. William Preston	Father Father-in-Law Grandfather	BG William Preston, CSA; Gen. Albert S. Johnston, CSA; Col. William P. Johnston, CSA[46]

WCP's son: 1d. Francis S. Preston	Father; Father-in-Law; Grandfather	BG John S. Preston, CSA; LTG Wade Hampton, CSA; Rev. R.J. Breckinridge, Sr., USA; Col. R.J. Breckinridge, Jr., CSA; Col. W.C.P. Breckinridge, CSA; Lt. Joseph C. Breckinridge, USA[47]
WCP's son: 1e. John Preston	Uncle Great-Uncle Great-Uncle-in-Law	Col. Richard C.W. Radford, CSA; RADM William Radford, USA; LTC John T. Radford, CSA; Col. Thomas T. Munford, CSA; Major William Kearny, CSA, BG Gabriel C. Wharton, CSA[48]

Patriots and Politicians, Signers and Soldiers—these fifty-nine Founding Fathers and their ninety-one Civil War descendants invite analysis. Yet caution must be exercised, because these 150 figures are not the total pool of personages.[17] There are, undoubtedly, still others in both centuries who are as yet unknown to this author. In the absence of such full data, there is little point in examining or comparing the average ages of these people in 1776 or 1861 or their total lifespans. Nor should any inference be drawn from the seeming supremacy of Southerners and Secessionists (fifty-eight Graycoats compared to thirty-three Yankees), since such statistics stand on surviving sources. They might well be significantly altered if fuller data were available. Yet even with that caveat, certain other perspectives may usefully be explored.[18] Consider, for instance, differences in the arenas

17 The analyses and numbers in the rest of this chapter apply to the fifty-nine Revolutionary War figures and ninety-one Civil Warriors mentioned in the text, including tables, plus Matthew Tilghman in endnote 29 for a total of 150. They do not include Eliza Gist Blair's connection to Nathaniel and Mordecai Gist and Charles Scott in the 18th Century or to her husband, children, and son-in-law in the Civil War, as mentioned in note 9 and endnote 21. Nor do they cover the Baylor-Armistead-Walker connection from endnote 13. Those linkages were found too late to be worked into this chapter. They are simply mentioned here as pieces of information. If they were added, they would raise the 18th Century total to sixty-two and the 19th Century number to ninety-eight, for a grand total of 160. That includes another one-generation separation of Francis P. Blair, Sr., as the son-in-law of Colonel Gist and the step-son-in-law of General Scott.

18 For instance, Table 5 on the Prestons was included because it demonstrated remarkable relationships between the Revolutionary War and Civil War generations. Not surprisingly,

of service between the two eras. Thirty of the Founding Fathers were statesmen, and twenty-nine were military officers.[19] Those proportions change markedly for the mid-19th Century personages. Only eight of them were mainly statesmen, and even Randolph was also a general.[20] The other eighty-three were military officers. Sixty per cent of the thirty military officers in blue, moreover, were professional soldiers or sailors, and two more had some prewar military experience.[21] For the fifty-three Butternut military men, in contrast, just fourteen were professionals, and an equal number had limited ante-bellum service.[22] Admittedly, this concentration on

---

this Virginia-Kentucky based family skewed the statistics toward the South. Of the twenty-one kinsmen of William C. Preston who served prominently in the Civil War (including Breckinridges, Johnstons, and Radfords), seventeen wore gray, and only four sided with the Union.

19 Those twenty-nine soldiers include McDonald, William C. Preston, and even Paul Revere, all of whom served in active operations under militia commissions. Those three "patriots" are listed in Tables 3 and 5, above. The other twenty-six military men were Allen, Blaine, Clark, George and James Clinton, Custis, Frazer, Gadsden, Gansevoort, Gist, Greene, Hamilton, Hampton, Huger, Knox, John Laurens, "Light Horse Harry" Lee, John and Thomas Marshall, Mercer, Pickens, Thomas Pinckney, Schuyler, Shelby, Tench Tilghman, and Washington. The thirty statesmen were John and John Quincy Adams, Braxton, Carroll, Drayton, Franklin, Gerry, Harrison, Henry, Hopkinson, Jefferson, Jenifer, King, Henry Laurens, four Lees (Arthur, Francis, Richard Henry, and William), Mason, Middleton, Morris, Nelson, Paine, Pendleton, C.C. Pinckney, Rush, Edward and John Rutledge, Stockton, and Matthew Tilghman.

20 Those civilian leaders include Minister Adams, Representative Blaine, and Reverend Breckinridge for the North and Governors Gist and Pickens, Minister Mason, Senator W.B. Preston, and Secretary Randolph for the South. John C. Breckinridge is not included here since he did not become Secretary of War until February, 1865. His main contribution to the Confederacy was commanding troops, 1861-64.

21 The eighteen Federal professionals were Carroll, Cullum, Doubleday, Emory, Halleck, Hamilton, Hitchcock, J. F. Lee, L.O. and W.W. Morris, Joseph Revere, Townsend, and Wheaton in the Army and Percival Drayton, Samuel Greene, S.P. Lee, William Radford, and Thatcher in the Navy. George Greene and Rufus King were both West Pointers, but they had been out of service for so long before 1861 that they are categorized as having "limited prewar experience." The ten Yankee citizen-soldiers were C.F. Adams, Jr.; Joseph Breckinridge, Clinton, Gansevoort, Harrison, Paine, Porter, Paul J. Revere, Rush, and Benjamin Tilghman.

22 The Confederate professionals were Armstrong, Cooper, Grayson, Benjamin and Frank Huger, Jenifer, A.S. Johnston, Kearny, Richard Radford, and three Lees (Fitz, Custis, Robert) in the Army and Ingraham and Smith Lee in the Navy. "Limited prewar-experience" officers were West Pointers Clark, T. F. Drayton, Gracie, Humphrey Marshall, McDonald, Mercer, William Pendleton, and Lloyd and Tench Tilghman and non-West Pointers John C. Breckinridge, S.R. Gist, W.H.F. Lee, Manigault, and William Preston.

commanders may reflect this author's interest in military history, but it is noteworthy, nonetheless, that of the fifty-nine Founding Fathers slightly under fifty per cent were soldiers, whereas their descendants were ninety-one per cent military (ninety-two per cent including General Randolph).

Noteworthy, as well, is the closeness of these "Greatest Generations" of the 18th and 19th Centuries. Four of the Founding Fathers literally were fathers or uncles of Civil War leaders. Three of their sons, a nephew, a step-nephew, and a nephew-in-law served in the 1860s.[23] Another thirty-four grandsons and ten grandsons-in-law served in the Civil War, descended from thirty leaders of the Revolution.[24] There were also twenty- eight great-grandsons and nine great-grandsons-in-law (scions of twenty-five earlier leaders),[25] plus three great-great-grandsons and one great-great-grandson-

---

The remaining twenty-five Secessionists—virtually half of the fifty-three officers in gray—were citizen-soldiers: Aylett, Braxton, young Robert and W.C.P. Breckinridge, Floyd, Frank and Wade Hampton, W.P. Johnston, Jones, E.G. Lee, Charles Marshall, Munford, Nelson, four Pattons (G.S., I.W., J.M., W.T.), A.S. Pendleton, John and Robert Preston, John Radford, Rutledge, Shelby, T.F. Tilghman, and Wharton.

23 For this first generation, Charles Francis Adams, Sr., was a son of John Quincy Adams, and Robert and Smith Lee were sons of "Light Horse Harry" Lee. George Rogers Clark was an uncle of Meriwether Lewis Clark and a step-uncle of William Radford. John Laurens was an uncle-in-law of Ingraham.

24 The Civil War grandsons were Charles Francis Adams, Sr. and Jr., Braxton, Floyd, Gansevoort, George Greene, Hamilton, Frank and Wade Hampton, Hitchcock, Benjamin Huger, King, five Lees (Fitz, G.W.C., W.H.F., J.F., S.P.), Manigault, Mason, McDonald, Mercer, W.W. Morris, Pickens, four Prestons (John S., Robert, William, and William B.), Randolph, J.W. and P.J. Revere, Rush, Thatcher, Tench Tilghman, and Townsend. They descended from John and John Quincy Adams, Braxton, WCP (five times), Gansevoort, Greene, Hamilton, Hampton, Allen, Thomas Pinckney, King, "Light Horse Harry" and Richard Henry Lee, Middleton, Mason, McDonald, Mercer, Morris, Pickens, Jefferson, Revere, Rush, Knox, Tench Tilghman, and Gerry, respectively. The grandsons-in-law were Rev. Breckinridge, Cooper, Cullum, Halleck, Wade Hampton, Ingraham, A.S. Johnston, Jones, and Robert and Smith Lee. Their respective 18th Century connections were WCP (thrice), Hamilton (twice), Henry Laurens, John Rutledge, John Marshall, Custis, Washington, and Mason.

25 The Civil War generation included great-grandsons C.F. Adams, Jr.; Armstrong, Aylett, Blaine, three Breckinridges (Joseph, Robert Jr., W.C.P.), Clinton, Percival and Thomas Drayton, S.D. Greene, Hamilton, Harrison, Frank Huger, W.P. Johnston, three Lees (Fitz, G.W.C., W.H.F.), Paine, four Pattons, (G.S., I.W., J.M., W.T.), W.N. Pendleton, Lewis Morris, Rush, and Lloyd and T.F. Tilghman. Great-grandsons-in-law were Cullum, Halleck, Doubleday, Emory, Jones, R.E. Lee, Manigault, Porter, and Wheaton. Direct ancestors of the first group were, respectively, John Adams, Frazer, Henry, Blaine, WCP (four times), James Clinton, Gadsden, Greene, Schuyler, Harrison, Thomas Pinckney, Mason, Custis (twice), Washington (twice), Paine, Mercer (four times), Pendleton, Morris,

in-law with ties to George Washington or Edmund Pendleton.[26] Twelve great-nephews, two great-nephews-in-law, fourteen great-great-nephews, two great-great-nephews-in-law, seven third-cousins, and one fourth-cousin (kin to twenty 18th Century personages) round out the relationships.[27]

Thus, six of those Civil War leaders were just one generation removed from the Revolutionary War generation, and fifty-three other Civil Warriors (sixty-five by category) were only two generations from there. Another thirty 19th Century people (fifty-four by category) were separated by three generations from the 1770s, and the remaining two Confederates (four by category) spanned four generations since the Revolution.[28]

Stockton, and Matthew and Tench Tilghman. Respective in-law connections three generations before the Civil War were Schuyler (twice), Hopkinson, Franklin, Thomas Marshall, Washington, Middleton, Morris, and Mason.

26 The great-great-grandsons and their ancestors were G.W.C. and W.H.F. Lee (George Washington) and A. S. Pendleton (Edmund Pendleton). The last-named personage from the 1700s may also be considered the great-great-grandfather-in-law of E.G. Lee.

27 The great-nephews were Reverend Breckinridge, Benjamin Huger, Jenifer, J.F. and S.P. Lee, Manigault (twice), Charles Marshall, Nelson, Richard and William Radford, Rutledge, and Lloyd Tilghman. Their respective great-uncles were WCP (three times), Huger, C.C. Pinckney, Jenifer, three Lees (Arthur, F.L., William), Middleton, Drayton, John Marshall, Nelson, Edward and John Rutledge, and Tench Tilghman. Gracie and Ingraham were great nephews-in-law to King and Edward Rutledge, respectively. The great-great-nephews were four Breckinridges (John C., Joseph, Robert Jr., and W.C.P.), Clinton, Emory, Grayson, Frank Huger, Kearny, Charles and Humphrey Marshall, Munford, Porter, and John Radford. Their 18th Century kin were WCP (nine times), George Clinton, Tench Tilghman, Huger, and Thomas Marshall (twice). Manigault and Wharton were great-great-nephews-in-law to Huger and WCP, respectively. Percival and Thomas Drayton were third-cousins to William Henry Drayton. Other such relatives were States Rights and William Gist to Mordecai Gist, Humphrey Marshall to John Marshall, Jo Shelby to Isaac Shelby, and B.C. Tilghman to Tench Tilghman. Finally, Samuel Carroll was fourth-cousin to Charles Carroll of Carrollton.

28 It is important to distinguish among *categories* of kinship, *numbers per category*, and *absolute numbers of different individual people*. As to categories, one generation of separation includes sons, sons-in-law, nephews, and nephews-in-law. Grandsons, grandsons-in-law, great nephews, great-nephews-in-law, and third-cousins are two generations apart. Three degrees of separation involve great-grandsons, great-grandsons-in-law, great-great-nephews, great-great-nephews-in-law, and fourth cousins. Finally, great-great-grandsons and great-great-grandsons-in-law are four levels removed from the Founding Fathers. Adding together the numbers for each of those categories, as specified in notes 23-27, comes to ninety-eight for the 18th Century and 129 for the 19th Century. Those total *numbers per category* far exceed the *absolute numbers* of fifty-nine Founding Fathers and ninety-one Civil Warriors. This discrepancy is caused by several individuals falling into two or more categories [William C. Preston (WCP), indeed, is counted in six different categories for Founding Fathers, and he accounts for twenty-six entries among Civil War

The closeness of those generations comes through clearly in the fact that eighteen of the ninety-one later leaders were alive during the life times of their Revolutionary relatives—General Carroll and Admiral Thatcher, admittedly, by only two and five months, respectively, but eight others as youngsters, six more as teenagers, and Charles Francis Adams, Sr., Benjamin Huger, and Humphrey Marshall as adults. Huger was in his twenties when his Pinckney kinsmen expired, and Marshall was twenty-three when the fourth Chief Justice died. Longest living overlap went to Adams, who was nearly nineteen years old when his grandfather passed away and forty years of age when his father died.[29]

---

categories—which themselves include five duplicates!] Eliminating thirty-nine repeats from the 1700s and thirty-eight duplicates from the 1800s produces the correct count in *absolute numbers* of fifty-nine and ninety-one, respectively. Allocating those absolute numbers over the four levels of separation and assigning each Civil Warrior to his particular generation closest to the Revolution produces the actual numbers shown in this paragraph of the text. Names as well as numbers for both eras are provided in the lists that follow: ONE GENERATION APART: Founding Fathers (4): John Quincy Adams, Clark, John Laurens, and "Light Horse Harry" Lee; Civil War (6): C.F. Adams, Sr.; Clark, Ingraham, R.E. and S.S. Lee, and William Radford. TWO GENERATIONS APART: Founding Fathers (39): John Adams, Allen, Braxton, Custis, Drayton, Gansevoort, Gerry, Gist, Greene, Hamilton, Hampton, Huger, Jefferson, Jenifer, King, Knox, Henry Laurens, four Lees (Arthur, Francis Lightfoot, Richard Henry, William), John Marshall, Mason, McDonald, Mercer, Middleton, Morris, Nelson, Pickens, C.C. and Thomas Pinckney, Preston, Revere, Rush, Edward and John Rutledge, Shelby, Tench Tilghman, and Washington; Civil War (53): C.F. Adams, Jr.; Braxton, Rev. Breckinridge, Cooper, Cullum, Percival and Thomas Drayton, Floyd, Gansevoort, S.R. and W.H. Gist, Gracie, G.S. Greene, Halleck, Hamilton, Frank and Wade Hampton, Hitchcock, Benjamin Huger, Jenifer, A.S. Johnston, Jones, King, five Lees (Fitz, G.W.C., W.H.F., J.F., S.P.), Manigault, Charles and Humphrey Marshall, Mason, McDonald, Mercer, W.W. Morris, Nelson, Pickens, four Prestons (J.S., R.T., W., W.B.), Richard Radford, Randolph, J. W. and P. J. Revere, Rush, Rutledge, Shelby, Thatcher, three Tilghmans (Benjamin, Lloyd, and Tench), and Townsend. THREE GENERATIONS APART: Founding Fathers (16): Blaine, Carroll, George and James Clinton, Franklin, Frazer, Gadsden, Harrison, Henry, Hopkinson, Thomas Marshall, Paine, Pendleton, Schuyler, Stockton, and Matthew Tilghman. Civil War (30): Armstrong, Aylett, Blaine, four Breckinridges (John C., Joseph, Robert Jr., W.C.P.), Carroll, Clinton, Doubleday, Emory, Grayson, S.D. Greene, Harrison, Frank Huger, W.P. Johnston, Kearny, L.O. Morris, Munford, Paine, four Pattons (G.S., I.W., J.M., W.T.), W.N. Pendleton, Porter, J.T. Radford, T.F. Tilghman, Wharton, and Wheaton. FOUR GENERATIONS APART: Civil War (2): E.G. Lee and A.S. Pendleton.

29 Besides Carroll and Thatcher, the other youths and their ages in the year when their famous forebears died are Jones (2), Charles Marshall (5), Frank Hampton and Joseph Revere (6), Randolph (8), Clark and William Radford (9), and Pickens (10). The teenagers and their ages are R.E. Lee (11), Charles Francis Adams, Jr., (for John Quincy Adams) and King (13), Smith Lee (16), and Wade Hampton (17). Charles Francis Adams, Sr., is counted twice: as a teenager (19) for his grandfather and as an adult for his father (40). The other

Such acquaintance accentuates the affinity between the "Greatest Generations" of the 18th and 19th Centuries. Some of those Civil War personages actually knew their acclaimed ancestors. All later leaders knew of them. Their very names united the generations—almost always the family names, sometimes the full names: the two Paul Reveres, the two Benjamin Harrisons, the two Rufus Kings, the two Wade Hamptons, or William C. Preston Breckinridge, Schuyler Hamilton, Ethan Allen Hitchcock, and Henry Knox Thatcher. Family counted for much in those years: it radiated glory, bestowed honor, imposed obligation. One of the greatest obligations was to uphold achievements of earlier generations of the family. Those accomplishments of the Patriots of 1776 were spectacular and special. They had declared, fought for, and won independence from the most powerful empire in the world. Many of their Civil War descendants fought to preserve the nation which their Revolutionary War ancestors had created. Many other Civil Warriors likened their own thirteen Confederate States to the Thirteen Colonies which their forebears had led in fighting for and gaining independence. From either perspective, family heritage reinforced the resolve of each side in the Civil War.

Abraham Lincoln understood how much this family connection with Revolutionary War ancestors meant to his generation. In the compelling conclusion of his First Inaugural Address, he expressed the hope that "the mystic chords of memory, stretching from every battle-field and patriot grave to every living heart and hearthstone, all over this broad land, will yet swell the chorus of the Union, when again touched, as surely they will be, by the better angels of our nature." How much more meaningful were "those mystic chords of memory" when they stretched from the "patriot graves" not just of patriots in the abstract but of patriot ancestors from only one generation or two or three before the Civil War—leaders who truly were the "Founding Fathers," the renowned Revolutionary War relatives of significant Civil War soldiers and statesmen.

---

adults, as mentioned in the text, were Benjamin Huger (20 for C.C. Pinckney and 23 for Thomas Pinckney) and Humphrey Marshall (23).

Endnotes, Tables 1 – 5:

1. Besides the twelve signers in this table, signers John Adams, Benjamin Franklin, Thomas Jefferson, and Francis and Richard Henry Lee have already been covered. Their respective Civil War kin are Charles Francis Adams, Sr. and Jr.; William H. Emory, George W. Randolph, and J. F. and S. P. Lee.

2. Carter Braxton (1736-97) of Virginia served in the Second Continental Congress, 1775-76. His namesake grandson (1836-98) commanded an artillery battalion in the II Corps/Army of Northern Virginia.

3. Charles Carroll of Carrollton (1737-1832) of Maryland was the last living signer of the Declaration. His first-cousin's great-grandson Samuel Carroll (1832-93) graduated from West Point in 1856 and served until 1869. In the Civil War, he led the 8th Ohio, then a famous fighting brigade, and finally a division.

4. Elbridge Gerry (1744-1814) signed the Declaration of Independence but was one of three delegates to the 1787 Philadelphia convention who refused to sign the Constitution because it lacked a Bill of Rights. Diplomat, Congressman, Governor of Massachusetts, and fifth Vice President of the United States (where he died in office), he is best remembered as the creator of "gerrymandered" voting districts. One of his grandsons, General Edward D. Townsend (1817-93) graduated from West Point in 1837 and served in the Second Seminole War. In the Civil War, he provided crucial army administration as Chief of Staff to Winfield Scott, March-November, 1861; Assistant Adjutant General of the Army, 1861-63; Acting Adjutant General of the Army, 1863-69; and Adjutant General of the Army, 1869-80. The assertion has also been made that the wife of Confederate Lieutenant General John C. Pemberton was related to Gerry. Since she was a Thompson and Gerry's wife was a Thompson, they may well be connected. However, proof of that relationship has not been found, so it is mentioned here only as an avenue for further exploration.

5. Benjamin Harrison V (1726-91) represented Virginia in both Continental Congresses, 1774-77, and served as Speaker of the House of Burgesses, and Virginia Governor. His son, Major General William Henry Harrison (1773-1841), was the ninth President of the United States. William Henry's grandson and Benjamin's great-grandson, another Benjamin (1833-1901), was the twenty-third President. In the Civil War, he rose from lieutenant to Colonel of the 70th Indiana and commanded two brigades in the West.

6. Francis Hopkinson (1737-91) of New Jersey designed the first official American flag. His great-granddaughter married Abner Doubleday (1819-93), who served in the Army, 1842-73, including at Fort Sumter in 1861; he led a brigade and division in the I Corps and briefly the corps itself at Gettysburg.

7. Arthur Middleton (1742-87) of South Carolina served in the Second Continental Congress, 1776-77, and was captured in Charleston in 1780. Through two of his daughters and a niece, he was connected triply to Confederate general Arthur M. Manigault (1824-86), who led the 10th South Carolina and then a brigade in the Army of Tennessee. One daughter was Manigault's step-mother. His actual mother was Middleton's niece. Another daughter was the grandmother of Manigault's wife. Two of A.M. Manigault's brothers were also prominent Confederate officers, Colonel Gabriel Manigault (1809-88) of the South Carolina Ordnance Department and Major Edward Manigault (1817-74) of the 18th South Carolina Heavy Artillery Battalion. They, too, were step-grandsons and great-nephews of Middleton. Those three brothers were also great-nephews of William Henry Drayton, who is covered in endnote 31.

8. Lewis Morris III (1726-98) of New York served in the Second Continental Congress, 1775-77. His grandson William W. Morris (1801-65), a career Army officer, 1815-65, served as Colonel of the 2nd U.S. Artillery throughout the Civil War. He led the Second Separate Brigade of the VIII Corps in Baltimore. Also serving in the city and temporarily heading that brigade was Colonel Peter A. Porter, who married the Signer's great-granddaughter. For more on Porter, see endnote 43. Still another senior artillery officer was Colonel Lewis O. Morris (1824-64), one of the Signer's great-grandsons. He was commissioned into U.S. service in 1847 following his father's death at Monterrey and continued in the Regular Army into the Civil War. He became Colonel of the 7th New York Heavy Artillery in 1862, guarded Washington until 1864, and fought in the field as infantry from Spotsylvania to Cold Harbor. Heavy casualties in the latter battle on June 3 caused brigade command to devolve on him. He survived that disastrous battle but only by one day. On June 4, a sharpshooter mortally wounded him, and he died within hours.

9. Thomas Nelson (1738-89) represented Virginia in the Second Continental Congress, 1775-77; served as Brigadier General commanding the Lower Virginia Militia, 1777-81; became governor in 1781; and as both Governor and General commanded the Virginia Militia during the Yorktown Siege. He was a great-uncle of Confederate Colonel William Nelson (1808-92), who led a light artillery battalion in Lee's army.

10. Robert Treat Paine (1731-1814) represented Massachusetts in the Continental Congresses, 1774-76, and later served as the Bay State's Speaker of the House and Attorney General. His great-grandson General Charles J. Paine (1833-1916) served as an officer in the 22nd and 30th Massachusetts, commanded the 2nd Louisiana, and led a division of Black troops in the XVIII, XXV, and X Corps.

11. Richard Stockton (1730-81) of New Jersey and his son-in-law Benjamin Rush (1746-1813) of Pennsylvania both served in the Second Continental Congress. Five months after signing the Declaration of Independence, Stockton was captured by Tories and turned over to the British. Although held for less than seven weeks, he was treated so brutally that he never recovered his health and died four years after being paroled. Rush, a prominent medical doctor and one of the leading intellectuals in the colonies, also served as Surgeon General and Physician General of the Middle Department for most of 1777 but resigned early in 1778. One of his sons, Richard Rush Sr. (1780-1859) was a cabinet officer, diplomat, and unsuccessful Vice-Presidential nominee in the early 19th Century. Richard's son, Colonel Richard Henry Rush, Jr. (1825-93), graduated from West Point in 1846 and served until resigning in 1854. He returned in 1861 as Colonel of the 6th Pennsylvania Cavalry, the best known of the few lancer regiments in the Civil War. He led a cavalry brigade at Antietam and two Veteran Reserve Corps brigades in 1864. He resigned, July 1, 1864. Thus, Colonel Rush was Dr. Rush's grandson and Stockton's great-grandson.

12. Edward Rutledge (1749-1800) of South Carolina was the youngest signer of the Declaration of Independence. He served in the Continental Congresses, 1774-76. As a LTC of artillery, he was captured in Charleston in 1780 and paroled the following year. He served as governor of South Carolina, 1798-1800. His great-nephew, Benjamin Huger Rutledge (1829-93), rose from captain to Colonel of the 4th South Carolina Cavalry and sometimes commanded the Butler/Dunovant South Carolina Cavalry Brigade as senior colonel. Also, Edward's grand-niece married Duncan Ingraham (1802-91), who rose from midshipman to Captain in the U.S. Navy, 1812-61, and who then served as a Confederate Navy Captain, commanding the Charleston Naval Squadron, which included three ironclads.

13. Besides the nineteen Revolutionary officers in this table, Nathanael Greene, Alexander Hamilton with Philip Schuyler, Henry Knox, "Light Horse Harry" Lee, and George Washington with Jackie Custis have already been covered. Their respective Civil War kin are George and Samuel Greene; Schuyler Hamilton, Henry Halleck, and George Cullum; Henry Thatcher; Smith and Fitz Lee and James M. Mason, and Robert, Custis, and W.H.F. Lee. Just as this book went to press, the author found that another of Washington's aides-de-camp, Brevet Brigadier General George Baylor, was great-uncle to Brigadier General Lewis A. Armistead (1817-63), Governor John R. Baylor (1822-94), and Colonel George Wythe Baylor (1832-1916) and great-great-uncle-in-law to Major General John G. Walker (1821-93)—all Confederates. That connection is mentioned here but is not further explored in this chapter.

14. Ethan Allen (1738-89) of Vermont served as brevet colonel in the Continental Army and as Major General in the army of the so-called "Republic of Vermont." He is best remembered for leading his Green Mountain Boys in seizing Fort Ticonderoga, May 10, 1775. Later that year, he was captured while invading Canada and held prisoner until 1778. His grandson Ethan Allen Hitchcock (1798-1870) graduated from West Point in 1817 and rose to colonel and brevet brigadier general by the time he resigned in 1855. He fought in the Second Seminole War and served on General-in-Chief Winfield Scott's staff during the Mexican War. He returned to service, 1862-67, as a Major General. He advised President Lincoln and served as Commissioner for Exchange of Prisoners of War and later as Commissary General of Prisoners.

15. Ephraim Blaine (1741-1804) of Pennsylvania served as Commissary of Purchases for George Washington's army, 1777-78, and for the entire Continental Army, 1780-82. His great-grandson, James G. Blaine (1830-93) of Maine, was elected to Congress in 1862 and served until 1876 (including as Speaker of the House, 1869-75), when he became Senator. He served twice as Secretary of State, 1881 and 1889-92, and was the unsuccessful Republican nominee for President in 1884.

16. George Rogers Clark (1752-1818) of Virginia commanded the Virginia militia in Kentucky. His captures of Kaskaskia, Cahokia, and Vincennes from the British gave credibility to American claims to the Illinois country. He was also a prominent Indian fighter on both sides of the Ohio River. His younger brother was Captain William Clark (1770-1838), the renowned explorer of the Louisiana Purchase. William's son, hence George's nephew, Meriwether Lewis Clark (1809-81), graduated from West Point in 1830 and served three years in the U.S. Army, including the Black Hawk War. He led a Missouri battalion in Doniphan's Expedition in the Mexican War and served as Commanding General of the pro-Secessionist 9th Division of Missouri State Guards in 1861. He was Chief of Artillery for Earl VanDorn at Pea Ridge and for Braxton Bragg at Perryville. He led a Provisional Brigade in the Department of Richmond, 1864-65, and was captured at Amelia Court House on April 5, 1865. After Meriwether's mother died, his father remarried the widow Radford in 1821 and thereby became the step-father of her son William Radford (1809-90), a future admiral in the Union Navy. That marriage made George Rogers Clark the admiral's step-uncle. For William Radford, see endnote 48 of Table 5.

17. Brevet Major General James Clinton (1736-1812) of New York commanded forces in the Hudson Highlands during the Saratoga Campaign and led a punitive expedition against the Iroquois two years later. His brother George (1739-1812) also commanded in the Hudson Highlands as a militia and Continental Brigadier General while simultaneously serving as New York Governor, 1777-95 and again 1801-04. He became Vice President from 1805 until he died in office in 1812. James' son (George's nephew) De Witt Clinton (1769-1828)—also a prominent New York political leader as Mayor, Senator, Lieutenant Governor, and Governor—is best remembered for building the Erie Canal. De Witt's grandson (thus, James' great-grandson and George's great-great-nephew) Major De Witt Clinton

(1833-73) entered the Civil War as a lieutenant in the 10th New York. As a Captain, he served as Aide-de-Camp to Major General John Wool, 1862-63, and to Major General E.R.S. Canby, 1864. Promoted to Major, he became Canby's Staff Judge Advocate in September, 1864, and held that position for the rest of the war. He transferred to the Regular Army in 1867 as Major and Judge Advocate and died in uniform in 1873.

18. LTC Persifor Frazer (1736-92) of the 5th Pennsylvania was captured at Brandywine. Exchanged, he led a brigade at Monmouth. In 1782, he was promoted Brigadier General commanding Pennsylvania Militia. His grandson, Brigadier General Persifor Frazer Smith (1798-1858), was one of the great fighting brigadiers of the Mexican War. Smith remained active in the 1850s against Comanches and Kansas rioters until he died in uniform in 1858. Four years before his death, he married the widow of Major Francis W. Armstrong (ca. 1783-1835), who had served in the U.S. Army, 1812-17, and who was the Choctaw Agent in the Indian Territory in 1835. Smith thereby became the step-father of her son, Francis C. Armstrong (1835-1909), who served in the U.S. Army, 1855-1861, and fought for the Federals at First Bull Run. He then resigned and rose from lieutenant to Brigadier General in Confederate service. He primarily led a cavalry brigade but had charge of a cavalry division at Chickamauga and East Tennessee.

19. Christopher Gadsden (1724-1805) was one of the most prominent Patriots in South Carolina. He served in the First and Second Continental Congresses but returned home early in 1776 to command the 1st South Carolina. A Continental Brigadier General, 1776-77, he helped save Charleston from the first British attack but, while Lieutenant Governor, was captured there in 1780 and held prisoner for almost a year. He designed the iconic Gadsden rattlesnake flag "Don't Tread on Me." His great-grandsons, Thomas and Percival Drayton, are covered in endnote 31.

20. As Colonel of the 3rd New York, Peter Gansevoort (1749-1812) successfully defended Fort Stanwix against British invaders. In 1781, he was promoted to Brigadier General of New York Militia. He left service at the end of the Revolutionary War but re-entered U.S. service as a Brigadier General from 1809 until his death three years later. His grandson, Henry S. Gansevoort (1834-71) entered the Civil War as a private in the 7th New York National Guard but was soon commissioned a lieutenant in the new 5th U.S. Artillery. He rose to LTC and then Colonel of the 13th New York Cavalry and was breveted Brigadier General. Postwar, he continued serving as a Captain in the 5th U.S. Artillery until his death in 1871.

21. Mordecai Gist (1743-92) served as Colonel of the 3rd Maryland, was promoted to Brigadier General in 1779, and led the Second Maryland Brigade in South Carolina in the 1780s. He settled in that state after the Revolution. There two of his third-cousins figured prominently in secession and civil war. William H. Gist (1807-74) served as Governor, 1858-60. In reaction against the election of Abraham Lincoln, he called the original secession convention for December of 1860, but his term expired six days before it passed the ordinance declaring that "The Union is dissolved." He was one of the signers of that ordinance. He served on the South Carolina Executive Council, 1861-62. William's first-cousin (hence also Mordecai's third-cousin), States Right Gist (1831-64), served as Adjutant General of South Carolina at the outbreak of the Civil War. He was an aide-de-camp to Brigadier General Barnard Bee at First Manassas and was promoted to Brigadier General in 1862. He led a brigade on the Carolinas coast and in the Vicksburg, Atlanta, and Nashville Campaigns, and a division at Chickamauga and Chattanooga. He lost his life during the heroic but disastrous assaults at Franklin, November 30, 1864. Mordecai was also second cousin to Eliza Blair (1794-1877); for her famous husband, children, and son-in-law, see n. 9.

22. Wade Hampton, Sr., (1752-1835) served as a captain in the 1st and 6th South Carolina and as LTC led a militia brigade, 1777-81. He returned to service in 1808 as Colonel of U.S. Light Dragoons, received his first star the following year, and was promoted to Major General in 1813. He resigned the following year after ignominiously failing in invading Canada. Much more successful was his namesake grandson, Wade Hampton III (1818-1902). He entered Confederate service as Colonel of Hampton's Legion and rose to Lieutenant General commanding all cavalry in the Carolinas, the first cavalry corps commander to earn that grade. From August, 1864, to January, 1865, he led the Cavalry Corps of Lee's army. Wade the Third's brother Frank Hampton (1829-63), also a grandson of Wade, Sr., was LTC of the 2nd South Carolina Cavalry when he was killed at Brandy Station. For Wade III's ties to the Prestons, see endnote 47.

23. Isaac Huger (1743-97) was LTC of the 1st South Carolina and Colonel of the 5th South Carolina, 1775-78, and was promoted to Brigadier General in 1779. He fought at Stono Ferry, Guilford Court House, and Hobkirk's Hill. More junior in the Revolutionary War (Major and aide-de-camp to Benjamin Lincoln and Horatio Gates, 1779-80) but more senior later (Major General, 1812-15) was Thomas Pinckney (1750-1828). He also served as Governor of South Carolina, Congressman, and diplomat. Pinckney's grandson and Huger's great-nephew was Benjamin Huger (1805-77). He graduated from West Point in 1825 and served in Ordnance (including Winfield Scott's Chief of Ordnance in Mexico) until resigning in 1861. As a Confederate Major General, he headed the Department of Norfolk and a division in the Army of Northern Virginia at Seven Pines and the Seven Days. Thereafter he performed ordnance duty at Mobile and the Trans-Mississippi. Benjamin's son (hence, Isaac's great-great-nephew and Pinckney's great-grandson) Frank Huger (1837-97) graduated from West Point in 1860, and the next year he followed his father into Confederate service. He served as his father's aide-de-camp at Norfolk and rose from captain to colonel commanding first a battery and then a battalion of light artillery in the Army of Northern Virginia. Besides his Huger kin, Isaac was also great-great-uncle-in-law to Arthur Manigault, CSA, who is covered in endnote 7.

24. John Laurens (1754-82) served as one of George Washington's aides-de-camp, 1777-79. He later fought at Savannah, Charleston, and Yorktown, and was killed in action on the Combahee River, August 27, 1782. His niece married Duncan Ingraham, U.S. and C.S. Navy. For Ingraham, see endnote 12.

25. Thomas Marshall (1730-1802) served as Colonel of the 3rd Virginia. His heroic stand at Brandywine saved the American army from disaster. He left Continental service in 1777 and led the Virginia State Artillery Regiment until 1781. His son John (1755-1835) served briefly in the 3rd and much longer in the 11th and 7th Virginia, 1776-81. Although rising no higher than captain and being more renowned for his service as Secretary of State, 1800-01, and as Chief Justice of the U.S. Supreme Court, 1801-35, John was prominent in the Revolution as one of five Deputy Judge Advocates General of the Army, 1777-78. Although John was a great nationalist, three of his relatives served prominently in the Confederacy. John's grandson-in-law (hence, Thomas's great-grandson-in-law) was Colonel Hilary P. Jones (1833-1913), who commanded an artillery battery and battalion in the Army of Northern Virginia, 1861-64, and who served as Chief of Artillery of the Department of North Carolina and Southern Virginia and the IV Corps, 1864-65. John and Thomas were also the respective great-uncle and great-great-uncle of Charles Marshall (1830-1902), who rose from Lieutenant to LTC on Robert E. Lee's staff, 1862-65. Another of Thomas's great-great-nephews and John's third-cousin was Humphrey Marshall (1812-72), who graduated from West Point in 1832 and served ten months in the U.S. Army. He returned to service as Colonel of the 1st Kentucky Cavalry in the Mexican War and served four terms in Congress. Commissioned a Confederate Brigadier General in 1861, he operated in eastern Kentucky and

southwestern Virginia, where he was defeated at Prestonburg but won at Princeton. Outraged at being overslaughed, he offered to resign three times. In June, 1863, his resignation was accepted. He then represented Kentucky in the Second Confederate Congress, 1864-65. General Marshall's mother was a sister of James G. Birney (1792-1857), the prominent abolitionist and Liberty Party nominee for president in 1840 and 1844. Humphrey Marshall thus was first-cousin to Birney's sons, including Major General David B. Birney (1825-64), who temporarily led the II and III Corps and permanently commanded the X Corps in the Union Army, and Brevet Major General William Birney (1819-1907), who headed a Black brigade and division in the Army of the James. First-cousins of Chief Justice John Marshall's third-cousin are too remote a relationship to rate a place in Table 2 for the Birney brothers and their father, but they are nevertheless an interesting connection to mention at least in a note.

26. Hugh Mercer (1726-77) fought in the Jacobite Rising of 1745 and, when it failed, fled his native Scotland for America. He served actively as a Pennsylvania colonel in the French and Indian War. He entered the Revolutionary War as Colonel of the 3rd Virginia and was promoted to Brigadier General in 1776. He fought at the surprise Battle of Trenton and was mortally wounded in preliminaries of the Battle of Princeton on January 3, 1777, and died January 12. His namesake grandson, Hugh Weedon Mercer (1808-77) graduated from West Point in 1828 and served until 1835. In 1861, he entered Confederate service as Colonel of the 1st Georgia Volunteers. Promoted to Brigadier General in October, 1861, he spent most of the war defending Savannah and the Georgia coast. In April, 1864, his brigade reinforced the Army of Tennessee. He served throughout the Atlanta Campaign and then returned to Savannah, where he commanded another brigade opposing William T. Sherman from November through February. He spent the final two months of the war at Macon, where he was paroled. In addition to that Georgia general, the hero of Princeton was great-grandfather to the famous Patton brothers of Virginia, seven of whom served in the Confederate Army. The four who made field grade are summarized here. Isaac W. Patton (1828-90) served as Colonel of a regiment variously designated the 22nd and 21st Louisiana at Vicksburg, where he was captured, and of another regiment called the 22nd Louisiana Consolidated at Mobile, 1864-65. John M. Patton, Jr. (1826-99) was the LTC and Colonel of the 21st Virginia in western Virginia and later the Stonewall Division until he resigned on August 8, 1862. He performed staff duty, 1862-63. Waller Tazewell Patton (1835-63) rose from captain to colonel of the 7th Virginia and was mortally wounded while leading that unit in Pickett's Charge. The most famous brother was George Smith Patton (1833-64), who became LTC of the 22nd Virginia in July of 1861 and Colonel of that regiment in January, 1863. He was commanding Brigadier General John Echols' Brigade when mortally wounded at Third Winchester. George S. Patton's namesake grandson, in turn, was the famous Four-Star General of World War II. Thus, that mid-20th Century officer was the great-great-great-grandson of Hugh Mercer of Revolutionary renown.

27. Andrew Pickens (1739-1817) rose from captain to Brigadier General in the South Carolina Militia and fought actively against British, Tories, and Cherokees. He played a key role in the turning point victory at Cowpens and was also engaged at Augusta and Eutaw Springs. Postwar, he served in the state legislature and one term in Congress. His grandson, Francis W. Pickens (ca. 1807-69), served in Congress, 1834-43, and was U.S. Minister to Russia, 1858-60 when he was elected Governor of South Carolina. He succeeded William H. Gist in that office, December 14, 1860, six days before their state seceded from the Union. He continued as Governor for two years during the Secession Crisis, the outbreak of the war at Fort Sumter, the raising of troops, and the defense of the state against initial Federal operations from Port Royal to Pocataligo.

28. Isaac Shelby (1750-1826) held commissions in the Virginia and North Carolina militia before and during the Revolutionary War, but his historical significance is not so much as a military officer but as a leader who rallied the frontier to the Patriot cause. He fought in Lord Dunmore's War and against Cherokees, Miami, and Shawnees. He was instrumental in winning the great American victory at King's Mountain. Fellow citizens elected him the first Governor of Kentucky in 1792. Twenty years later, he returned to the governorship and, as both Governor and Major General of militia, led Kentucky troops in the Battle of the Thames in 1814. By the mid-19th Century the frontier had moved beyond the Mississippi River. That was the arena for his third-cousin (the great-grandson of his father's brother John) Joseph O. Shelby (1830-97). He fought for the South in "Bleeding Kansas" and led a company, regiment, brigade, and division of Missouri cavalry in Confederate service. Promoted to Brigadier General in 1863 and Major General in the war's final weeks, he refused to surrender and led his troops across the Rio Grande into Mexico in July, 1865. Emperor Maximillian declined his services. Two years later he returned to Missouri.

29. LTC Tench Tilghman (1744-86) served as George Washington's aide-de-camp from August of 1776 to November of 1783. The general accorded his trusted staff officer the great honor of carrying official word about Lord Cornwallis's surrender at Yorktown to the Confederation Congress in Philadelphia. His health broken by long military service, the Marylander died just two and a half years after the war. His namesake grandson (1810-74) graduated from West Point in 1832 and served sixteen months in the U.S. Army. After resigning from Federal service, he was active in the Maryland militia and rose from LTC to Major General, commanding the Second Division. In that capacity, he ordered his troops to resist Federal forces moving through the Old-Line State in the spring of 1861. Some of his subordinates refused to obey, and Governor Thomas Hicks promptly removed him from command. He thus acted on behalf of the South, but no evidence has been found that he actually joined the Confederate Army. The situation of his son, Tench F. Tilghman (1833-67), is also anomalous. He is called "Colonel," but available sources do not show him in that or any grade in the Confederate Army. Perhaps, as with his father, his commission derived from the Maryland militia. Yet he unquestionably served the South by helping personally to escort President Davis from Richmond to Georgia in the spring of 1865. Better known than these two direct descendants is a great-nephew of the Revolutionary War officer, Lloyd Tilghman (1816-63). He graduated from West Point in 1836, served just three months, and resigned. He held Volunteer commissions in the Mexican War and entered Confederate service as Colonel of the 3rd Kentucky. Promoted to Brigadier General in October, 1861, he was captured at Fort Henry the following February. Exchanged just too late to fight at Second Corinth, he led a division and later a brigade in Mississippi. He was killed in action at Champion Hill, May 16, 1863. Besides his family ties to Washington's aide Tench Tilghman, the Butternut general was also the great-grandson of Tench's uncle Matthew Tilghman (1717-90)—the "Father of the Revolution" in Maryland. Matthew voted for the Declaration of Independence but just missed signing it because he left congress in late June, 1776, to preside over the Annapolis Convention. There he chaired the drafting of Maryland's first constitution. Not all of the Revolutionary War officer's Civil War kinsmen wore gray. Through his sister Anna Maria, Tench was the great-great-uncle of Major General William H. Emory (1811-87) of the Northern Army. Emory has already been covered in this chapter through his connection with Benjamin Franklin. Through his father's brother Edward, moreover, Tench was a third-cousin to Brevet Brigadier General Benjamin C. Tilghman (1821-1901). Benjamin rose from Captain to Colonel of the 26th Pennsylvania, 1861-63. Wounded out at Chancellorsville, he returned to service as Colonel of the 3rd USCT that August. That regiment served in South Carolina and Florida, where he commanded the post of Jacksonville and briefly

the District of Florida. With the war ended, he resigned in the late spring of 1865 with a brevet as Brigadier General. He is better known as an inventor for industry than as a soldier.

30. Besides the five Patriots in this table, John Quincy Adams, Patrick Henry, Arthur and William Lee, and Edmund Pendleton have already been covered in this chapter's text. Their respective Civil War kin are Charles Francis Adams, Sr. and Jr.; William Aylett; S.P. and J. F. Lee; and W.N. and A.S. Pendleton and Edwin Lee. Another Patriot, Matthew Tilghman, ancestor of Lloyd Tilghman, is covered in endnote 29.

31. William Henry Drayton (1742-79) helped design the Great Seal of South Carolina, served as the first Chief Justice of that state's Supreme Court, and was a delegate to the Second Continental Congress, 1778-79, where he died in office. His family illustrates how Revolution and Civil War disrupt not only empires and nations but also families. His maternal uncle and grandfather were both British Governors of South Carolina province, the loyalist uncle in 1775. Again in 1861, two of William Henry's third-cousins, Thomas and Percival, not just fought on opposite sides but directly against each other. Thomas (1809-91) graduated from West Point in 1828 and served in the U.S Army until 1836. Made a Confederate Brigadier General in September, 1861, he was defeated in his first battle, Port Royal, on November 7, 1861, where the U.S. Navy captured the great harbor from which it operated against Charleston and Savannah. Drayton led a brigade in Virginia in mid-1862 and a brigade and division in Arkansas and Texas in 1864-65. One of the warships attacking Port Royal, the USS *Pocahontas*, was commanded by Thomas's brother Percival (1812-65), a career Navy officer who rose from midshipman in 1827 to Captain in 1862. He later captained other vessels along the Carolina coast, including the ironclad USS *Passaic* at the Battle of Charleston Harbor, and he commanded the flagship USS *Hartford* while serving as Fleet Captain to Admiral David G. Farragut at the Battle of Mobile Bay. Ill health cut short his illustrious career just two months after the war. The Civil War Draytons were also Christopher Gadsden's great-grandsons (endnote 19). William Henry Drayton was also great-uncle to the Confederate Manigault brothers (endnote 7).

32. Henry Laurens (1724-92) served as the Fifth President of the Continental Congress, 1777-78, when the Articles of Confederation were passed. As U.S. Minister to the Netherlands, he negotiated Dutch participation in the Revolutionary War in 1780. On returning to America later that year, he was captured at sea by the British and was imprisoned in the Tower of London. In 1781, he was exchanged for Lord Cornwallis. His granddaughter married Captain Duncan Ingraham of the Confederate Navy, who is covered in endnote 12.

33. George Mason IV (1725-92), the author of the Virginia constitution and the father of the U.S. Bill of Rights, has already been covered in this chapter for his descendants Senator James M. Mason, Mrs. Smith Lee, and Fitz Lee. Another of his granddaughters (a sister to James M. Mason and Mrs. Smith Lee) married Samuel Cooper (1798-1876). After graduating from West Point in 1815, he rose to become the Adjutant General of the U.S. Army, 1851-61, and of the Confederate Army, 1861-65. He was the highest-ranking officer in Confederate service. Cooper's daughter Sarah (hence George Mason's great-granddaughter) married Lieutenant Frank Wheaton (1833-1903), who entered the U.S. Army in 1855, rose to become a Brevet Major General and division commander in the Union Army, and was Major General of Regulars when he retired in 1897. Sarah passed away one year into their marriage. Four years later, Wheaton married her first-cousin-once-removed Emma Mason, who was also a great-granddaughter of George Mason IV. Thus, Wheaton was doubly a great-grandson-in-law of the Father of the Bill of Rights through both wives. Emma, moreover, was the daughter of Brevet Brigadier General Richard B. Mason (1797-1850) of Mexican War renown. One year after Richard passed away, his widow married Captain, later Major General Don Carlos Buell (1818-98), who thus became the

step-father of Emma and her minor sister. Buell's link to the 18th Century patriot is too remote to rate a place in Table 3, but it does deserve mention in this note.

34. Angus McDonald (1727-78) fled Scotland after the failed Jacobite rising of 1745 and settled in Virginia. He served as a Virginia militia captain in the French and Indian War and major in Lord Dunmore's War, where he conducted a major punitive expedition into the Ohio country. Though an ardent Patriot, he declined a lieutenant-colonelcy in the Continental Army but served at that grade in the Virginia militia during that war until his death in 1778. His grandson Angus W. McDonald (1799-1864) graduated from West Point in 1817 and served until 1819. Thereafter the fur trade beckoned him far up the Missouri River. He was also active in public works for Virginia. He returned to service in 1861 and soon became Colonel of the 7th Virginia Cavalry, which he styled a brigade since he increased it to twenty-nine companies. He operated in the Shenandoah and South Branch Valleys but had to leave field service that November due to ill health. He later commanded various Virginia military posts including Lexington, near which he was captured, July 14, 1864. Being closely confined in irons in Wheeling worsened his bad health. Shortly after being exchanged and returning to Confederate lines, he died on December 1, 1864.

35. Paul Revere (1735-1818) was active in the Sons of Liberty and opposition to the British in Boston in the 1760s and early 1770s. He served as a field-grade Massachusetts militia officer in Boston harbor and in expeditions against Newport and Penobscot during the Revolutionary War. He is best remembered for his famous ride on the night of April 18-19, 1775, to alert the Patriots that British Regulars were moving against Lexington and Concord. Two of his grandsons were generals in the Civil War. Joseph Warren Revere (1812-80) served in the U.S. Navy, 1828-50, and entered the Civil War as Colonel of the 7th New Jersey. Promoted to Brigadier General in October, 1862, he led the Second Jersey Brigade at Fredericksburg and Chancellorsville. At the latter battle, he succeeded to command of the Second Division of the III Corps, which he inopportunely ordered to withdraw while the battle still raged. For that action, he was not merely relieved but court martialed and dismissed the service. President Lincoln mitigated the sentence to allow him to resign as of August, 1863. The military career of Joseph's cousin Paul Joseph Revere (1832-63), also a grandson of the renowned Revolutionary rider, ended more gloriously and more conclusively. He entered service in 1861 as the Major of the 20th Massachusetts and rose to the two higher grades in that regiment by 1863. He was mortally wounded at Gettysburg, July 2, 1863, and died two days later. He was breveted Brigadier General posthumously.

36. Besides the four Founding Fathers in this table, three other signers—Benjamin Franklin, Alexander Hamilton and George Washington—have been covered previously. Their respective Civil War kin are William H. Emory; Schuyler Hamilton, Henry Halleck, and George Cullum; and Robert, Custis, and W.H.F. Lee. Also addressed already are two other delegates to the constitutional convention who refused to sign because the Constitution contained no Bill of Rights: Elbridge Gerry and George Mason, kinsmen of Edward Townsend, James Mason, Samuel Cooper, Frank Wheaton, and Smith and Fitz Lee.

37. Daniel of St. Thomas Jenifer (1723-90) helped lead the Patriot cause in Maryland, held the Presidency of that state's Council of Safety in 1775-77, and served in the Continental Congress, 1778-82. As a replacement Maryland delegate to the Constitutional convention in Philadelphia in 1787, he signed that document. His great-nephew Walter H. Jenifer (1823-78) attended West Point, 1841-43, but did not graduate. He, nevertheless, served as a captain in the 3rd U.S. Dragoons, 1847-48, and a lieutenant in the 2nd U.S. Cavalry, 1855-61. He went south and served in the Confederate Army, 1861-65, including as

LTC commanding a cavalry battalion at First Manassas and Colonel of the 8th Virginia Cavalry, 1861-62. Postwar, he was among over forty ex- Northern and Southern officers who served in the Egyptian Army.

38. Rufus King (1755-1827) served as captain and aide-de-camp to Generals John Glover and John Sullivan in the Revolutionary War. He is better known for his later political and diplomatic contributions: Massachusetts representative to the Confederation Congress, 1784-87; U.S. Senator from New York, 1789-96 and 1813-25; and U.S. Minister to Great Britain, 1796-1803 and 1825-26. As a member of the Constitutional Convention of 1787, he signed the U.S. Constitution. In 1816, he had the dubious distinction of being the last Federalist candidate for President. His namesake grandson (1814-76) graduated from West Point in 1833 and served three years in the U.S. Army. He re-entered service in 1861 as a Brigadier General, the first commander of the Iron Brigade while it was still molten. He succeeded to command Irvin McDowell's division in the I Corps, which he led at Second Bull Run. He later led a division in the IV and XXII Corps. Because of continuing epilepsy, he resigned in October, 1863, and assumed his 1861 appointment as minister to the Papal States, which he held until 1867. While in Rome, he arranged to extradite John Surratt, one of the conspirators to kill Lincoln.

First-cousin to General Rufus King and great-nephew to Federalist Rufus King was Archibald Gracie III (1832-64). He graduated from West Point in 1854 and served two years in the U.S. Army. He entered Confederate service in 1861 and served as a junior officer in the 3rd and 11th Alabama. He recruited and became Colonel of the 43rd Alabama and was promoted to Brigadier General in 1862. His brigade was heavily engaged at Chickamauga and Second Drewry's Bluff. With his ample proportions, he famously shielded Robert E. Lee in a dangerous sector of Petersburg trenches in late October, 1864. Barely a month later, he was himself killed by Federal artillery fire during the siege, December 2, 1864.

39. An older brother of General Thomas Pinckney, Charles Cotesworth Pinckney (1746-1825) also served prominently in the military in the Revolutionary War, as Colonel of the 1st South Carolina and as a brigade commander in the Savannah Campaign. Captured at Charleston, he was held prisoner, 1780-82. A brevet of brigadier general came to him in November, 1783. Even higher substantive Two-Star grade was conferred on him during the Quasi-War, 1798-1800. Such military service would have justified listing him in Table 2. He is instead included in Table 4 because, as a South Carolina delegate to the Philadelphia convention, he signed the U.S. Constitution of 1787. He later served as U.S. Minister to France, 1796-98, during the XYZ Affair. He was the Federalist nominee for Vice President in 1800 and for President in 1804 and 1808 but was not elected. He was the great-uncle and great-great-uncle of Major General Benjamin Huger (1805-77) and Colonel Frank Huger (1837-97), respectively. Those two Graycoats are covered in endnote 23.

40. Like his younger brother Edward, John Rutledge (1739-1800) served in both Continental Congresses. However, John left Philadelphia in the spring of 1776 before the Declaration of Independence was proposed or signed. He departed to become President of South Carolina, 1776-78; he later served as its first governor, 1779-82. He returned to Philadelphia in 1787 for the Constitutional convention and signed that fundamental charter. He was an original Associate Justice of the U.S. Supreme Court, 1789-91, and was Chief Justice, June-December, 1795. However, when the Senate rejected his nomination, he immediately resigned and retired from public life. Like his brother Edward, John was a great-uncle of Confederate Colonel Benjamin Huger Rutledge (1829-93), and John was grandfather-in-law of Captain Duncan Ingraham of the Confederate Navy. Those two Secessionist officers are covered in endnote 12.

41. William C. Preston (1729-83) [abbreviated "WCP," #1], an Ulster migrant to Virginia in 1738, fought Indians in the French and Indian War and Lord Dunmore's War, suppressed Tories in southwestern Virginia, and battled British in North Carolina in the Revolutionary War. A member of the House of Burgesses in the 1760s, a signer of the Fincastle Resolutions in 1775, a founder of Liberty Hall Academy (now Washington and Lee University) in 1776, and a Virginia Militia Colonel during the Revolution, he could have been listed in Tables 2 or 3. However, he produced such a prodigious progeny that he rates a separate table. One of his six siblings and five of his twelve children are listed in the left column. Though not Founding Fathers themselves, they are entered in the left column simply for convenience of connecting with kin.

42. Throughout Table 5, the relationships shown in this column link the person in the left column with the Civil War personage in the right column. William C. Preston's relationship is one generation removed from whatever is specified in the middle column. Thus, as appears later in this table, he was grandfather to Confederate generals John S. Preston, William Preston, and John B. Floyd, grandfather-in-law to General Albert Sidney Johnston, and great-great-uncle to General John C. Breckinridge.

To facilitate following family relations, two family trees are provided. The one on p. 225 focuses on WCP, his sister Letitia (Preston) Breckinridge, and five of his children. The second tree emphasizes WCP's eldest son, John; John's wife, Mary (Radford) Preston; and her renowned Radford kin. Within those two trees, WCP carries the number "1," and his five children are "#1a-1e." His sister is number "2," and her son U.S. Attorney General [AG] John Breckinridge is "#2a." The Radfords carry the number "3," with John Preston's wife, Mary, as "#3a" and her sister and brothers as "#3b-3d." Those respective numbers are repeated in the left column and notes for Table 5. The table and trees show only children connected to prominent Civil War persons. Many other descendants who lack that link are not included.

43. WCP's sister Letitia (1728-98) [#2] married Robert P. Breckinridge (1720-73), an officer in the French and Indian War and the Revolutionary War. One of their sons John Breckinridge (1760-1806) [#2a] served briefly in the Virginia militia in the Revolution, played a major role in the Virginia and Kentucky Resolutions of 1798, and was U.S. Attorney General, 1805-06. He died while in the latter office. Four of John's nine children (Letitia's grandchildren) were parents of prominent Civil War personages.

The closest connection for Letitia was John's son (her grandson) Rev. Robert J. Breckinridge, Sr. (1800-71), himself prominent in the Civil War era as an influential Presbyterian minister and Moderator of the Presbyterian General Assembly in 1841. Equally influential was his support for keeping Kentucky in the Union, as a strong supporter of Abraham Lincoln for President, a gradual emancipationist, an editor, and the Chairman Pro Tempore of the National Union [Republican] Party national convention, which renominated Lincoln in 1864. Kentucky stayed in the Union, but his family did not stay together. Two of his sons, Robert J. Breckinridge, Jr. (1833-1915) and William C.P. Breckinridge (1837-1904), became Confederate colonels. William commanded the 9th Kentucky Cavalry and often led a cavalry brigade. Young Robert served first as a captain in the 2nd Kentucky, then was a Confederate Congressman from Kentucky, 1862-64, and was captured in February, 1865, while trying to raise a cavalry regiment in the Blue Grass State. Two of the reverend's other sons served in the Union Army. Neither attained high rank during the Civil War, but Joseph C. Breckinridge (1842-1920) is mentioned here because of his later prominence. Although only a lieutenant in the Civil War, he rose in the postwar Regular establishment to become Brigadier General and Inspector General of the U.S. Army, 1889-1903, and a Major General of Volunteers commanding the I Corps in the Spanish-American War. The mother of

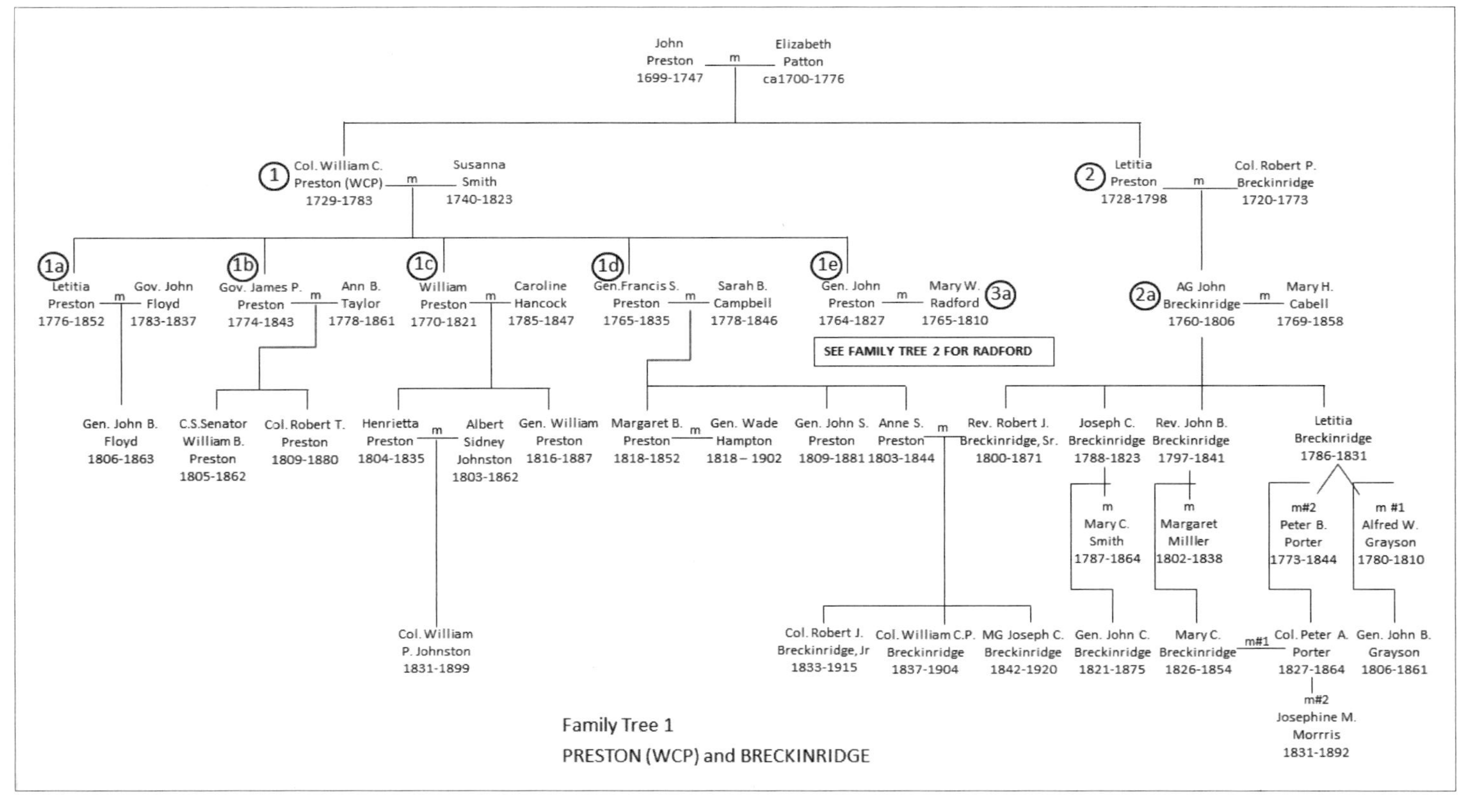
John Preston 1699-1747 m Elizabeth Patton ca1700-1776
1 Col. William C. Preston (WCP) 1729-1783 m Susanna Smith 1740-1823
2 Letitia Preston 1728-1798 m Col. Robert P. Breckinridge 1720-1773
1a Letitia Preston 1776-1852 m Gov. John Floyd 1783-1837
1b Gov. James P. Preston 1774-1843 m Ann B. Taylor 1778-1861
1c William Preston 1770-1821 m Caroline Hancock 1785-1847
1d Gen. Francis S. Preston 1765-1835 m Sarah B. Campbell 1778-1846
1e Gen. John Preston 1764-1827 m Mary W. Radford 1765-1810 3a
SEE FAMILY TREE 2 FOR RADFORD
2a AG John Breckinridge 1760-1806 m Mary H. Cabell 1769-1858
Gen. John B. Floyd 1806-1863
C.S.Senator William B. Preston 1805-1862
Col. Robert T. Preston 1809-1880
Henrietta Preston 1804-1835 m Albert Sidney Johnston 1803-1862
Gen. William Preston 1816-1887
Margaret B. Preston 1818-1852 m Gen. Wade Hampton 1818 – 1902
Gen. John S. Preston 1809-1881
Anne S. Preston 1803-1844 m Rev. Robert J. Breckinridge, Sr. 1800-1871
Joseph C. Breckinridge 1788-1823 m Mary C. Smith 1787-1864
Rev. John B. Breckinridge 1797-1841 m Margaret Milller 1802-1838
Letitia Breckinridge 1786-1831
m#2 Peter B. Porter 1773-1844
m #1 Alfred W. Grayson 1780-1810
Col. William P. Johnston 1831-1899
Col. Robert J. Breckinridge, Jr 1833-1915
Col. William C.P. Breckinridge 1837-1904
MG Joseph C. Breckinridge 1842-1920
Gen. John C. Breckinridge 1821-1875
Mary C. Breckinridge 1826-1854 m#1 Col. Peter A. Porter 1827-1864
m#2 Josephine M. Morrris 1831-1892
Gen. John B. Grayson 1806-1861
Family Tree 1
PRESTON (WCP) and BRECKINRIDGE

Joseph, William, and young Robert and the wife of Rev. Robert, Anne (1803-44), moreover, was herself a granddaughter of WCP [#1] as a child of his son Francis S. Preston [#1d]. Thus, Anne and her husband Robert, Sr., were first-cousins-once-removed. Their sons were great-grandchildren of WCP.

Besides Rev. Robert, three of the Attorney General's other children — Joseph, John, and Letitia — are notable as links to leaders in the 1860s. Son Joseph (1788-1823) was the father of John C. Breckinridge (1821-75). The latter served as the Major of the 3rd Kentucky in the Mexican War; Vice President of the United States, 1857-61; Southern Democrat nominee for President in 1860; Major General commanding a brigade, division, corps, and department in the Confederate Army; and the final Confederate Secretary of War, February-May, 1865. The Secretary's uncle Rev. John Breckinridge (1797-1841), another of the Attorney General's sons, was the father of Mary Breckinridge (1826-54), the first wife of Colonel Peter A. Porter, mentioned later in this note.

Porter was also connected to the Attorney General's oldest child, another Letitia (1786-1831). She married Alfred W. Grayson (1780-1810), the son of U.S. Senator William B. Grayson (1736-90) and himself Kentucky Secretary of State, 1807-08. Following Alfred's death, she married Peter B. Porter (1773-1844), a U.S. Congressman; U.S. Secretary of War, 1828-29; and a Major General with a distinguished combat record on the Niagara Frontier in the War of 1812. Among the children of her first marriage was John B. Grayson (1806-61), who graduated from West Point in 1826 and served in the U.S. Army (including the Second Seminole War and the Mexican War) until July of 1861, when he resigned to join Confederate service. Commissioned Brigadier General in August, he assumed command of the Department of Middle and Eastern Florida on September 4 and died of disease forty-seven days later.

His half-brother, Letitia's son by her second marriage, Peter A. Porter (1827-64), served longer in the Civil War and died more gloriously. He left the New York legislature in July, 1862, to become Colonel of a regiment soon designated the 8th New York Heavy Artillery. It served primarily in Baltimore, where he sometimes led a brigade, until May, 1864, when it took the field as infantry. He fought from Harris's Farm to Cold Harbor, where he was killed in the disastrous assault on June 3 while temporarily leading a brigade. His first wife was his first-cousin Mary Breckinridge (1826-54), a daughter of his mother's brother John (1797-1841). His second wife, Josephine Morris (1831-92), was the great-granddaughter of Lewis Morris III (1726-98), a Signer of the Declaration of Independence. He married her in 1859 and could have held a family reunion a few years later in Baltimore harbor, where her second-cousin, General William W. Morris, was his commanding officer. Grimmer connection came at Cold Harbor, where Porter was killed on June 3, and his wife's first-cousin-once-removed and fellow brigadier in the II Corps, Colonel Lewis O. Morris, was mortally wounded the next day. (William W. and Lewis O. Morris are covered in endnote 8.)

To summarize, WCP's sister Letitia Preston Breckinridge [#2] was the grandmother of Rev. Robert Breckinridge and the great-grandmother of Generals John C. Breckinridge and John Grayson, future General Joseph C. Breckinridge, and Colonels Robert J. Breckinridge, Jr., William C.P. Breckinridge, and Peter A. Porter. Through her, WCP [#1] was great-uncle to the minister and great-great-uncle to the other six officers. Through his son Francis Preston [#1d], moreover, WCP was grandfather-in-law to Rev. Breckinridge and great-grandfather to the minister's three sons, as shown in endnote 47.

44. WCP's daughter, yet another Letitia (1776-1852) [#1a], married John Floyd (1783-1837), a Virginia Militia Brigadier General in the War of 1812, a Congressman, 1817-29; and Governor of Virginia, 1830-34, during Nat Turner's Rebellion. Their son and WCP's grandson, John B. Floyd (1806-63), also served as Governor of Virginia, 1849-52, and as Secretary of War, 1857-60. He resigned

that office during the secession crisis because President James Buchanan refused to order Major Robert Anderson to return to Fort Moultrie from Fort Sumter.

Though previously a Unionist, he was commissioned a Brigadier General in Confederate service. His operations in the Kanawha Valley in 1861 were unsuccessful, and his command at Fort Donelson the following February proved disastrous. He escaped from there with his own division hours before the surrender, only to be relieved from command by President Davis on March 11, 1862. Two months later, he was commissioned a Major General of Virginia forces to organize and command the Virginia State Line in the southwestern part of the commonwealth. Supposedly recruited only from non-conscriptable men, the Virginia State Line actually competed with the national government for manpower. It was discontinued in February, 1863, and its few remaining soldiers were nominally turned over to the Confederacy the following month. Floyd himself expired on August 26 of that year. On learning of his passing, Northern Colonel John T. Wilder, commanding the Lightning Brigade, informed Army of the Cumberland headquarters on August 31 that "it is commonly reported that the rebel general J.B. Floyd is dead, having succeeded in cheating everything but Satan" (*OR*, v. XXX, pt. 3, pp. 251-52).

45. WCP's son James Patton Preston (1774-1843) [#1b] served as a colonel in the War of 1812 and as Governor of Virginia, 1816-19. One of his sons William Ballard Preston (1805-62) was Secretary of the Navy, 1849-50, and a Confederate Congressman and Senator from Virginia from 1861 until his death in 1862. In the commonwealth's secession convention, he proposed the ordinance of secession which took Virginia out of the Union. Ballard's brother Robert (1809-80) served as Colonel of the 28th Virginia, the 5th Virginia State Line, and the 4th Virginia Reserves, and commanded the Virginia Reserve Brigade in southwestern Virginia in 1865. Robert and Ballard Preston, thus, were grandsons of WCP [#1].

46. WCP's son William Preston (1770-1821) [#1c], a captain in the U.S. Army, 1792-98, had only one son (1816-87), who carried the given name William into the Civil War generation. The younger William served as LTC of the 4th Kentucky in the Mexican War, as a two-term U.S. Congressman, as U.S. Minister to Spain, and as a Brigadier General commanding a brigade and division in the Confederate Army. His final, uncompleted mission was as envoy to Emperor Maximilian of Mexico.

His early Civil War service was on the staff of General Albert Sidney Johnston (1803-62), who was not only his commanding general but also his brother-in-law, the husband of William's sister Henrietta (1804-35). Johnston graduated from West Point in 1826 and served in the U.S. Army until 1834, including the Black Hawk War. He became Adjutant General and Secretary of War of the independent Republic of Texas, fought in the Mexican War, re-entered the U.S. Army in 1849 and rose from major to Brevet Brigadier General. He became the second-ranking general in the Confederate Army, commanded in the Western Theater, and was killed at Shiloh. His son, William Preston Johnston (1831-99), held field grade commissions in the Graycoat 1st, 2nd, and 3rd Kentucky and served primarily as aide-de-camp to Jefferson Davis. Faithful to the end, young Johnston was captured with the President in Georgia, May 10, 1865. For these three kinsmen, WCP [#1] was grandfather to General Preston, grandfather-in-law to General Johnston, and great-grandfather to Colonel Johnston.

47. WCP's son Francis Smith Preston (1765-1836) [#1d] served as a Virginia Militia Colonel, Brigadier General, and Major General in the War of 1812, and a Congressman, 1793-97. One of his sons (hence, WCP's grandson) John Smith Preston (1809-81) served on General P.G.T. Beauregard's staff at Fort Sumter and First Manassas and headed the Confederate Conscription Bureau as a colonel and brigadier general. Francis' daughter Anne (1803-44) married Rev. Robert J. Breckinridge, who is described in endnote 43 along with three of his sons. Another daughter, Margaret (1818-52) married

Wade Hampton III (see endnote 22). Thus, through Francis, three of WCP's grandchildren and three of his great-grandchildren were prominent in the Civil War in their own right or through their husbands.

48. WCP's son John Preston (1764-1827) [#1e] served as a Virginia Militia General and the Treasurer of Virginia. In addition to being uncle to his siblings' famous children, as described in the four preceding notes, he was uncle or great-uncle to his wife's nephews, as shown in the family tree on p. 229. She was Mary Radford (1765-1810) [#3a]. Her sister Sarah [#3b] was the grandmother of Thomas T. Munford (1831-1918), Colonel of the 2nd Virginia Cavalry, frequent brigade commander, and head of the Second Cavalry Division in the war's final weeks. Though often called "General" because of his senior commands, he ranked no higher than colonel. That grade was also held by Munford's cousin and predecessor as Colonel of the 2nd Virginia Cavalry, Richard C.W. Radford (1822-86), the son of Mary's brother William [#3c]. After graduating from West Point in 1845, he served eleven years in the U.S. Army. He commanded General Beauregard's cavalry at First Manassas. Not re-elected as colonel in 1862, he later commanded the 1st Regiment and then the First Brigade of John B. Floyd's Virginia State Line. Richard's brother, Dr. John Blair Radford, had two children of note as Civil Warriors. His son, John Taylor Radford (1838-64), was LTC of the 22nd Virginia Cavalry when killed in action in the Shenandoah Valley, November 12, 1864. He previously served as aide to his brother-in-law, Brigadier General Gabriel C. Wharton (1824-1906), who led the 51st Virginia and later a brigade and division. Wharton was the fiancé and husband of Dr. Radford's daughter, Anne. Not all Radfords wore gray. Another of Mary Radford Preston's brothers, John [#3d], had two children with Union connections. His son Admiral William Radford (1808-90) served in the U.S. Navy, 1825-70. He had the bridge of the U.S.S. *New Ironsides*, commanded the ironclad naval division in attacking Fort Fisher, and took command of the North Atlantic Squadron as Acting Rear Admiral on May 1, 1865. The admiral's sister Mary, moreover, was the wife of General Stephen W. Kearny (1794-1848) of Mexican War renown. He died before the Civil War, but his nephew, Major General Philip Kearny (1815-62), commanded a brigade and division in the Union Army until killed at Chantilly. In contrast to Phil Kearny, Stephen's and Mary's own son, Major William Kearny (1833-93), left the U.S. Army in 1861 and served on the staffs of Southern generals William J. Hardee, John B. Magruder, and Thomas F. Drayton. The admiral's step-brother, moreover, the aforementioned Brigadier General Meriwether Lewis Clark, also fought for the Confederacy. (For Clark and Drayton, see endnotes 16 and 31.)

In summary, John Preston [#1e] through his wife, Mary [#3a], was uncle to Richard and William Radford, uncle-in-law to Stephen Kearny, great-uncle to John Taylor Radford, Thomas T. Munford, and William Kearny, and great-uncle-in-law to Gabriel Wharton. In turn, WCP [#1] was great-uncle to the first two officers, great-uncle-in-law to S. W. Kearny, great-great-uncle to the next three, and great-great-uncle-in-law to Wharton.

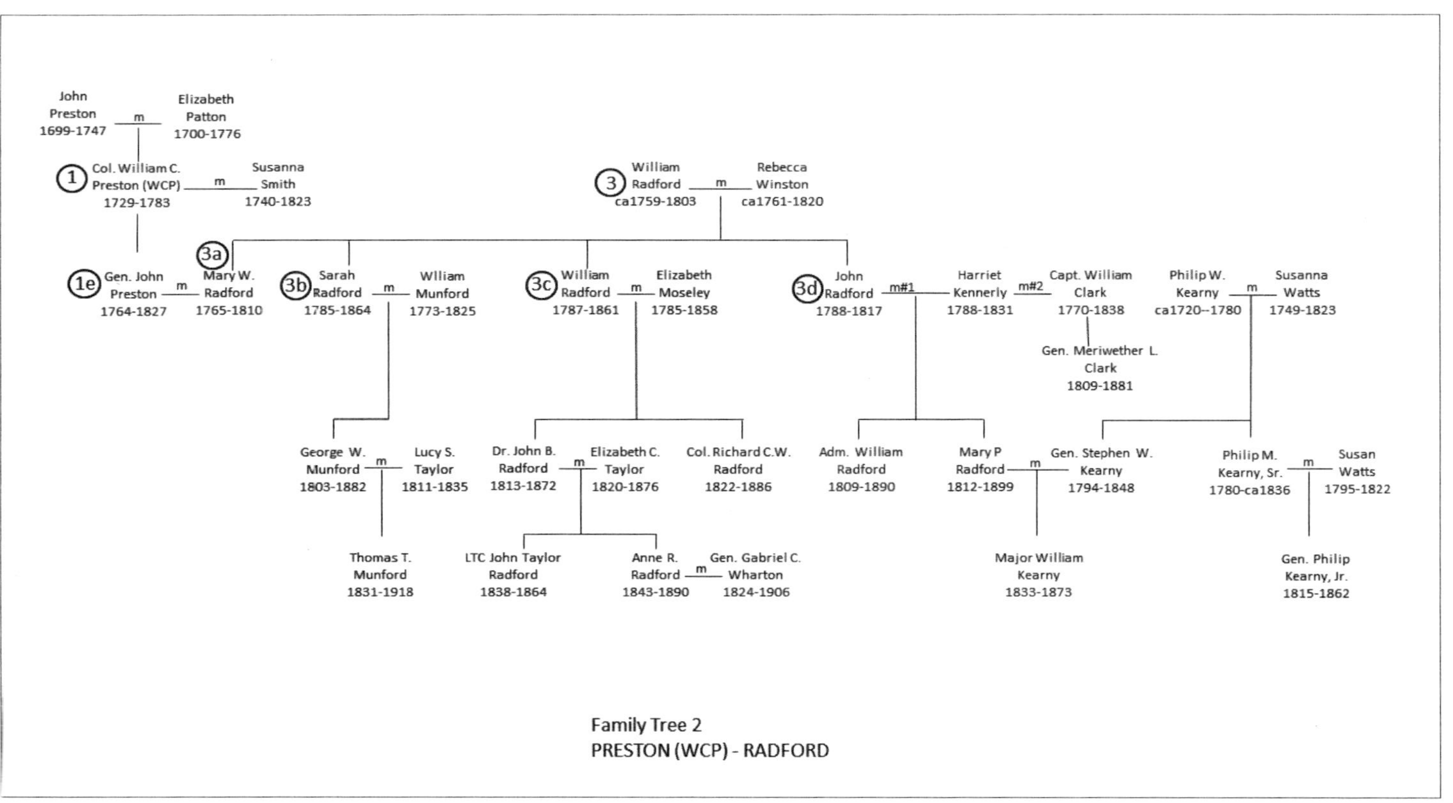

Family Tree 2
PRESTON (WCP) - RADFORD

71. John Quincy Adams.
National Portrait Gallery

72. Charles Francis Adams, Sr. LOC

73. "Light Horse Harry" Lee. *Wikipedia*

74. Sydney Smith Lee. LOC

75. Robert E. Lee. LOC

76. George Rogers Clark. *Filson Club*

77. Meriwether Lewis Clark. *Wikipedia*

78. William Radford. *Wikipedia Commons*

79. John Laurens. *Wikiwand*

80. Duncan N. Ingraham. *LOC*

Epilogue

This first volume of *Challenges of Command* analyzes the generalship of Ulysses S. Grant and Robert E. Lee throughout the Civil War, particularly during the great Virginia Campaign of 1864-65. The volume also offers new ways of looking at Federal corps commanders—such commanders as citizen-soldiers in general and such commanders at Antietam, Gettysburg, and Petersburg in particular. And the volume provides original research revealing family relations that bound Civil War leaders to the Revolutionary War generation.

All ten chapters concentrate on individuals—Grant and Lee, various corps commanders, leaders who helped create the United States and leaders who helped preserve the United States or who tried to create the Confederate States. This focus is not surprising because history is about individuals, separately and collectively, and about how their actions and inactions, for good or for ill, shape the course of events.

Individuals continue to figure prominently in the upcoming second volume of *Challenges of Command*. There, however, the perspective broadens to cover the very nature of war. Grand strategy, strategy, and operations throughout the Civil War, at Gettysburg, and in the Virginia Campaign of 1864-65, are assessed. And military organizations—sometimes specific to one unit or campaign, other times spanning the war—are explored. Chapters on the following topics are projected:

- "'Fear, Honor, and Interest:' Thucydides and the Outbreak of the American Civil War";
- "War Aims in a Civil War between Two Nation States";

- "Converging Conquest: Federal Grand Strategy and the Winning of the Civil War";
- "Penetrating the Void: Confederate Strategy and Federal Strategic Response in the Gettysburg Campaign";
- "Strategic Imperatives and Tactical Realities: Confederate Generalship in the Gettysburg Campaign";
- "The Four Fighting Fronts of Virginia, 1864-1865";
- "'That Maryland Raid Upset My Plans:' Ulysses S. Grant and Early's Raid, June-August, 1864";
- "Continuity of Command Structure from Bull Run to Appomattox";
- "Forth with the Fourth: An Overview of the Overlooked Federal IV Corps in the Eastern Theater, March, 1862-August, 1863";
- "Federal and Confederate Engineers in the Gettysburg Campaign";
- "Carlisle Barracks in the Civil War Era";
- "The Armies of Appomattox."

Readers who find these titles intriguing and who have found this first volume stimulating are invited to read Volume II, which will be published soon. Through both volumes, *Challenges of Command* encourages readers to think anew about the people and events of America's most fascinating era, the Civil War.

Richard J. Sommers, Ph.D.
Carlisle, Pennsylvania
December 28, 2017
RichmondRedeemed@aol.com

Bibliography

List of Abbreviations

AHEC: U.S. Army Heritage and Education Center, Carlisle Barracks, PA
CWTI: *Civil War Times Illustrated*
LOC: Library of Congress, Washington, DC
NA: National Archives, Washington, DC
OR: *The War of the Rebellion: A Compilation of the Official Records of the Union and Confederate Armies*

Books and Articles

Official Documents

Heitman, Francis B. *Historical Register and Dictionary of the United States Army, from Its Organization, September 29, 1789, to March 2, 1903.* Washington, DC: U.S. Government Printing Office, 1903.

———. *Historical Register of Officers of the Continental Army during the War of the Revolution, April, 1775 to December, 1783.* Washington, DC: U.S. Government Printing Office, 1893.

Official Records of the Union and Confederate Navies in the War of the Rebellion. Washington, DC: U.S. Government Printing Office, 1894-1922.

Supplement to the Official Records of the Union and Confederate Armies. Wilmington, NC: Broadfoot Publishing Company, 1997.

U.S. Census Bureau. *Census for 1860.* Washington, DC: Government Printing Office, 1860.

The War of the Rebellion: A Compilation of the Official Records of the Union and Confederate Armies. Washington, DC: U.S. Government Printing Office, 1880-1901.

Autobiographies, Biographies, Published Personal Papers

Alexander, Edward P. *Military Memoirs of a Confederate.* Bloomington: Indiana University Press, 1962.

Allardice, Bruce S. *Confederate Colonels: A Biographical Register.* Columbia: University of Missouri Press, 2008.

———. *More Confederate Generals.* Baton Rouge: Louisiana State University Press, 1995.

Anders, Curt. *Injustice on Trial: Second Bull Run, General Fitz John Porter's Court-Martial, and the Schofield Board Investigation That Restored His Good Name.* Zionsville, IN: Guild Press/Emmis Publishing, 2002.

Badeau, Adam. *Military History of Ulysses S. Grant: From April, 1861, to April, 1865.* New York: D. Appleton, 1868-1881.

Banks, Raymond. *King of Louisiana, 1862-1865, and Other Government Work: A Biography of Major General Nathaniel Prentice Banks, Speaker of the U.S. House of Representatives*. Las Vegas, NV: Raymond H. Banks, 2005.

Barthel, Thomas. *Abner Doubleday: A Civil War Biography*. Jefferson, NC: McFarland & Company, Inc., Publishers, 2010.

Bartlett, JoAnn. *Abner Doubleday: His Life and Times—Looking Beyond the Myth.* Bloomington, IN: Xlibris, 2009.

Basler, Roy P., ed. *The Collected Works of Abraham Lincoln.* New Brunswick, NJ: Rutgers University Press, 1953-55.

Bretzger, Paul. *Observing Hancock at Gettysburg: The General's Leadership through Eyewitness Accounts.* Jefferson, NC: McFarland & Company, Inc., Publishers, 2016.

Brinton, John H. *Personal Memoirs of John H. Brinton: Civil War Surgeon, 1861-1865.* Carbondale: Southern Illinois University Press, 1996.

Burgess, Milton V. *David Gregg: Pennsylvania Cavalryman.* State College, PA: Nittany Valley Offset, 1984.

Butler, Benjamin F. *Butler's Book: A Review of His Legal, Political and Military Career.* Boston: Thayer, 1892.

Butterfield, Julia, comp. *A Biographical Memorial of General Daniel Butterfield: Including Many Addresses and Military Writings*. New York: Grafton Press, 1904.

Carmichael, Peter S., ed. *Audacity Personified: The Generalship of Robert E. Lee.* Baton Rouge: Louisiana State University Press, 2004.

Carpenter, John. *Sword and Olive Branch, Oliver Otis Howard.* Pittsburgh: University of Pittsburgh Press, 1964.

Catton, Bruce. *Grant Moves South*. Boston: Little, Brown, 1960.

———. *Grant Takes Command*. Boston: Little, Brown, 1969.

Chance, Joseph, ed. *My Life in the Old Army: The Reminiscences of Abner Doubleday.* Ft. Worth: Texas Christian University Press, 1998.

Chernow, Ron. *Grant*. New York: Penguin Press, 2017.

Cleaves, Freeman. *Meade of Gettysburg*. Norman: University of Oklahoma Press, 1960.

Connelly, Thomas L. *The Marble Man, Robert E. Lee and His Image in American Society*. New York: Knopf, 1977.

Cox, Jacob D. *Military Reminiscences of the Civil War*. New York: C. Scribner's Sons, 1900.

Crawford, Samuel W. *The Genesis of the Civil War: The Story of Sumter, 1860-1861.* New York: C. L. Webster & Company, 1887.

Cresap, Bernarr. *Appomattox Commander: The Story of General E.O.C. Ord.* San Diego: A. S. Barnes, 1981.

Cullum, George W. *Biographical Register of the Officers and Graduates of the U.S. Military Academy at West Point, N.Y. since Its Establishment in 1802.* Cambridge, MA: Riverside Press, 1901.

Davis, Oliver W. *Life of David Bell Birney, Major-General United States Volunteers.* Philadelphia: King & Baird, 1867.

Davis, William C. *Breckinridge: Statesman, Soldier, Symbol.* Baton Rouge: Louisiana State University Press, 1974.

———. *Crucible of Command: Ulysses S. Grant and Robert E. Lee, The War They Fought, The Peace They Forged.* Boston, MA: Da Capo Press, 2014.

DeTrobriand, Philippe Regis Denis de Keredern. *Four Years with the Army of the Potomac.* Boston: Ticknor and Company, 1889.

Dinges, Bruce, and Leckie, Shirley, eds. *A Just and Righteous Cause: Benjamin H. Grierson's Civil War Memoir.* Carbondale: Southern Illinois University Press, 2008.

Dodge, Grenville M. *The Battle of Atlanta and Other Campaigns, Addresses, etc.* Council Bluffs, IA: Monarch Printing Co., 1910.

Doubleday, Abner. *Reminiscences of Forts Sumter and Moultrie in 1860-61.* New York: Harper & Brothers, 1876.

Ecelbarger, Gary. *Black Jack Logan: An Extraordinary Life in Peace and War.* Guilford, CT: Lyons Press, 2005.

Eisenschiml, Otto. *The Celebrated Case of Fitz John Porter: An American Dreyfus Affair.* Indianapolis: Bobbs-Merrill, 1950.

Eubank, Damon. *In the Shadow of the Patriarch: The John J. Crittenden Family in War and Peace.* Macon: Mercer University Press, 2009.

Freeman, Douglas Southall. *R.E. Lee: A Biography.* New York: Charles Scribner's Sons, 1935.

———. *Lee's Lieutenants: A Study in Command.* New York: Charles Scribner's Sons, 1944.

Gallagher, Gary W., ed. *Fighting for the Confederacy: The Personal Recollections of General Edward Porter Alexander*. Chapel Hill: University of North Carolina Press, 1989.

———. ed., *Lee the Soldier*. Lincoln: University of Nebraska Press, 1996.

Gambone, Albert M. *Major-General Darius Nash Couch: Enigmatic Valor.* Baltimore, MD: Butternut & Blue, 2000.

Gibbon, John. *Personal Recollections of the Civil War.* New York: G.P. Putnam's, 1928.

Gould, John M. *Joseph K. F. Mansfield, Brigadier General of the U.S. Army: A Narrative of Events Connected with His Mortal Wounding at Antietam, Sharpsburg, Maryland, September 17, 1862.* Portland, ME: S. Berry, printer, 1895.

Grant, Ulysses S. *Personal Memoirs of U.S. Grant.* New York: Charles L. Webster & Company, 1886.

Hancock, Almira R. *Reminiscences of Winfield Scott Hancock by His Wife*. New York: C.L. Webster & Co., 1887.

Harrington, Fred. *Fighting Politician: Major General N. P. Banks*. Philadelphia: University of Pennsylvania Press, 1948.

Harsh, Joseph L. *Confederate Tide Rising: Robert E. Lee and the Making of Southern Strategy, 1861-1862*. Kent: Kent State University Press, 1998.

———. *Taken at the Flood: Robert E. Lee and Confederate Strategy in the Maryland Campaign of 1862.* Kent: Kent State University Press, 1999.

Hebert, Walter H. *Fighting Joe Hooker.* Lincoln: University of Nebraska Press, 1999.

Hessler, James A. *Sickles at Gettysburg: The Controversial Civil War General Who Committed Murder, Abandoned Little Round Top, and Declared Himself the Hero of Gettysburg*. El Dorado Hills, CA: Savas Beatie, 2009.

Hirshson, Stanley. *Grenville M. Dodge: Soldier, Politician, Railroad Pioneer.* Bloomington: Indiana University Press, 1967.

Hollandsworth, James. *Pretense of Glory: The Life of General Nathaniel P. Banks.* Baton Rouge: Louisiana State University Press, 1998.

Holzman, Richard. *Stormy Ben Butler.* New York: Macmillan, 1954.

Howard, Oliver Otis. *Autobiography of Oliver Otis Howard, Major General, United States Army.* New York: Baker & Taylor Co., 1907.

Hunt, Gaillard. *Israel, Elihu, and Cadwallader Washburn: A Chapter in American Biography.* New York: The Macmillan Company, 1925.

Hunt, Roger D. *Brevet Brigadier Generals in Blue.* Gaithersburg, MD: Olde Soldier Books, 1990.

Huntington, Tom. *Searching for George Gordon Meade: The Forgotten Victor of Gettysburg.* Mechanicsburg, PA: Stackpole Books, 2013.

In Memoriam: Henry Warner Slocum, 1826-1894. Albany: J.B. Lyon, 1904.

Jamieson, Perry D. *Winfield Scott Hancock: Gettysburg Hero.* Abilene, TX: McWhiney Foundation Press, 2003.

Jermann, Donald R. *Fitz-John Porter, Scapegoat of Second Manassas: The Rise, Fall, and Rise of the General Accused of Disobedience.* Jefferson, NC: McFarland & Company, Inc., Publishers, 2009.

———. *Union General Gouverneur Warren: Hero at Little Round Top, Disgrace at Five Forks.* Jefferson, NC: McFarland & Company, Inc., Publishers, 2015.

Jones, James Pickett. *Black Jack: John A. Logan and Southern Illinois in the Civil War Era.* Carbondale: Southern Illinois University Press, 1995.

Jones, Keith Marshall. *"Congress as My Government:" Chief Justice John Marshall in the American Revolution (1775-1781).* New York: Connecticut Colonel Publishing Company, 2008.

Jordan, David M. *Winfield Scott Hancock: A Soldier's Life.* Bloomington: Indiana University Press, 1988.

———. *"Happiness Is Not My Companion": The Life of General G. K. Warren.* Bloomington: Indiana University Press, 2001.

Kautz, Lawrence G. *August Valentine Kautz, USA: Biography of a Civil War General.* Jefferson, NC: McFarland & Company, Inc., Publishers, 2008.

Keneally, Thomas. *American Scoundrel: The Life of the Notorious Civil War General Dan Sickles.* New York: Nan A. Talese/Doubleday, 2002.

Kiper, Richard. *Major General John Alexander McClernand: Politician in Uniform.* Kent: Kent State University Press, 1999.

Korda, Michael. *Ulysses S. Grant: The Unlikely Hero.* New York: Atlas Books/HarperCollins, 2004.

Krick, Robert E. Lee. *Staff Officers in Gray: A Biographical Register of the Staff Officers in the Army of Northern Virginia.* Chapel Hill: University of North Carolina Press, 2003.

Krick, Robert K. *Lee's Colonels: A Biographical Register of the Field Officers of the Army of Northern Virginia.* Dayton, OH: Morningside, 1992.

Laas, Virginia, ed. *Wartime Washington: The Civil War Letters of Elizabeth Blair Lee.* Urbana: University of Illinois Press, 1991.

Lash, Jeffrey. *A Politician Turned General: The Civil War Career of Stephen Augustus Hurlbut.* Kent: Kent State University Press, 2003.

Lavery, Dennis and Mark Jordan. *Iron Brigade General: John Gibbon, A Rebel in Blue.* Westport, CT: Greenwood Press, 1993.

Leckie, William. *Unlikely Warriors: General Benjamin H. Grierson and His Family.* Norman: University of Oklahoma Press, 1984.

Lee, Fitzhugh. *General Lee.* New York: D. Appleton and Co., 1894.

Lee, Robert E., Jr. *Recollections and Letters of General Robert E. Lee.* Garden City, NY: Garden City Publishing, 1924.

Lewis, Lloyd. *Captain Sam Grant.* Boston: Little, Brown, 1950.

Long, Armistead L. *Memoirs of Robert E. Lee: His Military and Personal History, Embracing a Large Amount of Information Hitherto Unpublished.* New York: J.M. Stoddart, 1886.

Long, William W. *A Biography of Major General Edwin Vose Sumner, U.S.A., 1797-1863.* n.p., 1971.

Marshall, Jessie Ames, ed. *Private and Official Correspondence of Gen. Benjamin F. Butler during the Period of the Civil War.* Norwood, MA: Plimpton Press, 1917.

Marvel, William. *Burnside.* Chapel Hill: University of North Carolina Press, 1991.

Maurice, Frederick, ed. *An Aide-de-Camp of Lee: Being the Papers of Colonel Charles Marshall, Sometime Aide-de-Camp, Military Secretary and Assistant Adjutant General on the Staff of Robert E. Lee, 1862-1865.* Boston: Little, Brown, and Co., 1927.

McClellan, George B. *McClellan's Own Story: The War for the Union, the Soldiers Who Fought It, the Civilians Who Directed It and His Relations to It and to Them.* New York: C. L. Webster & Company, 1887.

McConnell, W.F. *Remember Reno: A Biography of Major General Jesse Lee Reno.* Shippensburg, PA: White Mane Publishing, 1996.

Meade, George, ed. *The Life and Letters of George Gordon Meade: Major-General, United States Army.* New York: Charles Scribner's Sons, 1913.

Melton, Brian C. *Sherman's Forgotten General: Henry W. Slocum.* Columbia: University of Missouri Press, 2007.

Memorial of Gen. J. K. F. Mansfield, United States Army, Who Fell in Battle at Sharpsburg, Md., Sept 17, 1862. Boston: Press of T. R. Marvin & Sons, 1862.

Meyers, Christopher C. *Union General John A. McClernand and the Politics of Command.* Jefferson, NC: McFarland & Company, Inc., Publishers, 2010.

Monroe, Haskell M.; McIntosh, James T.; and Crist, Lynda L., eds. *The Papers of Jefferson Davis.* Baton Rouge: Louisiana State University Press, 1971-2015.

Morgan, James P. *Grenville Mellen Dodge in the Civil War: Union Spymaster, Railroad Builder and Organizer of the Fourth Iowa Volunteer Infantry.* Jefferson, NC: McFarland & Company, Inc., Publishers, 2016.

Nagel, Paul C. *The Lees of Virginia: Seven Generations of an American Family.* New York: Oxford University Press, 1990.

Nash, Howard P. *Stormy Petrel: The Life and Times of General Benjamin F. Butler, 1818-1893.* Rutherford: Fairleigh Dickinson University Press, 1969.

Nevins, Allan, ed. *A Diary of Battle: The Personal Journals of Colonel Charles S. Wainwright, 1861-1865.* New York: Harcourt, Brace & World, 1962.

Nichols, Edward J. *Toward Gettysburg: A Biography of General John F. Reynolds.* University Park: Pennsylvania State University Press, 1958.

Nolan, Alan T. *Lee Considered: General Robert E. Lee and Civil War History*. Chapel Hill: University of North Carolina Press, 1991.

Nolan, Dick. *Benjamin Franklin Butler: The Damnedest Yankee.* Novato, CA: Presidio Press, 1991.

Palmer, George T. *A Conscientious Turncoat: The Story of John M. Palmer, 1817-1900.* Whitefish, MT: Kessinger Publishing, LLC, 2008.

Palmer, John M. *Personal Recollections of John M. Palmer: The Story of an Earnest Life*. Cincinnati: R. Clarke Co., 1901.

Patton, Robert H. *The Pattons: A Personal History of an American Family*. New York: Crown Publishers, 1994.

Pinchon, Edgcumb. *Dan Sickles, Hero of Gettysburg and "Yankee King of Spain."* Garden City, NY: Doubleday, Doran and Company, Inc., 1945.

Poore, Benjamin Perley. *The Life and Public Services of Ambrose E. Burnside: Soldier, Citizen, Statesman.* Providence, RI: J.A. & R.A. Reid, 1882.

Porter, Horace. *Campaigning with Grant*. New York: Century, 1897.

Quaife, Milo, ed. *From the Cannon's Mouth: The Civil War Letters of General Alpheus S. Williams.* Detroit: Wayne State University Press, 1959.

Quatman, G. William. *A Young General and the Fall of Richmond: The Life and Career of Godfrey Weitzel.* Athens: Ohio University Press, 2015.

Rafuse, Ethan. *Fitz John Porter, the Campaign of Second Manassas, and the Problem of Command and Control in the 19th Century: A Scholarly Monograph*. The Papers of the Blue & Gray Education Society, No. 7; Saline, MI: McNaughton and Gunn, 1998.

———. *George Gordon Meade and the War in the East.* Abilene, TX: McWhiney Foundation Press, 2003.

Sauers, Richard A. *Gettysburg: The Meade-Sickles Controversy.* Washington, DC: Brassey's, 2003.

———. *Meade: Victor of Gettysburg.* Washington, DC: Brassey's, 2003.

Schmiel, Eugene. *Citizen General: Jacob Dolson Cox and the Civil War Era*. Athens: Ohio University Press, 2014.

Schurz, Carl. *Intimate Letters of Carl Schurz, 1841-1869*. Madison: State Historical Society of Wisconsin, 1928.

———. *The Reminiscences of Carl Schurz.* New York: McClure Co., 1907-08.

Sedgwick, John. *Correspondence of John Sedgwick, Major-General.* New York: Printed for C. and E.B. Stoeckel, 1902-1903.

Simon, John Y., and Marszalek, John C., eds. *The Papers of Ulysses S. Grant.* Carbondale: Southern Illinois University Press, 1967-2012.

Simpson, Brooks D. *Let Us Have Peace: General Ulysses S. Grant and the Politics of War and Reconstruction, 1861-1868.* Chapel Hill: University of North Carolina Press, 1991.

_____, ed. *Sherman's Civil War: Selected Correspondence of William T. Sherman, 1860-1865*. Chapel Hill: University of North Carolina Press, 1999.

———. *Ulysses S. Grant: Triumph Over Adversity, 1822-1865*. Boston: Houghton Mifflin, 2000.

Slocum, Charles Elihu. *The Life and Services of Major-General Henry Warner Slocum*. Toledo, OH: Slocum Publishing Company, 1913.

Smith, William E. *The Francis Preston Blair Family in Politics.* New York: Macmillan Co., 1933.

Snell, Mark. *From First to Last: The Life of Major General William B. Franklin*. New York: Fordham University Press, 2002.

Sommers, Richard J. "George T. Anderson," "Alfred M. Scales," and seventeen other entries in William C. Davis, ed., *The Confederate General*. Harrisburg: National Historical Society, 1991-92.

———. "Richard Heron Anderson" in David C. Roller and Robert W. Twyman, eds., *The Encyclopedia of Southern History*. Baton Rouge: Louisiana State University Press, 1979.

———. "Romeyn B. Ayres," "Horatio G. Wright," and eight other entries in John T. Hubbell and James W. Geary, eds., *Biographical Dictionary of the Union: Northern Leaders of the Civil War*. Westport, CT: Greenwood Press, 1995.

———. Foreword for Volume XI of Lynda L. Crist, ed., *The Papers of Jefferson Davis*. Baton Rouge: Louisiana State University Press, 2003.

———. "Grant, Ulysses Simpson (1822-1885)," in David S. and Jeanne T. Heidler, eds., *Encyclopedia of the American Civil War*, v. II. Santa Barbara: ABC-CLIO, 2000.

———. "'Stonewall' Jackson," "George G. Meade," and "William T. Sherman" in Volume II of Andrew Roberts, ed., *The Art of War: Great Commanders of the Modern World*. London: Quercus, 2009.

———. "The Men Who Led," in William C. Davis, ed., *Touched by Fire, a Photographic Portrait of the Civil War*, v. I. Boston: Little, Brown, 1985.

"Stanley, Francis" [psued. for Stanley Francis L. Crocchiola]. *E. V. Sumner: Major-General United States Army, 1797-1863.* Borger, TX: Jim Hess Printers, 1968.

Styple, William. *Generals in Bronze: Interviewing the Commanders of the Civil War.* Kearny, NJ: Belle Grove Publishing Co., 2005.

———, ed. *Our Noble Blood: The Civil War Letters of Régis de Trobriand, Major-General, U.S.V.* Kearny, NJ: Belle Grove Publishing Co., 1997.

Swanberg, W.A. *Sickles the Incredible*. New York: Scribner, 1956.

Tate, Thomas K. *General Edwin Vose Sumner, USA: A Civil War Biography*. Jefferson, NC: McFarland & Company, Inc., Publishers, 2013.

Taylor, Emerson G. *Gouverneur Kemble Warren: The Life and Letters of an American Soldier, 1830-1882.* Boston: Houghton Mifflin, 1932.

Trefousse, Hans. *Carl Schurz, A Biography*. Knoxville: University of Tennessee Press, 1982.

———. *Ben Butler: The South Called Him Beast!* New York: Octagon Books, 1957.

Tucker, Glenn. *Hancock the Superb.* Indianapolis: Bobbs-Merrill, 1960.

U.S. Military Academy. Association of Graduates. *Annual Reunion of the Association of Graduates of the United States Military Academy.* Saginaw, MI: Seamann & Peters, various dates annually.

Wagner, Richard. *For Honor, Flag, and Family: Civil War Major General Samuel W. Crawford, 1827-1892.* Shippensburg, PA: White Mane Books, 2005.

Walker, Francis A. *General Hancock*. New York: D. Appleton, 1894.

Warner, Ezra. *Generals in Blue: Lives of the Union Commanders*. Baton Rouge: Louisiana State University Press, 1964.

———. *Generals in Gray: Lives of the Confederate Commanders*. Baton Rouge: Louisiana State University Press, 1959.

Weland, Gerald. *O.O. Howard, Union General.* Jefferson, NC: McFarland & Company, Inc., Publishers, 1995.

Welsh, Jack D. *Medical Histories of Confederate Generals.* Kent: Kent State University Press, 1995.

———. *Medical Histories of Union Generals.* Kent: Kent State University Press, 1996.

Werlich, Robert. *"Beast" Butler: The Incredible Career of Major General Benjamin Franklin Butler.* Washington, DC: Quaker Press, 1962.

West, Richard. *Lincoln's Scapegoat General: A Life of Benjamin F. Butler, 1818-1893.* Boston: Houghton Mifflin, 1965.

White, Ronald C. *American Ulysses: A Life of Ulysses S. Grant.* New York: Random House, 2016.

Winslow, Richard Elliott. *General John Sedgwick, The Story of a Union Corps Commander.* Novato, CA: Presidio Press, 1982.

Campaigns and Battles

Bearss, Edwin C., and Suderow, Bryce A. *The Petersburg Campaign.* El Dorado Hills, CA: Savas Beatie, 2012-2014.

Broadwater, Robert, ed. *Gettysburg as the Generals Remembered It: Postwar Perspectives of Ten Commanders.* Jefferson, NC: McFarland & Company, Inc., Publishers, 2010.

Calkins, Christopher M. *The Appomattox Campaign: March 29-April 9, 1865.* Conshohocken, PA: Combined Books, 1997.

Cavanaugh, Michael A. *The Petersburg Campaign: The Battle of the Crater, "The Horrid Pit," June 25-August 6, 1864.* Lynchburg, VA: H.E. Howard, 1989.

Doubleday, Abner. *Chancellorsville and Gettysburg.* New York: C. Scribner's Sons, 1882.

Greene, A. Wilson. *The Final Battles of the Petersburg Campaign: Breaking the Backbone of the Rebellion.* Knoxville: University of Tennessee Press, 2008.

———. *A Campaign of Giants: The Battle for Petersburg.* Chapel Hill: The University of North Carolina Press, 2018.

Greene, Samuel Dana. "In the 'Monitor' Turret," in Buel, Clarence C., and Johnson, Robert U., eds. *Battles and Leaders of the Civil War*, v. 1. New York: Thomas Yoseloff, 1956.

Hess, Earl J. *In the Trenches at Petersburg: Field Fortifications and Confederate Defeat.* Chapel Hill: University of North Carolina Press, 2009.

———. *Trench Warfare under Grant and Lee: Field Fortifications in the Overland Campaign.* Chapel Hill: University of North Carolina Press, 2007.

Horn, John. *The Siege of Petersburg: The Battles for the Weldon Railroad, August 1864.* El Dorado Hills, CA: Savas Beatie, 2015.

Howe, Thomas. *The Petersburg Campaign: Wasted Valor, June 15-18, 1864.* Lynchburg, VA: H. E. Howard, 1988.

Jamieson, Perry D. *Spring 1865: The Closing Campaigns of the Civil War.* Lincoln: University of Nebraska Press, 2015.

Marvel, William. *Lee's Last Retreat: The Flight to Appomattox.* Chapel Hill: University of North Carolina Press, 2002.

Matter, William D. *If It Takes All Summer: The Battle of Spotsylvania*. Chapel Hill: University of North Carolina Press, 1988.

Miller, J. Michael. *The North Anna Campaign: "Even to Hell Itself," May 21-26, 1864*. Lynchburg, VA: H. E. Howard, 1989.

Newsome, Hampton. *Richmond Must Fall: The Richmond-Petersburg Campaign, October 1864*. Kent: Kent State University Press, 2013.

Price, James S. *The Battle of First Deep Bottom*. Charleston, SC: The History Press, 2014.

Rhea, Gordon C. *The Battle of the Wilderness, May 5-6, 1864*. Baton Rouge: Louisiana State University Press, 1994.

———. *The Battles for Spotsylvania Court House and the Road to Yellow Tavern, May 7-12, 1864*. Baton Rouge: Louisiana State University Press, 1997.

———. *To the North Anna River: Grant and Lee, May 13-25, 1864*. Baton Rouge: Louisiana State University Press, 2000.

———. *Cold Harbor: Grant and Lee, May 26-June 3, 1864*. Baton Rouge: Louisiana State University Press, 2002.

———. *On to Petersburg: Grant and Lee, June 4-15, 1864*. Baton Rouge: Louisiana State University Press, 2017.

Sommers, Richard J. "The Battle No One Wanted [Second Squirrel Level Road]," *Civil War Times Illustrated*, v. XIV, No. 5 (August, 1975), pp. 10-18.

———. "The Battle of the Boydton Plank Road, October 27-28, 1864," *Civil War Magazine*, No. LXVII (April, 1998), pp. 35-38.

———. "The Battles of Pegram's Farm and First Squirrel Level Road, September 29-October 2, 1864," *Civil War Magazine*, No. LXVII (April, 1998), pp. 31-35.

———. "Cold Harbor," "Trevilian Station," and "Samaria Church" in Frances H. Kennedy, ed., *The Civil War Battlefield Guide*. Boston: Houghton Mifflin, 1998.

———. "The Dutch Gap Affair: Military Atrocities and Rights of Negro Soldiers," *Civil War History*, v. XXI, no. 1 (March, 1975), pp. 51-64.

———. "1864," in William B. Styple, ed., *Writing and Fighting the Civil War: Soldier Correspondence to the New York Sunday Mercury*. Kearny, NJ: Belle Grove Publishing Company, 2000.

———. "Fury at Fort Harrison," *Civil War Times Illustrated*, v. XIX, No. 6 (October, 1980), pp. 12-23.

———. "Hatcher's Run, Battle of (October 27-28, 1864)," in David C. Roller and Robert W. Twyman, eds., *The Encyclopedia of Southern History*. Baton Rouge: Louisiana State University Press, 1979.

———. "Land Operations in Virginia in 1864," in William C. Davis, ed., *Virginia at War, 1864*, v. IV, *The Tightening Noose*. Lexington: University Press of Kentucky, 2009.

———. "Petersburg Autumn: The Battle of Poplar Spring Church," in Roman J. Heleniak and Lawrence L. Hewitt, eds., *The Confederate High Command & Related Topics; The 1988 Deep Delta Civil War Symposium: Themes in Honor of T. Harry Williams*. Shippensburg, PA: White Mane Publishing Company, 1990.

———. "Petersburg Besieged," in William C. Davis, ed., *The Image of War, 1861-1865*, v. VI, *The End of an Era*. Garden City: Doubleday, 1984.

———. "Petersburg Campaign, 15 June 1864-3 April 1865," in David S. and Jeanne T. Heidler, eds., *Encyclopedia of the American Civil War*, v. III. Santa Barbara: ABC-CLIO, 2000.

———. *Richmond Redeemed: The Siege at Petersburg* [First Edition]. Garden City, NY: Doubleday, 1981.

———. *Richmond Redeemed: The Siege at Petersburg; The Battles of Chaffin's Bluff and Poplar Spring Church, September 29-October 2, 1864* [Expanded 150th Anniversary Edition]. El Dorado Hills, CA: Savas Beatie, 2014.

Trudeau, Noah Andre. *Out of the Storm: The End of the Civil War, April-June 1865.* Boston: Little, Brown, 1994.

Varon, Elizabeth. *Appomattox: Victory, Defeat, and Freedom at the End of the Civil War.* New York: Oxford University Press, 2014.

Unit Histories

Armstrong, Marion. *Unfurl Those Colors!: McClellan, Sumner, and the Second Army Corps in the Antietam Campaign.* Tuscaloosa: University of Alabama Press, 2008.

Catton, Bruce. *Mr. Lincoln's Army*. Garden City, NY: Doubleday, 1951.

———. *Glory Road: The Bloody Route from Fredericksburg to Gettysburg*. Garden City, NY: Doubleday, 1952.

———. *A Stillness at Appomattox*. Garden City, NY: Doubleday, 1953.

Glatthaar, Joseph T. *General Lee's Army: From Victory to Collapse*. New York: Free Press, 2008.

Gregg, David M. *The Second Cavalry Division of the Army of the Potomac in the Gettysburg Campaign*. Philadelphia: Military Order of the Loyal Legion of the United States; Commandery of the State of Pennsylvania, 1907.

Harrison, Kathy Georg, and Busey, John W. *Nothing but Glory: Pickett's Division at Gettysburg.* Hightstown, NJ: Longstreet House, 1987.

Huffstodt, Jim. *Hard Dying Men: The Story of General W.H.L. Wallace, General T.E.G. Ransom, and Their "Old Eleventh" Illinois Infantry in the American Civil War (1861-1865).* Bowie, MD: Heritage Books, 1991.

Hyde, Thomas W. *Following the Greek Cross, or, Memories of the Sixth Army Corps.* Columbia: University of South Carolina Press, 2005.

Kreiser, Lawrence. *Defeating Lee: A History of the Second Corps, Army of the Potomac.* Bloomington: Indiana University Press, 2011.

Longacre, Edward G. *Army of Amateurs: General Benjamin F. Butler and the Army of the James, 1863-1865.* Mechanicsburg, PA: Stackpole Books, 1997.

Powell, William H. *The Fifth Army Corps (Army of the Potomac): A Record of Operations during the Civil War in the United States of America, 1861-1865.* New York: G. P. Putnam's Sons, 1896.

Pula, James. *Under the Crescent Moon with the XI Corps in the Civil War. Volume 1: From the Defenses of Washington to Chancellorsville, 1862-1863.* El Dorado Hills, CA: Savas Beatie, 2017.

Reese, Timothy J. *Sykes' Regular Infantry Division, 1861-1864: A History of Regular United States Infantry Operations in the Civil War's Eastern Theater.* Jefferson, NC: McFarland & Company, Inc., Publishers, 1990.

Starr, Stephen Z. *The Union Cavalry in the Civil War*. Baton Rouge: Louisiana State University Press, 1979-85.

Stevens, George T. *Three Years in the Sixth Corps: A Concise Narrative of Events in the Army of the Potomac from 1861 to the Close of the Rebellion, April, 1865.* New York: D. Van Nostrand, 1870.

Swinton, William. *Campaigns of the Army of the Potomac: A Critical History of Operations in Virginia, Maryland and Pennsylvania, from the Commencement to the Close of the War, 1861-1865.* New York: C. Scribner's Sons, 1882.

Walker, Francis A. *History of the Second Army Corps in the Army of the Potomac.* New York: C. Scribner's Sons, 1886.

Wallace, Lee. *A Guide to Virginia Military Organizations, 1861-1865*. Lynchburg, VA: H. E. Howard, Inc., 1986.

Welcher, Frank. *The Union Army, 1861-1865: Organization and Operations.* Bloomington: Indiana University Press, 1989-93.

Wert, Jeffry. *A Glorious Army: Robert E. Lee's Triumph, 1862-1863.* New York: Simon & Schuster, 2011.

———. *The Sword of Lincoln: The Army of the Potomac*. New York: Simon & Schuster, 2005.

Woodbury, Augustus. *Major General Ambrose E. Burnside and the Ninth Army Corps: A Narrative of Campaigns in North Carolina, Maryland, Virginia, Ohio, Kentucky, Mississippi and Tennessee, During the War for the Preservation of the Republic*. Providence, RI: S.S. Rider & Brother, 1867.

Young, Alfred C. *Lee's Army during the Overland Campaign: A Numerical Study.* Baton Rouge: Louisiana State University Press, 2013.

Other

Dyer, Frederick H. *A Compendium of the War of the Rebellion.* New York: T. Yoseloff, 1959.

Greene, A. Wilson. *Civil War Petersburg: Confederate City in the Crucible of War.* Charlottesville: University of Virginia Press, 2006.

Hess, Earl J. *Field Armies and Fortifications in the Civil War: The Eastern Campaigns, 1861-1864.* Chapel Hill: University of North Carolina Press, 2005.

McWhiney, Grady. *Attack and Die: Civil War Military Tactics and the Southern Heritage.* Tuscaloosa: University of Alabama Press, 1982.

Myers, Jr., Minor. *Liberty without Anarchy: A History of the Society of the Cincinnati.* Charlottesville: University Press of Virginia, 1983.

Sommers, Richard J. "American Military History, 1816-1916" in John E. Jessup and Robert W. Coakley, eds., *A Guide to the Study and Use of Military History.* Washington, DC: U.S. Army Center of Military History, 1979.

———. "Civil War Soldiers: The Henderson Brothers" and "Robert McQuin Black," in Richard L. Tritt, ed., *Here Lyes the Body: The Story of Meeting House Springs*. Carlisle, PA: First Presbyterian Church, 2009.

———. "Civil War Strategy," "Civil War Tactics," and thirty other entries in Patricia Faust, ed., *The Historical Times Illustrated Encyclopedia of the Civil War.* New York: Harper & Row, 1986.

———. "'They Fired into Us an Awful Fire:' The Civil War Diary of Private Charles C. Perkins, 1st Massachusetts Infantry Regiment, June 4-July 4, 1862," in William J. Miller, ed., *Campaign Chronicles: The Peninsula Campaign: Yorktown to the Seven Days*, v. 1. Campbell, CA: Savas Woodbury, 1993.

———. "Union Strategy in the Eastern Theater, 1861-1862" in James I. Robertson, Jr., ed., *Military Strategy in the American Civil War*. Richmond: Virginia Sesquicentennial of the American Civil War Commission, 2012.

———. The U.S. Army and Military Thinking in 1861," in James I. Robertson, Jr., ed., *Military Strategy in the American Civil War*. Richmond: Virginia Sesquicentennial of the American Civil War Commission, 2012.

———, ed. *Vignettes of Military History*, 3 vols. Carlisle Barracks, PA: U.S. Army Military History Institute, 1976-82.

Wright, Marcus J., and Simpson, Harold B. *Texas in the War, 1861-1865*. Hillsboro, TX: The Hill Junior College Press, 1965.

Dissertations

Bower, Jerry. "The Civil War Career of Jacob Dolson Cox," Ph.D. dissertation, Michigan State University, 1970.

Charnley, Jeffrey. "Neglected Honor: The Life of General A.S. Williams of Michigan (1810-1878)," Ph.D. dissertation, Michigan State University, 1983.

Dinges, Bruce. "The Making of a Cavalryman: Benjamin H. Grierson and the Civil War Along the Mississippi, 1861-1865," Ph.D. dissertation, Rice University, 1978.

Losson, Christopher. "Jacob Dolson Cox: A Military Biography," Ph.D. dissertation, University of Mississippi, 1993.

Marino, Carl. "General Alfred Howe Terry: Soldier from Connecticut," Ph.D. dissertation, New York University, 1968.

McDonald, JoAnna M. "R. E. Lee: A Paradoxical Paradigm," Ph.D. dissertation, Morgan State University, 2013.

Sommers, Richard J. "Grant's Fifth Offensive at Petersburg, A Study in Strategy, Tactics, and Generalship," Ph.D. dissertation, Rice University, 1970.

Websites

www.ancestry.com
www.en.wikipedia.org
www.findagrave.com
www.geni.com
Www.suddenlink.net
www.wikitree.com

Index

Dr. Richard J. Sommers has contributed extensively to Civil War and military history. He retired recently as the Senior Historian of the Army Heritage and Education Center, where he served for more than four decades. In addition to *Richmond Redeemed* and *Challenges of Civil War Command*, he has authored more than 100 chapters, articles, entries, and reviews on a wide variety of Civil War topics.

Dr. Sommers is the recipient of a host of awards, including the Bell Wiley Prize for the best Civil War book published in 1981-82, the Harrisburg Civil War Round Table General John F. Hartranft Award "for meritorious service," and the Army Heritage Center Foundation General John Armstrong Award "for significant contributions." The U.S. Army War College has recognized him as a "Distinguished Fellow." He is a popular speaker to Civil War audiences, including the Civil War Round Table circuit, and continues to teach at the War College in Carlisle, Pennsylvania.

Born in Indiana and educated at Carleton College (B.A.) and Rice University (Ph.D.), Dr. Sommers resides in Carlisle with his wife, Tracy.